PENGUIN BOOKS

IN BANKS WE TRUST

Penny Lernoux, whose *Cry of the People* won widespread acclaim, is an investigative reporter who received the Maria Moors Cabot Award from Columbia University and the Sidney Hillman Foundation Book Award. She has written about Latin America for *Newsweek, Harper's, Business Week, The Nation, The Atlantic, The National Catholic Reporter*, and was the Hubert Humphrey Visiting Professor at Macalester College. She lives in Bogotá, Colombia.

In Banks We Trust

PENNY LERNOUX

PENGUIN BOOKS

PENGUIN BOOKS
Viking Penguin Inc., 40 West 23rd Street,
New York, New York 10010, U.S.A.
Penguin Books Ltd, Harmondsworth, Middlesex, England
Penguin Books Australia Ltd, Ringwood, Victoria, Australia
Penguin Books Canada Limited, 2801 John Street,
Markham, Ontario, Canada L3R 1B4
Penguin Books (N.Z.) Ltd, 182–190 Wairau Road,
Auckland 10, New Zealand

First published in the United States of America by
Anchor Press / Doubleday & Company, Inc., 1984
Published with a new introduction in Penguin Books 1986

Published simultaneously in Canada

Printed in the United States of America by
R. R. Donnelley & Sons Company, Harrisonburg, Virginia
Set in Times Roman

To DENIS

ACKNOWLEDGMENTS

First acknowledgment must go to Arthur Jones, former editor of the *National Catholic Reporter,* who encouraged me to write this book by asking me to do a series of investigative articles on banking. His concern for the ethical issues of international finance coincided with a plea to scholars, economists, and journalists by a man who has much influenced me, Cardinal Paulo Evaristo Arns, the archbishop of São Paulo. Like Jones, the cardinal felt a need for much deeper investigation into economic developments affecting human rights.

The hardest part of my task proved to be focusing the investigation, and for that I owe much to Victor Navasky, editor of *The Nation,* who patiently guided me through the first stages of research and provided me with the invaluable services of *Nation* intern David Corn, who ferreted out congressional files, bank statements, and much other background material.

I am indebted to the Fund for Investigative Journalism, which gave me a grant to continue the research; to Beverly Putnam Landrey and Natalie Watson, who worked untiringly to help complete the final, crucial part of the research; to Betty Pego for the typing; and to my friend and mentor Robert Hatch, *The Nation*'s film critic, who was responsible for the editing.

Special thanks must go to my husband Denis for his critical insights and unswerving commitment. I am also grateful to Alvaro Escallón Villa for leading me through the labyrinth of Colombian banking, and to Professor Emily Rosenberg for helping me with the historical background of American banking.

Many bankers and government officials spoke frankly to me about the problems dealt with in the book. Chief among them are the anonymous bankers who supplied answers to several banking puzzles. Among government officials, I am particularly grateful to Richard E. Jaffe, of the Criminal Investigation Division of the Florida State Attorney's Office in Miami, and to George Shaffner, an investigator with the Organized Crime Bureau of the Dade County Police Department. I am also grateful to Miami lawyers R. Jerome Sanford and Richard L. Williams, and to private investigator Wayne B. Black.

Acknowledgment also is due to the investigative unit of Colombia's most influential daily, *El Tiempo,* for its work in exposing the criminal activities of Colombian bankers and their U.S. connections; to Tom Fox, editor of the *National Catholic Reporter,* for pursuing the Vatican Bank's links to criminal interests; and to *The Wall Street Journal* for its penetrating profiles of American bankers.

Finally, I would like to thank Philip Pochoda, Editorial Director at Doubleday, for his trust and support.

CONTENTS

"What is robbing a bank compared to owning a bank!"

BERTOLT BRECHT, *The Threepenny Opera*

INTRODUCTION

In December 1984 I received an unexpected Christmas card from a high-ranking executive of a large U.S. bank. He wrote that he had "approached *In Banks We Trust* skeptically and even with a bit of a defensive attitude." But on reading the book, he found himself "alternately amazed, amused, appalled and left apprehensive. If anything, events subsequent to publication showed you to be too mild on your subjects. We [bankers] can only hope the examples of such institutional failures as Franklin National, Banco Ambrosiano and Continental will make those responsible for management and regulation of banks sit up and take notice. Sadly though, we appear to learn only slowly, if ever, from previous errors."

Such pessimism reflects the traumatic events that have occurred since *In Banks We Trust* was written. The following update covers some of those developments, including the collapse of various banks described in the book, and the fate of their directors. It also details such recent dramas as the Ohio and Maryland panics and the discovery of widespread illegal practices by the United States' most respected financial institutions. Those who have followed the banking crisis will not be surprised to learn of the sharp increase in bank failures. The major cause is perhaps less well-known: investigations by the Federal Deposit Insurance Corporation (FDIC) show that at least half of the recent bank disasters resulted from criminal activities.

Among the issues raised in the book is the go-go atmosphere

in banking, which has encouraged executives to risk their institutions' stability by gambling on loans and by bending or breaking laws designed to ensure the safety of deposits. The Penn Square Bank in Oklahoma City, described in Chapter 1, was a classic example of such hanky-panky. But the fallout from its failure in 1982 was not limited to Oklahoma: it also brought down Continental Illinois National Bank, once the nation's sixth largest, and nearly scuttled Seattle-First National Bank.

Both banks had lent heavily to the brash Oklahoma institution, and when the details of their exposure became public, investors shunned them. The strain on Continental, which also held a large portfolio of dubious Latin-American loans, proved insupportable, and in May of 1984, following a run on Continental by institutional investors, the government was forced to intervene to save the bank. The FDIC hurriedly put together a $7.5 billion rescue package ($1.5 billion from the FDIC and $5.5 billion from sixteen large banks). But attempts to find a buyer for the crippled institution proved futile since not even the megabanks could swallow Continental's $4.5 billion portfolio of bad loans. In the end the FDIC was forced to pick up the tab in exchange for 80 percent of Continental's equity, effectively nationalizing the bank.

Several influential bankers who appear in Chapter 1 subsequently lost their jobs due to the Penn Square debacle. Roger Anderson, Continental's chairman for eleven years, opted for early retirement amid a growing scandal over responsibility for the Penn Square loans. Three Continental executives were forced to leave because of their part in the affair. A subsequent internal bank investigation found that they had held interests in a Colorado oil company which had borrowed $500 million from the bank.[1] Meanwhile, a former executive at Seattle-First National admitted that the bank had been a party to a loan shuttle scheme to deceive bank examiners about the extent of Penn Square's exposure to oil and gas investments. Banks frequently buy and sell loans to beef up their balance sheets, but the practice is illegal if the aim is to mislead government regulators. According to the executive, Penn Square regularly

moved questionable loans "out the back door to Seafirst" prior
to bank examinations; when the danger of detection had passed,
the loans were returned to Penn Square.[2] John R. Boyd, the
fun-loving Seafirst senior vice president in charge of the Penn
Square merry-go-round, was among the first to be axed when
the scandal broke. Stanford C. Stoddard, chairman of Michigan
National Corporation, also paid for his bank's involvement in
Penn Square loans. Although Michigan National was pulled
into the vortex by following Continental's lead, the spotlight
shifted to Stoddard when it became known that his bank had
engaged in extensive self-lending—a practice also common at
Penn Square. With bank examiners swarming over Michigan
National, Stoddard opted to take an indefinite leave of absence.

Little people were also hurt by the Penn Square disaster.
Credit unions and savings and loan associations lost millions
of dollars on uninsured deposits, and it is unlikely they will
ever see the money again. (Almost two hundred suits have
been filed against the bank for claims of $1.06 billion, although
Penn Square's remaining assets are valued at only $200 mil-
lion.) Continental's failure added to the public's nervousness
despite the FDIC's promise to make good on all accounts,
including those that were uninsured. Thus in the spring of 1985,
when news broke that an Ohio savings and loan had lost $145.5
million on a government-securities trading operation, there was
a run on the state's sixty-nine savings institutions, most of which
did not carry government insurance. For six days worried depositors besieged the thrifts, camping outside their closed doors
in a scene from the depths of the Great Depression. Calm was
restored only after Ohio Governor Richard Celeste declared a
bank holiday and the state legislature passed emergency relief
measures. More than two-thirds of the savings institutions subsequently reopened, and by June most had obtained federal
insurance. But the thrifts are still sifting through the wreckage.
Smaller or less sound savings institutions which did not qualify
for government coverage were put on the block for mergers,
and some depositors were limited in the amounts they could
withdraw. In addition to individual distress—hapless depositors were forced to postpone important purchases or trim their

living expenses—Ohio taxpayers were stuck with a $245 million bill for the thrifts' bailout.

Several factors contributed to the Ohio panic. One was the trend among some thrifts to range far beyond their traditional role of providing home mortgages to gamble on such seemingly fast-buck investments as oil wells and racehorses. Home State Savings' failure, which set off the Ohio thrift run, was caused by heavy losses arising from an alleged fraud in a government-securities dealership in Fort Lauderdale, Florida, known as the E.S.M. Group Inc. Not only is the trade in government securities a complex specialty, but those who bet on the game can also sustain enormous losses because of sudden fluctuations in interest rates. Home State invested heavily in the exotic business after Marvin Warner, a Cincinnati financier who held a 96 percent stake in the thrift, was introduced to one of E.S.M.'s founders by his son-in-law, Miami lawyer Stephen Arky.[3]* But in 1983 state savings and loan regulators became alarmed at the thrift's exposure to the government-securities business and won a promise from Home State's board that it would wind down its dealings with E.S.M. In fact, Home State continued to buy securities through E.S.M., increasing its exposure to $700 million while also doubling its own assets, or loans, to a precarious $1.4 billion.

The house of cards collapsed in March 1985, when E.S.M. went under. Investors in the firm were stuck with $315 million in losses since many of the securities had disappeared. Government investigations indicate that the company pledged the same securities to different investors. E.S.M.'s court-appointed receiver is suing Alexander Grant & Co., the Chicago-based accounting firm that gave the firm a clean bill of health, even though it was hemorrhaging from losses. The Securities and Exchange Commission (SEC) also charged that an Alexander Grant auditor had taken $125,000 in bribes from E.S.M. to improve its books.

*Arky committed suicide in July 1985, leaving a note behind in which he disclaimed any responsibility for the E.S.M. disaster.

Warner, who was the U.S. ambassador to Switzerland under the Carter administration, denied that he had any knowledge of the goings-on at E.S.M. or Home State. He told *Newsweek* that he had been a victim of the scheme, although he said he had recovered a $4.5 million investment he had made in E.S.M. "On a day-to-day basis I did not know what was going on in my own bank," he said.[4] A group of Home State depositors took another view: they filed a $432 million suit claiming the bank had invested in E.S.M. "not because it was prudent or even safe to do so, but rather because of the illicit financial benefits conferred upon Warner."[5]

Home State was not the first Warner institution to suffer from management's apparent inattention. Great American Banks, a South Florida bank holding company of which Warner was chairman and Arky a director and legal counsel, was earlier charged with laundering more than $94 million in illegal drug money for Colombian drug traffickers (see Chapter 7). In April 1984, a year before E.S.M. collapsed, Great American pleaded guilty on four counts of failing to inform the Treasury of cash transactions of $10,000 or more. At the time of the federal indictment Great American's management claimed the bank had been "a victim."[6]

A second factor in the Ohio panic was the thrifts' dependence on privately owned insurance pools which proved insufficient to stem the flood. Although most state savings and loan associations have federal insurance, thrifts in Maryland, North Carolina, and Massachusetts remained the exceptions. Events in Ohio increased depositors' wariness, and two months later Maryland savings institutions were hit by a similar run. As in Ohio, the panic was precipitated by reports that one of the thrifts, Baltimore's Old Court Savings & Loan, was in financial trouble because of its investments, in this case primarily in real estate. A probe by Maryland's attorney general also showed that Old Court's management had received lavish consulting fees and large overdrafts.[7] Although the state government hurriedly ordered the thrifts to apply for federal insurance, and savings institutions in Massachusetts and North Carolina did likewise, the measure brought little consolation to Maryland depositors, whose withdrawals from the thrifts were limited to $1,000 a month.

The advantage of private insurance is that it enables the holder to engage in activities that might not be acceptable to federal insurers, particularly in cases where local regulation is known to be weak. In Maryland, for example, state regulators did not obtain authority to police the thrifts until after the panic. In Ohio three different savings and loan superintendents were unable to stop Home State from investing in E.S.M. Some states, such as California, have actually encouraged such dealings through excessive deregulation. Although the Federal Home Loan Bank Board moved to plug the holes following the Ohio and Maryland thrift runs, a number of savings and loan institutions are still in shaky condition due to excessive lending and competition with commercial banks in the interest-rate war. Costly rescues of failed thrifts have so depleted the federal insurance fund that it amounts to less than 0.7 percent of the value of deposits, and government officials expect reserves to decline further unless Washington comes to the rescue.

Federal regulators want Congress to give them legal authority to clean up the mess, but most legislators are reluctant to sponsor a frontal attack on states' rights, particularly when it involves complex financial issues. As admitted by congressional staffers, few of their bosses have the knowledge or interest to deal with esoteric money matters, although stricter congressional oversight is badly needed in several sectors, including the largely unregulated government-securities market, which deals daily in hundreds of billions of dollars. The securities roulette, which was another ingredient in the Ohio scandal, earlier cost Chase Manhattan $285 million in losses through the collapse of a high-flying New York trader known as Drysdale Government Securities (Chapter 1). Two top Drysdale officials later pleaded guilty to stealing more than $270 million through computer fraud and other schemes to milk the banks. (Among the latter was an E.S.M.–style operation in which securities were not delivered to customers.)

As noted in Chapter 1, financial speculation in government

securities has made a mockery of attempts to control the money supply. It has also led to a rash of fraudulent practices which often go undetected because regulators lack the expertise or the clout to deal with the problem. In Ohio, for instance, most of the state thrift examiners had no understanding of the securities business, according to a former Ohio examiner,[8] and thus they apparently did not realize the extent of the risk to Home State. While the Federal Home Loan Bank Board knew E.S.M. was poorly capitalized, and had even ordered an Illinois savings institution to divest itself of E.S.M. investments, this information was not passed on to Ohio regulators—yet another example of the failure in communications among bank regulators (see Chapters 2, 3, and 5). A month after the E.S.M. fiasco several divisions of Bevill, Bresler & Schulman, a New Jersey firm trading in government securities, went under. Customers lost at least $198 million, and the SEC charged the company with fraud.[9] Subsequently it was discovered that Old Court, the Maryland savings and loan that had set off the thrift run, had also been involved in government-securities trading.

One result of the Ohio and Maryland panics was a sharp drop in the percentage of people voicing confidence in the economy. Polsters reported that depositors were "shocked" and "expect many more banking problems." To judge by government bank statistics, that fear was not unfounded. The number of institutions on the FDIC's problem list rose from two hundred in 1975 to nearly eight hundred a decade later, and bank failures increased significantly. Seventy-nine banks collapsed in 1984, the highest rate since 1937. Fifty-nine went under in the first seven months of 1985 when bank failures were running at eight times the average in 1981. Since then, the FDIC has had to pump billions of dollars into the banking system compared with only $500 million in the previous forty-seven years. Public queasiness has also taken a toll of bank stocks, which plummet with the slightest rumor. Perhaps most telling, U.S. banks, which used to be considered impeccable credit risks, are now paying significantly higher rates for loans than European banks.

*   *   *

In the wake of Penn Square, Continental, and other disasters, troubleshooting became a flourishing business. Bank regulators were treated to courses on everything from "junk" bonds to interest-rate swaps, and bankers hired consultants to teach them how to avoid the pitfalls of an E.S.M. or a Drysdale. One St. Louis consulting firm headed by a former bank president produced an underground best-seller, a videotape called "The Worst Loan I Ever Made."[10] Its message: "If the crooks don't get you, your friends will."

It was a warning that Deak & Co. should have heeded. Deak is the owner of Deak-Perera U.S. Inc., one of the country's largest nonbank foreign currency and metals trading firms. When it became known that a Deak-Perera account had been used for a Colombian drug-money laundering operation, the parent company lost so many customers that it was forced to file for bankruptcy proceedings.

The Brahmin First National Bank of Boston also underwent humiliating scrutiny because of illegal cash transactions involving the Angiulo family, a reputed organized-crime group in New England. In an effort to stop the U.S. narcotics traffic, which now earns $100 billion a year, a Justice Department strike force opened investigations in New England, where drug business has moved because of the heat on South Florida banks (Chapter 7). Government investigators found that the Angiulo family had bought more than $1.7 million in cashier's checks— the most common method of laundering money—from a Bank of Boston branch, often paying for the checks in cash. Although a 1970 bank regulation requires financial institutions to report all cash transactions of $10,000 and more, the Bank of Boston gave cash-reporting exemptions to two companies allegedly connected with the Angiulos. As a result of these discoveries, the Treasury also became involved in the investigation, uncovering unreported cash shipments of $1.2 billion by the bank. In 1985 the Bank of Boston pleaded guilty to a felony charge and paid a $500,000 fine.

Although the fine was a pittance for New England's largest banking company, the bad publicity caused important customers, including several townships, to withdraw their deposits. Nor did the bank's haughty dismissal of any wrongdoing help its image. The bank's characterization of the problem as a "systems failure" drew a sharp retort from Treasury officials, who pointed out that cash-reporting requirements have been well-publicized within the banking community. As bankers themselves admit, the movement of large sums of cash is hardly routine and frequently points to a money-laundering scheme (see Chapter 7). Bank of Boston Chairman William L. Brown also angered stockholders by denying that the currency violations had surfaced through an investigation of organized crime. "We didn't see that the public wouldn't believe us," the bank's director of corporate communications explained to *Business Week*.[11]

After the shocking revelations at the Bank of Boston, Treasury officials said they could no longer "assume, and the bank examiners cannot assume, that any bank, no matter how large, is in compliance with the law." Just how many important banks had failed to comply was soon revealed by the admission of the American Bankers Association that forty-five important banks were seeking criminal immunity from the Treasury Department in exchange for full disclosure of cash-transfer violations. Among the first to come clean were Shawmut Bank of Boston, the city's third-largest bank, which admitted to Treasury that it had failed to report more than $190 million in cash transactions, and Boston's second-largest bank, Bank of New England, which acknowledged two sets of unreported cash transactions. Following more such revelations, the Treasury in June 1985 imposed $1.2 million in fines on Chase Manhattan, Manufacturers Hanover, Irving Trust, and Chemical Bank. It also announced that it was investigating 140 other banks for similar cash-reporting violations.

Treasury's get-tough attitude reflects a growing awareness of the importance of banks to the drug traffic—another premise of this book (Chapters 4 through 8). Cash, said James D. Harmon, executive director of the President's Commission on Organized Crime, is "the life-support system without which organized crime cannot exist. If [bankers] choose not to help in the efforts to prevent narcotics trafficking, they should know that every dose of heroin or cocaine, every bribe and every bullet which finds its way into the bodies of federal agents, is paid for by the cash which they never opened their eyes wide enough to see."[12]

As the government investigation of the Angiulo family continued, other important financial institutions were caught in the web, including the Boston branch of E. F. Hutton & Co., a large national brokerage house. But revelations that Hutton had managed accounts for some of the Angiulos caused hardly a ripple compared to the storm that broke following the firm's admission of guilt to 2,000 counts of fraud in bilking dozens of small banks of $8 million over a twenty-month period. Although Hutton was forced to pay $2.7 million in court costs and reimburse the banks, no individual was charged with a crime. As many as twenty-five employees were involved in the fraud, but the Justice Department refused to prosecute on the ground that the abuses were largely due to overzealous branch and regional managers whose bonuses depended on higher cash flows. (A similar practice of tying bonuses to profits led to enormous losses at Chase Manhattan: see Chapter 1.) Wall Streeters found it hard to swallow the claim that senior management had not known what was going on. Their skepticism was shared by New York Mayor Edward I. Koch, who dropped Hutton as comanager of a bond issue, and by fifteen prominent Senate Democrats, who complained to Attorney General Edwin Meese III about Justice's "blatant failure to find individual liability."

In failing to pin down the blame, government officials encouraged the belief that fines for corporate crimes should be treated as operating expenses. The Justice Department also provided support for the theory that "systems failures" can be held responsible for wrongdoing. But people run systems, and they can only be deterred from criminal activity through enforcement of the law. *Business Week* columnist William B. Glaberson summed up the feelings of many by noting that government investigators, "with great fanfare, announced a crime without a criminal. The notion denies logic and challenges the most rudimentary concepts of how justice ought to work."[13]

Though infrequent, corporate crimes can catch up with those responsible. Jake Butcher, for example, who controlled eleven banks in Tennessee and Kentucky, faced a stiff prison sentence after pleading guilty to charges of misusing his banks' money to make illegal loans to himself and associates (Chapter 2). Jaime Michelsen, who once controlled Colombia's largest private bank as well as a medium-sized Miami bank (Chapter 7), fled to Miami rather than face penal charges for his part in the collapse of the Bank of Colombia. Subsequent investigations[14] showed that Michelsen and his managers had been involved in massive self-lending and the evasion of foreign exchange regulations.

Juan Vicente Pérez Sandoval (Chapter 8), who presided over the shotgun wedding of Florida's Flagship and Sun banks, also fled to Miami after the Venezuelan government intervened in his Banco de Comercio (Bancomer) in mid-1985. A go-go financier with influential contacts in Venezuela and Florida, Pérez bought up huge blocks of Flagship stock in an attempt to gain control of the bank. While Flagship's management successfully beat off the Venezuelan's takeover bid, it was unable to resist Pérez's insistence on the merger with Sun after he threatened a bloody court battle. Throughout the bank's troubles with Pérez, Flagship lawyers kept insisting that he had not fully disclosed his business relationships in Venezuela, including an earlier association with the notorious World Finance Corporation (Chapter 8). But bank regulators did not want to listen. Two years later Flagship was justified by events in Caracas when the government was forced to take over Bancomer, following some $85 million in losses. Official investigations showed that part of the losses stemmed from loans made to Pérez's own businesses. The government also reported that Bancomer had paid illegal commissions of 2 to 5 percent to individuals who brought state agency accounts to the bank. Justice Minister José Manzo González said Venezuela would seek Pérez's extradition from the United States.[15]

Foreign banks had $300 million on loan to Venezuela's Bancomer when it went under and more than twice that much to Michelsen's Bank of Colombia. In both cases the governments were pressured by their foreign creditors to repay the money. While the Venezuelans and Colombians balked at using public funds to paper over the crimes of individuals, governments often have no choice but to underwrite such bailouts: either they pay or there are no more loans.

Colombia is a good example of how crooked bankers can send the economy into a nosedive. In 1982 newspaper revelations of massive self-lending led to the imprisonment of two bank presidents whose activities turned out to be typical of the country's bankers (Chapters 5 and 8). Their arrest set off a tidal wave that engulfed the country's financial system, bringing down bank after bank despite frantic efforts by the government to pick up the pieces. By the time Michelsen fled to Miami at the end of 1983 the system was bust. Up to that point the Colombian government had been considered a model borrower on the international loan markets with a relatively small (for its population), conservatively managed foreign debt. But the banking scandal so unnerved New York bankers that they began to reexamine their credit arrangements with Colombia. Like European institutions that upped the cost of loans to U.S. banks because of Continental and other debacles, Colombia was forced to pay higher rates to obtain loans. Then it was unable to get any loans at all. To compensate for the credit crunch, the government ran down its foreign reserves, and by the fall of 1984 Colombia faced a major economic crisis. The government had no choice but to go to the International Monetary Fund (IMF), which serves as policeman for the First World's bankers. The result was a tough austerity program that led to the collapse of dozens of industries, an unprecedented rise in unemployment, and a sharp erosion in real earnings. It will take the country years to recover from the shock, and many Colombian banks may not recover at all. Among those to suffer was the local Chase Manhattan affiliate, Banco de Comercio, which had also engaged in extensive self-lending (Chapter 7). Although Chase and its local representative, James Therrien (later president of Comercio), persistently evaded the issue of Comercio's questionable loans, the figures spoke for themselves: in 1985 the Bogotá Stock Exchange reported that nearly half of Comercio's lending portfolio contained overdue or dubious loans—the worst record of any Colombian financial institution, even the crippled Bank of Colombia.[16]

As shown by Penn Square, problems at a small local bank can spread throughout the financial system, hurting depositors in faraway states. But a bank failure in Colombia or Venezuela, for example, can also have repercussions in California or Nebraska because so many U.S. banks, even small ones, joined the Latin-American lending spree in the 1970s, thereby tying American pocketbooks to the Latin-American debt (Part III). Although Penn Square was the immediate cause of Continental's demise, the bank sustained huge losses in Latin America as well. Other banks have also taken a beating because of their exposure to the region. For instance, in May 1984, when Argentina seemed unlikely to pay interest on its foreign debt, nervous investors knocked 11 percent off the stock of Manufacturers Hanover because it had more on loan to Argentina ($1.3 billion) than any other U.S. bank. According to *The Economist*, had the bank followed the Europeans' example by setting aside a loan-loss reserve of 10 percent of its loans to Argentina in the previous year, Manufacturers would have suffered a 22 percent drop in net profits. "Similar provisions against all their loans to Latin America's four largest debtors [Brazil, Mexico, Argentina and Venezuela] would have wiped out most of the 1983 earnings of America's big banks."[17]

Bank of America offers a cautionary tale of what can happen to a bank when it underestimates such loan provisions. In the second quarter of 1985 BankAmerica posted a $338 million loss, surpassed in U.S. banking history only by Continental's $1.1 billion bath in 1984. Samuel Armacost, the bank's chairman since 1981, had made a herculean effort to shake up the behemoth by eliminating nearly 10,000 employees (mostly through attrition) and slashing costs. But the cumulation of more than a decade of sloppy management could not be wiped out in just a few years, and even under Armacost, Bank-

America made some unwise moves. Among the latter was the acquisition of Seattle-First National, which needed a large capital infusion to survive its losses from Penn Square. Although BankAmerica spent $150 million on the bank, Seafirst continued to lose money, and in late 1984 the Comptroller of the Currency forced BankAmerica to raise new capital because of an increase in loan losses and problem loans, particularly at Seafirst. (Bank management was also hit by a shareholder lawsuit which charged that BankAmerica had "recklessly" purchased the Seattle bank.[18])

In addition to Seafirst's hangover, BankAmerica had to contend with a $95 million loss arising from an apparently phony mortgage-loan scheme in which its employees acted as escrow agents. The bank also suffered a $60 million loss at its subsidiary in Paraguay, where local bank officials made unauthorized loans to agricultural producers which headquarters did not learn about for two years. Meanwhile in Argentina, BankAmerica purchased a local bank at a sealed-bid auction for $150 million—nearly three times the next highest bid—just when the country was entering the worst recession since the 1930s.

Paraguay and Argentina are not the bank's only headaches in Latin America, where it is heavily exposed. When a team of tough New York examiners from the Comptroller of the Currency went over BankAmerica's books, they questioned the lack of reserves for many apparently shaky loans, including high-risk credits to Latin-American borrowers. Thus instead of confirming an expected profit for the second quarter of 1985, the bank was forced to take a huge loss in order to add $527 million to its loan-loss reserves.

Despite BankAmerica's decision to sell up to thirty-five of its affiliates in Latin America, it could be hit by more shocks. The bank has loaned heavily to Brazil, where the foreign debt has become a political football (Chapter 11), but even more to Mexico, where it has over $2.7 billion invested. After Mexico's near default in 1982 the bankers put Humpty-Dumpty together again by refinancing the country's debts, and within months of the restructuring they were claiming that the Latin-American debt crisis was over. That was not the view in Latin America, however, where economic conditions went from bad to worse because of the transfer of billions of dollars in desperately needed capital to First World bankers for debt repayment. Most of the region, Mexico included, slid into such deep recession that the U.S. economic recovery could not pull it out of the hole, in contrast to other areas of the world. Notwithstanding the bankers' optimism, debt has become a structural problem in Latin America, and such temporary cures as loan restructuring do not deal with the root causes of the sickness, which is why so many countries are in chronic crisis.

Though the Mexican bailout (Chapter 11) supposedly demonstrated that the international banking community could bring the dead back to life, Mexico proved no different from other Latin-American countries: in 1985 it was again on the danger list. A sharp drop in prices for oil, which supplies nearly half of government revenues, and parallel declines in nonoil exports, cost the country billions of dollars, making it unlikely that Mexico would meet its debt payment schedule. For the first time since the 1982 scare, bankers admitted that their solutions were not working and that they might have to go through the Mexican drama all over again. But there was a notable difference in the replay. After three years of harsh debt-imposed austerity the Mexican people were exhausted, and the knowledge that they had sacrificed for nothing made them angry and frustrated. Wondered Mary Williams Walsh, a *Wall Street Journal* reporter in Mexico, "How much more pain can the nation take?"[19]

U.S. bankers in Mexico privately admitted that the situation was worse than in 1982, when the country still had memories of the oil boom. Although none believed Mexico would declare a moratorium, there was a sense of rebellion in the air, signaled by Mexico's more responsive attitude toward a Latin-American debt club, which it originally opposed. Other countries also became more militant. Peru's young reformist President Alan García Pérez said he would not sacrifice his country to repay Peru's $14 billion debt and refused to have anything to do with the IMF. When he assumed the presidency in July 1985, Peru was already $500 million in arrears on interest payments, and there seemed no way it could catch up: debt payments due that year were $3.7 billion compared to exports of only $3.1 billion.

The suffering caused by Peru's debt crisis is apparent even to casual visitors to Lima, which is beginning to look like Calcutta. Thousands of poor people descend on the downtown area daily hawking peanuts, fruit, eggs, hats, telephone tokens, individual cigarettes, even rocks. The peddlers, many of them women, are lucky if they earn enough in a day to pay for the two-hour bus ride to their slum homes and a bag of potatoes to feed their families. While they work, their babies lie on newspapers on the street under the merciless sun, and toddlers play in the dirty water in the gutters. The people are dressed in tattered clothing, and they look infinitely tired and sad. According to a two-year study by local economists, such street vendors and other underemployed people account for two-thirds of the city's economic activities.

The situation is even worse in Bolivia, which has given up any attempt to pay its $5 billion debt. In 1985 inflation was running at a mind-boggling 5,000 percent, the economy was in the fifth consecutive year of decline, and real wages had fallen by 25 percent. Conditions in Bolivia are so bad that the World Bank now classifies it in the same category with the starving countries of Africa. Seventy percent of the children die before the age of fifteen, making Bolivia's infant mortality rate the highest in Latin America. Life expectancy is only forty-seven years. Half of the six million people are undernourished, and most of the deaths are due to "diseases of poverty," such as diarrhea, dehydration, enteritis, and tuberculosis.

Most foreign banks, including BankAmerica, have "written off" Bolivia, but how does one write off six million suffering people? Hard-nosed bankers argue that it is the Bolivians' own fault. In fact, a major reason for Bolivia's economic problems is the depressed price of its principal export commodity, tin, which in turn is due to the dumping of U.S. Government tin stocks on the international market every time the price is about to rise. Like other Latin-American countries, Bolivia has also suffered from the growth in U.S. protectionism, which cost the region $4.8 billion in lost trade in 1985. At the same time, the

Latin-American economies have been hammered by high U.S. interest rates, thanks to the Reagan administration's increased borrowing to finance the budget deficit. Why should the Latin Americans pay for U.S. deficits? asked the Washington *Post* (May 29, 1984). "It is a political reality that Latin [American] governments can't go much farther in imposing hardships on their own people without evidence that Americans are going to take action at least to limit the burden."

The *Post* was not the only institution to question whether the Latin Americans' suffering was to any avail. Some bankers, particularly in Europe, began to suggest that it was time to consider long-term structural solutions. Support for a change in thinking came from such unexpected places as the Federal Reserve, where vice-chairman Preston Martin aired the possibility despite the Fed's long-held belief that a few years of economic austerity would do the trick. Henry Kissinger, of all people, took up the same theme by proposing a cap on interest rates and a Marshall Plan for Latin America to be financed by Europe and the United States. Though hardly known for his sensitivity to Third World issues, Kissinger echoed the opinion of many Latin-American leaders when he said that if Washington did not do something about the debt crisis, the United States "would find itself on the political defensive in its own geographic backyard."[20]

There comes a time when even the most powerful nation can no longer behave as though the rest of the world were its piggy bank. Such was Jacques de Larosière's message to Washington in the summer of 1985. The IMF's director said that the U.S. budget deficit was endangering the international economic system by draining capital from other countries to pay for excessive spending and a growing trade imbalance that had put U.S. export industries in the red. Federal Reserve Chairman Paul Volcker agreed that debt growth was "much faster than is consistent with the long-run health of our economy and financial system." Put bluntly by the Treasury: the United States was living beyond its means.

In an ironic twist the United States became a debtor nation

in 1985 for the first time since 1917. Attracted by high interest rates, foreign capital poured into the country in the early 1980s, fueling the United States' economic recovery. Spurred on by the government's own spendthrift example, individuals and corporations were encouraged to borrow by a plethora of lending facilities. In their race for consumer business, banks often paid little heed to customers' creditworthiness—much as they had failed to check the collateral of Latin-American borrowers during the lending binge in the 1970s (Chapter 11). Thus loan delinquencies sharply increased; in some sectors, such as home mortgages, they hit an all-time high. Just as individuals went into debt for nonessential items like vacations in Europe and expensive club memberships, corporations built up enormous liabilities largely because of the merger mania. To add to their holdings or prevent a takeover, they contracted billions of dollars in debt. Banks were no exception, a good example being Florida's Southeast Banking Corp., which had to spend more than $148 million to buy back its stock from unwanted shareholders (Chapter 3). The most worrying aspect of the debt buildup, however, was the enormous surge in the budget deficit, which has been rising at the staggering annual rate of $200 billion.

Like the Latin-American countries, Uncle Sam has become deeply indebted to foreigners in order to finance government spending. U.S. economists calculate that the United States' foreign debt will hit the $1 trillion mark by 1990 and that total debt (including internal liabilities) will top $2 trillion. The figures are so astronomical that they are like Bolivia's 5,000 percent inflation—beyond the ken of ordinary people and apparently most legislators, who cannot come to grips with the problem. Nevertheless, it is obvious that no nation can go on living with debts of such magnitude. As noted by the IMF, the scenario suggests one or all of three unpleasant possibilities—higher taxes, higher interest rates, and/or higher inflation. More taxes will be needed for interest payments on the debt, and because debt is pegged to floating interest rates, the United States could end up in the same position as the Latin Americans, who have had to pay far more for loans than originally anticipated (see Chapter 11). Foreign lenders could also demand higher rates for their money because of lower credit ratings, as has already happened to many U.S. banks. Forced to earmark ever larger portions of their incomes for debt repayment, government, corporations, and individuals will find it increasingly difficult to make ends meet. Interest payments to the United States' foreign creditors, for example, were $18 billion in 1984 and are expected to top $30 billion by the end of the decade. If foreign capital flees the country, as the IMF has warned, interest rates will skyrocket as government, corporations, and consumers compete for scarce resources, producing an even worse recession than that during the Carter administration when high interest rates sharply curtailed business investment. The experience of other countries shows that, when interest costs become so burdensome that no amount of budget cuts or tax hikes can make a dent in the debt, governments are tempted to increase the money supply in order to buy back, or "monetize," the debt. But the consequence is hyperinflation.

Unlike fairy tales in which good inevitably triumphs over evil, in real life there is no magical formula for greed. The most that society can expect is just laws and an efficient system of enforcement based on the common good. While many bankers are law-abiding citizens who provide a service to the community, others have been exclusively concerned with individual or corporate gain, often at enormous cost to taxpayers and depositors. Banking, more than any other industry, is based on public trust. If we cannot trust in banks, how can we have confidence in our economic prosperity?

1. *The Wall Street Journal,* Feb. 13, 1984.
2. *The Wall Street Journal,* June 16, 1983.
3. *Newsweek,* April 1, 1985.
4. Ibid.
5. *Time,* April 8, 1985.
6. *Florida Bank Directory* (Florida Bankers Association, Spring 1982); Miami

Herald, Dec. 14, 1982; Miami *News,* Dec. 14 and 15, 1982; Preliminary Report by the President's Commission on Organized Crime and Money-Laundering (Washington, 1984).

7. *Time,* May 27, 1985.

8. *The Wall Street Journal,* July 16, 1985.

9. *Time,* June 10, 1985.

10. Available from Bankers Training & Consulting, 1695 South Brentwood, St. Louis, MO, 63144.

11. *Business Week,* March 4, 1985.

12. *Business Week,* March 18, 1985.

13. William B. Glaberson, "The Punishment of Hutton Doesn't Fit the Crime," *Business Week,* June 3, 1985.

14. Donadío, Alberto, *¿Por qué cayó Jaime Michelsen?* (Bogotá: El Ancora Editores), 1984; *El Espectador,* March 21, 1985; *El Tiempo,* June 16, 1985.

15. *Latin American Regional Reports: Andean Group Report,* June 21, 1985; Associated Press, June 10, 1985; *The Wall Street Journal,* Dec. 29, 1983; New York *Times,* May 14, 1983.

16. First-quarter results of 1985 as reported to the Bolsa de Bogotá, published in *El Tiempo,* June 24, 1985.

17. *The Economist,* June 2, 1984.

18. *The Wall Street Journal,* July 22, 1985.

19. Ibid.

20. *Latin America Weekly Report,* June 28, 1985.

HOW TO FOLLOW THE BANK TRAIL

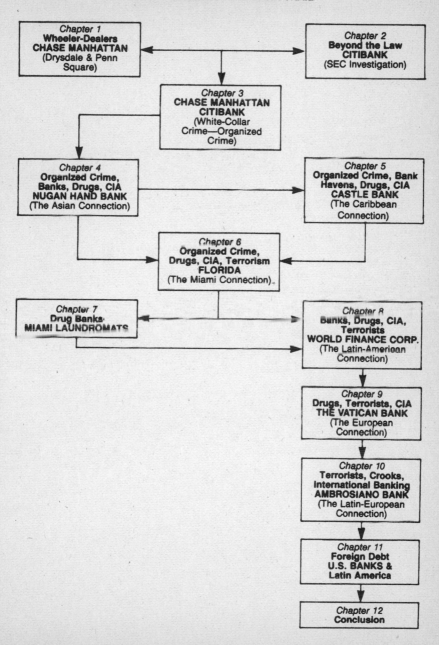

GUIDE TO TRAIL

PART I

CHAPTER 1 describes how Chase Manhattan, through loose management, lost $542 million on a securities gamble and a high-flying bank in an Oklahoma shopping center. Supporting cast: Continental Illinois and Seattle-First National.

CHAPTER 2 documents how such disasters occur through lax regulation and auditing procedures encouraged by "bank reserve," and how such "reserve" enabled Citibank to evade tax and prudential regulations, as revealed by the shocking results of a three-year Securities and Exchange Commission investigation.

CHAPTER 3 links Chase's loose management and Citibank's failure to check employees' backgrounds to the $20.3 million "Outrigger" real estate scam involving organized-crime figures.

PART II

CHAPTER 4 reveals how a Sydney merchant bank became the fulcrum for organized crime, covert action, and the politics of heroin in Southeast Asia. Cast includes a Who's Who of the CIA.

CHAPTER 5 connects Southeast Asian heroin traffic, the CIA, and organized crime in Caribbean bank havens.

CHAPTER 6 shows how Miami has become a center for "hot" money, drugs, and international intrigue.

Chapter 7 names Miami banks in drug traffic and explains money laundering and regulators' failure to stop it.

CHAPTER 8 tells of the rise and fall of an international laundromat with CIA, drug, terrorist, and organized-crime connections.

CHAPTER 9 documents the links among European and Latin-American fascists and Nazis, the cocaine traffic, organized crime, and the Vatican Bank.

Part I

ROGUES' GALLERY—Chapter 1

BILL "BEEP" JENNINGS, the go-for-broke owner of the Penn Square Bank in Oklahoma City, which collapsed in 1982.

WILLIAM G. PATTERSON, Penn Square's fun-loving executive vice president in charge of energy loans.

CARL W. SWAN, an Oklahoma oilman who was a director of and the second largest stockholder in Penn Square; Swan and his companies received $200 million in loans through Penn Square.

Chapter 1

From Chase Manhattan's basement to a storefront bank in an Oklahoma shopping center. The hazards of gambling with other people's money.

When David Rockefeller took over the Chase Manhattan Bank in 1969, it was running neck and neck with Citibank for second place in U.S. banking, after Bank of America. Within three years Citibank had drawn ahead, and Chase was moving into one of its worst economic storms. Attempting to play catch-up, it led all banks in real estate loans, but during the 1973–74 recession the market collapsed, and Chase was among the hardest hit. Its real estate investment business went bankrupt in 1979, and by 1980 Chase had written off nearly $630 million in real estate losses.

In addition to that debacle, the bank's bond traders found themselves on the wrong side of massive interest-rate bets. In 1974 Chase discovered that one or more of its managers, hoping to hide trading losses, had cooked the books to the tune of $34 million. A senior vice president was blamed and fired in one of more than a dozen management shake-ups during Rockefeller's chairmanship. By the end of 1974 Chase had insufficient capital to cover its bad loans and was placed on the bank regulators' list of troubled banks. It was accused of poor management and controls, with $4 billion outstanding in such loans. Thus when Chase faltered again in 1982, there was no great surprise. The question on everyone's mind, reported *The Banker,* was: Who's minding the shop?[1]

Like the State Department, which from time to time the Rockefellers have also attempted to run, Chase is governed by a mass of minute regulations that often don't work or are ignored

by the staff. In the main, they are overridden by the tacit understanding that bank officers who earn good profits need not bother
with rules. To be sure, Chase is by no means the only U.S. bank
that ignores its own rules in pursuit of profit, but it does seem to
get stung more often. "Chase has a long record of being on the
wrong side of a position, having people do unauthorized things,"
said one financial analyst. "Every three to five years they get
caught with their pants down."[2]

Though an inelegant indictment of so aristocratic an institution, it characterizes the arrogance of ignorance that has become
the posture of Chase and other large U.S. banks. Believing that
their size and political connections make them immune to any
reversal, they have embarked on a series of financial adventures
so reckless in conception and sloppy in execution that a first-year
accounting student might blush to propose them. Yet the big
banks never seem to learn from their mistakes—and that is why
they were so hard-pressed in 1982, when institutions and corporations to which they had carelessly lent money were falling like
trees in a gale.

Chase's problems were bound up with the private goals of
David Rockefeller, who tended to treat the bank as an instrument of his political ambitions. Unlike his brother, Nelson,
David Rockefeller was interested not in public office but in the
political power conferred by international finance. He saw himself as a white knight, charging about the world's capitals to slay
socialist dragons. But, as one observer noted, when so engaged
Rockefeller often seemed like a caricature of an international
capitalist: He was a man capable of describing himself as "the
spider in the center of a web of international intrigue."[3]

Actually, Rockefeller was no better at intrigue than at banking. His Trilateral Commission,* founded in 1973 with an all-star
cast of businessmen and politicians from the First World (it included Jimmy Carter), was supposed to plan strategy for out-
smarting the Third World. Instead it was soon overwhelmed by
the political and economic differences that divided the triangle of
Japan, Europe, and the United States. While the commission
managed to provoke considerable wrath in the developing coun-

---

* See Chapter 11, p. 241.

tries, its only evident contribution to the North-South dialogue was a book suggesting that democracy was bad for business.[4]

Rockefeller's relations with Iran and Argentina proved notably shortsighted. As the "Shah's banker," Rockefeller was on warm terms with Mohammed Reza Pahlavi, and Chase made more loans to Iran than did any other U.S. bank. But when the Shah was deposed in 1979, Chase became an Iranian symbol for the hated "Yankee imperialism." Rockefeller hardly helped matters by persuading the Carter administration to admit the Shah to the United States, thereby precipitating the hostage crisis.

Nor were European bankers amused by Chase's decision to declare a $500 million syndicated loan to Iran in default. Ten days earlier the Iranian Government had instructed Chase to pay the interest on the loan out of Iran's London deposits, and the European banks in the syndicate protested that Chase had no right to call a default. They said that Chase was following its own narrow interests to the detriment of the syndicate and the whole global banking system, because Rockefeller, mixing his personal brand of politics with banking, was bent on punishing the revolutionary government in Iran. In retrospect the Europeans were right: Iran repaid all other bankers without such arm-twisting, and Chase was left with a black eye.

Rockefeller proved similarly indiscreet in Argentina, where he went out of his way to praise the policies of his good friend, Economy Minister José Martínez de Hoz, who was shortly to be sacked by Argentina's military government for bringing on the worst economic debacle since the Depression. Rockefeller is also remembered by thousands of victims of the military's repression as the American banker who told Argentina's generals not to worry about human rights.[5]

Thus, when Rockefeller turned over the bank's management to Willard C. Butcher in 1980, there was a sense of relief among Chase staffers, who expected that the bank would be run in a more professional manner, without reference to Rockefeller's political causes. A tall, stooped man in his late fifties, the blustery, raspy-voiced Butcher had risen through the ranks of Chase by a hard-driving, ruthless dedication to the bank. A "hands-on" manager, he lacked the polish and aristocratic urbanity of Rockefeller, but he was a better banker. The problem was that Chase had been known for years as "David's Bank," and when Butcher took over he apparently thought he had to emulate Rockefeller by spending a good deal of time in Washington and foreign capitals. (Or, as he once told *Newsweek*, "David's job is to play the music, and mine is to see that the bank dances to it.") At the same time, Butcher decentralized authority at Chase in an attempt to "add a spirit of aggressiveness" to the bank.[6] But the aggressiveness and lack of control at the top led to the same sort of debacles caused by Rockefeller's indifference to management detail, and while Butcher was away, telling foreign governments how to run *their* economies, Chase once again ran aground.

Trouble erupted in a basement of Chase's Wall Street headquarters in May 1982—at the same time that two Chase executives were being indicted for fraud.† The basement was the headquarters for Chase's institutional-banking unit, set up as a service operation for big financial customers. It was intended not to show a large profit but to provide expert advice in such technical areas as the safekeeping of securities. However, in the late 1970s, when Chase was trying to bolster its profitability in the wake of the real estate disaster, the institutional-banking unit was seized by a moneymaking euphoria. The bright young men in the basement, having discovered that money could be made much faster by lending than by charging service fees, had embarked on a spree that would eventually cost the bank $542 million and nine of its executives their jobs. According to Chase insiders, the bank was as much at fault as the basement gamblers. "There was pressure from the top to produce profits and growth," said one officer. "You would have to stretch."[7] Corner cutting was also encouraged by tying the bonuses and promotions of those in the institutional-banking unit to the volume of business they generated, a practice other bankers called "incredible."

Among the institutional unit's biggest growth accounts was a small New York firm, Drysdale Government Securities, Inc., which dealt in the little-understood practice of lending and borrowing government securities through so-called repurchase agreements, or "repos." In the most elementary of repo maneuvers, a government-securities dealer borrows short-term money

† See Chapter 3.

by selling securities, simultaneously agreeing to repurchase them in a few days. The money is often used to meet the firm's obligations.

Though Drysdale, a brash, four-month-old newcomer, was shunned by other New York banks, the basement team at Chase were gung ho to do business. Some thirty banks and brokerage firms had placed government securities with Chase in return for cash facilities or to keep on deposit. Chase, as agent for the owners, in turn lent the securities to Drysdale, which apparently used the borrowed securities to parlay its $5 million capital into security holdings estimated at as much as $4 billion. The firm's aggressive president, Richard Taaffe, gambled that he could sustain this high-wire act with a change in U.S. interest rates, which came too late. When the gamble failed, Drysdale could not repay Chase the $285 million in interest that was due the thirty banks and brokers on the bonds they had placed with Chase.

Although Butcher and other top Chase managers were taken unawares by the default, people inside the bank said that there had been signs of trouble for some time, certain middle managers having voiced concern that the government-securities lending business had grown too big. "There was an indication there could be a problem, but no one thought it would be this serious or this sudden," one Chase officer said.[8] Outsiders were less charitable. "This was not a fluke," commented a bank analyst. "What kind of controls can the bank have if it does business with a firm trading in billions on so small a capital?"[9]

"Drysdale came to us," said an official of a rival bank, "but we wouldn't deal with them. They didn't tell us what their business background was; they didn't tell us who else they were dealing with; they didn't tell us anything. That is what is so amazing. How could Chase get into deals this size if they didn't know what they were dealing with?"[10]

If Chase had checked with other government-securities brokers, it would have seen immediately that it was being gulled into acting as a front for a securities firm with a decidedly shady reputation.[11] Nor did Chase consult with the New York Stock Exchange, although Drysdale Government Securities, Inc., was spun off from Drysdale Securities Corporation when the Stock Exchange objected that the latter's government-securities division was growing too large for its capital base. But perhaps the biggest sign of folly is that other departments of Chase had declined to do business with Drysdale because it was considered too great a credit risk.

Chase's chairman was the first to be blamed. Bank analysts complained that in trying to copy Rockefeller's globe-trotting style, Butcher was spending too little time at his management job in New York. Butcher himself admitted that he didn't even know Chase was lending government securities. Nor were the risks of the complex, $150 billion-a-day business clear to Butcher's subordinates. The basement crowd that dealt with Drysdale came from sales and operations backgrounds and lacked the prudence of experienced credit officers or securities traders. It is a fundamental rule in banking that a second officer with higher authority must approve a loan made by his junior, and loans by Chase's institutional-banking unit were supposed to be checked by another group of officers in the corporate-banking section. These regulations were ignored.[12]

To the neophytes in the basement, Drysdale seemed to offer profits in the form of fees for Chase's role as middleman. Apparently believing that the business was risk-free, they failed to consult with Chase's money market experts and operated "in their own little world," in the words of a Chase executive.[13] Credit checks were sloppy because the people in the institutional-banking unit assumed that they would not be held responsible if a customer failed to meet his obligations. Indeed, when Butcher first learned the bad news, he refused to make good on the loss to the brokerage firms and banks that had entrusted securities to Chase. Only after the Federal Reserve intervened did the bank agree to swallow the $285 million loss. "What the hell could Chase do?" wondered a Federal Reserve official. "They wouldn't have had ten customers left anywhere in the world if they had left the brokers holding the bag."[14]

In the days after the Drysdale scandal broke, terror reigned in the basement. Peter Demmer, the vice president in charge of the Drysdale operation, remained incommunicado, unable to touch a file unless accompanied by someone else. "He's like an Argentine political prisoner," said one Chase insider. "We don't hear anything from him."[15] Nine Chase officials were subsequently sacked, including three executive vice presidents—and still the bad news continued.

Within weeks of Drysdale's collapse, another government-securities trader, Lombard-Wall, went under. Its two largest unsecured creditors were Chase Manhattan and the New York State Dormitory Authority, which finances construction of local universities and hospitals. Chase stood to lose $45 million, again because the bank's management had not been watching the store.[16] While Chase was trying to clean house by firing scapegoats, bank regulators were also being criticized for allowing the government-securities business to run amok. The booming market in repos clearly showed that financial speculation was making a mockery of government attempts to control the nation's money supply. One of the ways the Federal Reserve contracts the money supply is to sell Treasury securities. The Fed gets ready money—which is thus removed from circulation—while purchasers of securities get bonds they cannot use as cash. Or so say the textbooks. In the real world a broker can turn in the securities to a bank and get a corresponding cash advance without forfeiting interest on the securities. And repos are only one of many methods devised by financiers to evade attempts to control them or the money supply. The lesson of the runaway repos is hardly new. As shown in the years leading up to the crash of '29, if given half a chance financial markets will drive themselves into a crisis, spurred on by competition and unscrupulous Wall Street gamblers.

***

Just how unscrupulous banking has become was revealed with the crash of a small, high-flying Oklahoma bank. Again Chase's basement operations were involved, but this time Chase was not alone: Other big losers were Continental Illinois National Bank, the nation's sixth largest bank and previously thought to be one of the best managed; Seattle-First National Bank, which enjoyed a similar reputation; and the Michigan National Corporation, whose own past behavior had been somewhat odd. "If you're not concerned about the banking system after all this, you would have to be unconscious," remarked Lawrence R. Fuller, vice president and bank-stock analyst of Drexel Burnham Lambert.[17]

When the Penn Square Bank of Oklahoma City failed in July 1982, its creditors were stuck with some $2 billion in loans so shaky that they could only be described as reckless gambling. And the other banks knew it: At Continental Illinois, according to a Chicago banker, the decision to take risks was corporate policy.[18] This was true also of Chase, which was prepared to trade safety for growth. Other Penn Square investors saw the bank as an easy means of tax write-offs: Four fifths of the bank's loans were for oil and gas projects, and until 1981, when the tax laws changed, oil and gas investments were tax shelters for high-income investors. "These people aren't in here to look for oil, only to keep their money away from Uncle Sam," commented a local oilman. "And when they find out they can actually lose it, they start squealing like pigs stuck under a fence."[19] But the greediest people of all were Penn Square's directors, who illegally used the bank for their personal interests and hustled for loans to promote their own businesses.

Anyone visiting Penn Square's headquarters in a tiny, windowless office at the bank of a residential shopping center might have wondered at the nerve of its promoters. When it was shut down, the bank had assets of $525 million, seventeen times the level eight years earlier, when Bill "Beep" Jennings took over. A go-for-broke financier, Jennings changed Penn Square from a modest operation dealing mostly in loans to farmers and real estate developers into a merchant bank for the region's rapidly expanding gas and oil industry. In a typical deal Penn Square would set up a loan that would extend the bank beyond its legal lending limit. To avoid that situation Penn Square would invite bigger banks to share the pie. In those days the oil business was booming and the big banks were delighted to oblige. To be sure, there was some risk, but Oklahoma's small energy producers were willing to pay premium interest rates, and the oil or gas was there in the ground as collateral—or so it was assumed. Since the oilmen were a clannish group whose flashy style somewhat confused the typical New York or Chicago loan officer, Penn Square was useful as a middleman in the heart of what bankers call the "Oil Patch." Continental Illinois, located in the depressed Great Lakes region, could not get enough of Penn Square's loans: It had $1 billion in loans on its books when the bank collapsed.

Chase Manhattan's basement housed another $212 million, while Seattle-First National, also in a depressed area, committed itself to $400 million.

The key man in Penn Square's lucrative business was William G. Patterson, the bank's young, fun-loving executive vice president in charge of oil and gas loans. By all accounts Patterson was a real card. Around the office he frequently wore a Mickey Mouse beanie or a hollowed-out duck decoy. Among his more commented-upon eccentricities were food fights in the fancy restaurants of Chicago and New York. The crowd at Cowboys, a popular country and western disco in Oklahoma City, remembers the high times when he would show up with an entourage. "He would sometimes drink beer out of his boot or stuff a whole roast quail in his pocket," one waiter recalled. An officer from Manufacturers Hanover Trust Company of New York was in Cowboys one evening when Patterson pulled his boot stunt. "There's no way we'll ever do business with this guy," the stunned banker was heard to remark.[20]

Out-of-state bankers often joined the fun. To solicit business from Penn Square, Seattle-First National outfitted officers with ten-gallon hats, rakishly accented with $40 ostrich feathers, so they would feel more at home with "the good ol' boys" from Oklahoma. According to one Seattle-First source, they would "sit around hotel rooms at 4 A.M. drinking Wild Turkey out of water glasses." The Seattle platoon was headed by the bank's senior vice president, John R. Boyd, in charge of energy loans. A "consummate deal maker," according to a former associate, Boyd got on well with Patterson. Like the Penn Square whiz kid, he entertained lavishly and loved a prank. He once startled Seattle-First's "gray hairs"—his name for the bank's staid credit committee—by striding into a meeting wearing a sheik's robe and Arab headdress he had picked up in Abu Dhabi.[21]

But the fun and games ended abruptly when the Comptroller of the Currency declared Penn Square insolvent, with $46 million in losses as compared to a net capital of only $37 million—and a further $2 billion in loans owed the big banks in the North. It was only the third time since the Depression that the federal government had shut down a bank. (A more common and less painful course for a bankrupt bank is to merge with a bigger institution.) Although the regulators were loathe to put Penn Square to the wall, they had no choice, given the violations of banking law, shoddy record keeping, a large portfolio of bad loans, and a flurry of lawsuits that will tie up the bank's remaining assets for years to come.

Penn Square's problems were first attributed to the woes of the oil industry, which suffered a severe setback in 1981 after ten fat years. Because average prices had risen by a factor of ten in a decade, more oil and gas became available. At the same time, the demand dropped because of the higher cost and the worldwide recession. However, until the bottom fell out of the market, good luck and fast bucks intoxicated the petroleum stronghold of Oklahoma City. Diamond rings shaped like oil derricks became a common sight, a Rolls-Royce dealership opened and thrived, and the price of deep natural gas reached more than fifty times the level of the 1960s.[22] In such an atmosphere Bill Patterson's antics hardly seemed out of place.

In fact, Patterson and Penn Square were guilty of more than corny humor and heedless optimism—but that became known only after the bank collapsed. Unlike other Oklahoma City banks, which lent no more than 20 percent of their portfolios to the oil and gas industry, Penn Square concentrated 80 percent of its loans in that sector. And while other banks of comparable size increased their assets at a steady 15 percent a year from 1978 to 1981, Penn Square's annual growth never dropped below 40 percent. In the eight months before its failure, the bank's own loans and those it handed on to other banks increased by $1.1 billion.[23] Almost all the money dispensed in the last days before the bank closed went to companies involved in oil and gas, several of them owned by Penn Square directors or stockholders. "It was street knowledge that you could get a loan at Penn Square easier than anywhere else," said a local geologist.

Although the thirty-four-year-old Patterson was then in charge of 80 percent of the bank's loans, he had no previous lending experience. The only limit on his lending activities was a legal restriction imposed on the bank: no more than 15 percent of its capital to any one borrower. But even that was no real restriction, since Penn Square could originate much bigger loans as long as it sloughed off the excess before the paperwork was completed and the loans reached its books. For a fee Penn Square syndicated its loans—$2 billion of them—to Chase, Continental, Seattle, and others. Syndication is common in specialized areas such as real estate and energy, which have large capital requirements, but prudent banks check the loans in which they participate.

In Penn Square's case the brash led the blind. Continental and Chase trusted Patterson and his small team of officers to check collateral for loans and to keep an eye on the borrowers. Seattle-First National, Michigan National, and other smaller banks sheepishly followed the big ones over the Penn Square cliff. Seattle-First National "looked at Continental and Chase and thought it was in good company," observed a former high-ranking officer of that bank.[24] Apparently no one at these banks thought to check Patterson's paperwork on the loans they took through syndication. It later turned out that many were so poorly documented that the only information provided was a name and an address. Missing were routine credit reports on the borrowers, formal lending agreements, and legal papers to secure collateral. Nor did the bankers ask the bank regulators about Penn Square's credit standing. Had they done so, they would have discovered that the bank was on the "problem" list of the Comptroller of the Currency—which fact, however, the Comptroller never bothered to pass on to the banks!

Patterson poured out money as though he owned the mint. One borrower of $7 million said that on the day he met with Patterson to propose a large, unsecured loan, the banker was wearing his Mickey Mouse cap. "He just listened and said, 'I think we can handle that' "—all the while "tugging on those strings on each side of the hat that make the ears wiggle."[25]

The same borrower, who claimed he had never been in default on any of his Penn Square loans, said, "I was a good bet. But, golly, you should see some of the other loans that Bill made. Once I introduced him to a friend of mine who had a second mortgage on his house and lost all his money in a drilling program. Then he lost his job and had missed two house payments by the time I introduced him to Bill. But Bill chatted with him for a half hour and gave him a $100,000 credit line at Penn Square."[26]

Sloppy credit checks were the least of it. Bank and public records show that self-lending, or insider loans, weighed heavily in Penn Square's failure. According to investigations by the Tulsa *Tribune* and the bank's own records, the bank arranged loans totaling several hundred million dollars for its senior officials and directors, and for companies in which the officers and directors had an interest. Documentation in a lawsuit against Penn Square also alleged that Patterson acted as huckster for a bank director's company to obtain money from outside investors.[27] "There will be a number of people going to jail out of Penn Square," predicted a government investigator. "This was so corrupt; there were so many kickbacks, payoffs. It will take months to sort them out."[28]‡

Among those who benefited most from Penn Square's generosity was Carl W. Swan, an Oklahoma oilman who was a director and the second largest shareholder in the bank. Swan borrowed more than $200 million through Penn Square for himself or for groups in which he had controlling or significant interests. Bank records show that some of the concerns for which Swan borrowed ended in bankruptcy, and that several repaid little or no principal on short-term loans before the bank collapsed. On the day before that happened, Continental Illinois and Penn Square refinanced $48.9 million in loans to the Longhorn Oil and Gas Company, in which Swan held a 40 percent stake. The records also show that Seattle-First lent $32 million in 1981 to a Swan-related partnership that owned a twenty-two-story office building that was to house Penn Square's new headquarters. Another Penn Square director and large shareholder had organized the partnership and was to have managed the building; still another director controlled the company constructing the building.[29]

In addition to Longhorn Oil, Swan's petroleum interests included the Continental Drilling Company, Inc., which borrowed

‡ The FBI has produced evidence that a Penn Square vice president misappropriated a third of a million dollars on behalf of developer Allen Senall, a former business associate of Allen Wolfson, who was convicted for defrauding the Key Bank of Tampa and was linked to the collapse of the Metropolitan Bank in Tampa and the Mob-looted Northern Ohio Bank. *Parapolitics/USA* [March 1, 1983], citing Tampa *Tribune* [Sept. 10, 1982], St. Petersburg *Times* [Sept. 10, 1982], and Oklahoma City *Times* [Aug. 23, 1982].

more than $90 million from Penn Square and three correspondent banks; the High Plains Drilling Company, which was loaned more than $25 million by Penn Square and its correspondents; and T.O.S. Industries, which owed more than $16 million to Penn Square and Continental Illinois when it filed for reorganization under federal bankruptcy laws.[30]

Chairman "Beep" Jennings, according to bank records, received at least $18 million in loans from Penn Square and its correspondent banks for himself and his business interests. One of these Jennings-related companies later went bust; others repaid little or no principal on short-term borrowings, and some had almost no collateral. Furthermore, when reporting to the Federal Reserve Board, Penn Square's parent holding company omitted several of Jennings' outside business interests from forms that required such disclosure. Jennings and Swan together engaged in more than a half dozen business ventures, and Swan was active in management of the bank.[31]

J. B. Allen, another Oklahoma oilman who invested in the Penn Square office building, was also a principal in Continental Drilling and Longhorn Oil. In addition, Allen had other oil interests that, along with his personal borrowings, accounted for at least another $20 million in Penn Square–related loans. A third investor in the office building was oilman Robert A. Hefner III, whose G.H.K. Company borrowed some $125 million from Penn Square and its correspondent banks.[32]

Investors in Swan's Longhorn Oil and Gas Company also alleged that Swan and Patterson enticed them into buying into the company with false assertions. In a suit against Penn Square, the investors said that the sales pitch was that they needed to invest only 25 percent of the $150,000 price for one unit of participation in certain oil-drilling schemes. The 75 percent balance was to be covered by standby letters of credit (i.e., bank guarantee of payment) from the customers' own banks to Penn Square. The investors said they were told that Penn Square would not call the letters of credit, but in May 1982, when the bank was desperate, it did so, thereby immediately transforming the letters into actual loan obligations to their banks by the investors. The latter won a temporary injunction against such payment on the ground that the "letters of credit were induced by fraud."[33]

In the aftermath of the Penn Square debacle, people took to shaking their heads and wondering, as did the chairman of the House Banking Committee, how "some of the nation's most sophisticated financial institutions, with all variety of expertise at hand, were lured like moths to the glow of this go-go bank sitting in a shopping center in Oklahoma City?" But William M. Jenkins, the sheepish chairman of Seattle-First National, summed it up best: "We look dumb."[34]

Like Continental and Chase, the Seattle bank was hungry for growth and profits. "There was a balancing act going on there," recalled a former officer in the bank's energy department. "In the end, they sacrificed a good, clean portfolio for growth." The Seattle bank and its people suffered for that imprudence: Two senior officers were dismissed, including the happy-go-lucky Boyd, and four hundred other employees were laid off. The bank reported a second-quarter net operating loss of $55.4 million. Jenkins, the patrician banker who by aggressive lending catapulted Seattle-First into the ranks of the nation's top twenty banks, concluded, "I should have retired last year."[35]

At Continental Illinois the repercussions were even worse, constraining Roger D. Anderson, Continental's chairman, to make an extraordinary public confession of the bank's bad debts. If nothing else, the list was impressive: In addition to a $200 million loss on the Penn Square loans, the bank had $1.3 billion in "problem loans" out to such foundering or bankrupt companies as International Harvester, Braniff, Massey Ferguson, Canada's Dome Petroleum Company, and the Mexican conglomerate Alfa (Seattle-First also had investments in Alfa).[36] It came as no surprise, then, when Continental declared a $61 million loss for the second quarter of 1982.

Though Continental projected a highly conservative image, it was an overzealous lender in every sector of the economy. For example, in energy, where it had a reputation for "expertise," the bank became a national leader, with $5 billion in loans. Later it turned out that much of Continental's savvy was actually Penn Square's. Thus, Continental followed Penn Square's lead by attaching a worth greater than other banks would grant to underground oil and gas resources, and thus was willing to lend more against them.

The extent of Continental's culpability was raised in a class-action lawsuit filed in the summer of 1982 by an irate Continental stockholder. He charged the bank and its senior officers with fraud, claiming that they "did not disclose the extent to which reckless and wholly imprudent loan and investment decisions by the bank had jeopardized the assets, earnings, and net worth of the . . . bank." The suit charged that although Continental's officers knew there had been serious difficulties at the bank, they continued to assert publicly that there were no significant problems. According to legal sources, Continental's management was reluctant to speak, primarily because its officers and directors could be held personally liable for losses. Like most banks, Continental's officers are insured against fraud, but the question posed by Penn Square was whether an insurance company would be obliged to pay if it were shown that losses had been caused by gross negligence. Either way, said one bank analyst, "the situation is deplorable. . . . In fairness to Continental, the likelihood they were defrauded must also be considered. However, the possibility that they were duped does not strike us as being much better [than the other alternative]."[37]

That it sometimes comes down to the same thing is illustrated by the Michigan National Corporation, a $6.2 billion holding company. Michigan National had $53 million in questionable loans to Penn Square—a stake that far exceeded its 1981 earnings of $37.8 million. And, like Penn Square, Michigan National engaged regularly in self-lending—sometimes at the multimillion-dollar level—that involved bank officers, directors, or entities with which they were associated. Both the Securities and Exchange Commission and the Office of the Comptroller of the Currency have criticized Michigan National for "inadequate" disclosures on insider lending and for violation of banking laws forbidding large loans to bank officials. Data from analysts and public and bank records show that the corporation lent more than $100 million to companies owned by or associated with bank officials; more than half these loans had gone to companies in serious trouble or in bankruptcy proceedings.[38] As at Penn Square, Michigan National's director, Stanford C. Stoddard, used the corporation to make questionable deals in which he and his friends held an interest. Bank examiners also uncovered $59 million in loans to companies associated with four Michigan National bank directors.[39]

***

Quite a few reputations were buried in the collapse of Penn Square, but, as pointed out by banker Michael Thomas in *Someone Else's Money,*[40] a thinly disguised fictional account of goings-on in Wall Street, the greedy pursuit of profits has become a threat to probity and common sense throughout today's financial world. Thomas' story describes an individualistic billionaire who avenges himself on the financiers by luring them into a pair of phony industries—one of them in oil. So eager are the bankers for a piece of the action that they fail to make any checks.

The facts are at least as shocking as Thomas' fiction: One of Penn Square's conditions for selling loans to Chase, Continental, and the others was that they would not investigate them—and, incredibly, the banks agreed. With bonuses tied to the amount of business they generated, Chase's basement gang was obviously more interested in volume than detail work. Chairman Butcher's failure to attend to details also contributed to the disaster. By encouraging aggressiveness without a complementary dose of prudence, he showed that Chase had not really changed since the 1970s, when it had gambled recklessly in the real estate market; in the 1980s Chase was again involved in shaky real estate deals.[41] Neither bigness nor political clout could disguise the fact that "David's Bank" was an extraordinarily slack place where cocksure young bankers could lose more than a half billion dollars on a roll of the dice in a basement.

ROGUES' GALLERY—Chapter 2

PEAT MARWICK, MITCHELL AND COMPANY, the largest bank auditors in the United States; the auditors for Penn Square.

ELDON L. BELLER, the president of Penn Square, who claimed he had no authority.

WALTER B. WRISTON, the chairman of Citibank, under whom "rinky-dink deals" were authorized to enable the bank to evade tax and bank reserve regulations on three continents.

SHEARMAN AND STERLING, the law firm employed by Citibank to "whitewash" the "rinky-dink deals."

Chapter 2

The arrogance of Citibank, or how bankers hoodwink their regulators and endanger the U.S. economy.

When Penn Square collapsed in July 1982, large numbers of depositors lost money, including 150 credit unions and pension funds around the country. It was the first time since the Depression that such a thing had happened. Because bank deposits in the United States are protected by federal insurance, many people believe that Uncle Sam will come to the rescue if a bank fails. But that is true only for financial institutions covered by the Federal Deposit Insurance Corporation (FDIC) and only for deposits up to $100,000. In Penn Square's case, savings and loan associations had $22.4 million on deposit; credit unions had $107 million. Most of these individual accounts went over the $100,000 insurance limit (altogether, Penn Square had $190 million in uninsured deposits). According to the FDIC, which took over administration of the bank, these depositors probably would get back eighty cents on the dollar, but even that was not certain because Penn Square's major bank creditors, like Chase, were suing for a bigger share of its $37 million capital.

Penn Square underscored the precariousness of government insurance: Had there been a succession of such failures or a chain reaction, with one bank pulling down another, the FDIC would not have had enough money to cover even deposits up to $100,000. In 1974, when the Long Island–based Franklin National Bank collapsed, the FDIC's rescue package cost the corporation 40 percent of its funds. And in 1982 and 1983 the number and size of bank failures increased substantially. In February 1983, for example, Knoxville's United American Bank went under with an even bigger splash than Penn Square because it had more assets, or loans.* The ratio of insurance to deposits is about $1 to $81, and some congressmen think that safety net insufficient.

Because the FDIC loses money when it declares a bank insolvent, it will do almost anything, short of illegal loans, to avoid a bankruptcy. Thus it tends to ignore shoddy practices and funny deals in the hope that a troubled bank will somehow muddle through. Nor is the FDIC the only regulatory agency that delays beyond the point where preventive medicine can be effective. All three federal bank regulatory agencies are haunted by the fear that if they move decisively word will get out that a bank is in trouble, causing a run on the bank by panicky depositors. So for the most part they limit themselves to chiding bank offenders "not to do it anymore," which naturally only encourages management to go on gambling. Of the three—the FDIC, the Federal Reserve, and the Office of the Comptroller of the Currency—the Comptroller is generally cited as the most efficient, though its record is hardly reassuring. A study by the Government Accounting Office (GAO) found that 201 banks stayed on the Comptroller's problem list for two years or more between 1971 and 1975. "We noted a tendency by each supervisory agency," said GAO, "to delay formal action until a bank's problems had become so severe as to be difficult at best to correct."[1]

Dithering is also caused by bureaucratic inflexibility. Bank examiners should have been on Penn Square's premises, more or less continuously, beginning in 1980, when problems were first spotted, but examiners in the district were toiling away in other banks with impeccable records. As noted by a former deputy comptroller of the currency, "The general rule is that problem banks are underexamined and average banks overexamined."[2]

Ironically, the plethora of regulators contributes to laxity. In

---

* Bank regulators said that the principal cause of the bank's failure was insider loans to members of United America's board of directors and friends of chairman Jake Butcher, including Bert Lance, President Carter's director of the Office of Management and Budget. United American was later merged with First Tennessee National Corporation, the state's largest bank holding company.

addition to the FDIC, the Fed, and the Comptroller, every state has its own bank regulatory agency, and there are specialized agencies for certain institutions, like the Federal Home Loan Bank Board for savings and loan associations. A state-chartered bank, for instance, may be regulated by the Federal Reserve, the FDIC, and the state, but each agency tends to work independently, jealously guarding its prerogatives and information. In the Penn Square case the Comptroller failed to warn the Federal Reserve of the bank's problems, although the banks most affected, such as Chase Manhattan and Continental Illinois, are supervised by the Federal Reserve and the Fed should have been informed.[3]

Bankers complain that they are overregulated, and there is some truth in the contention that the duplication of agencies multiplies the paperwork. But when a real problem arises, none of the regulators wants to take responsibility.

Many bank regulators come from and often return to the industry they are supposed to discipline; they thus share the bankers' attitude that their institutions' internal rules are the best guarantee of regulation since, as one Federal Reserve director stated, "a banker is not going to cut off his nose" by engaging in dangerous lending practices. But, as shown by Chase Manhattan's experience with Drysdale and Penn Square,† this is precisely what greedy bankers do. If the regulators do not stop such practices—either out of fear that disciplinary action may call attention to a bank's plight or because they are too chummy with management—the bank's problems will likely worsen: It is the rare gambler who knows when to stop. Such was the case of Citibank, which ignored U.S. laws and engaged in a gambling spree in Latin America that made Penn Square seem like a minor folly.‡ A former deputy comptroller said that his office argued against such loans, only to be overruled by the Federal Reserve Board, which contended that they should not be challenged. The board's chairman, Paul Volcker, is an alumnus of Chase Manhattan and a member of the old-boy network of New York banks led by Chase and Citibank. In the dispute over foreign loans he has

† See previous chapter.
‡ See pp. 29–39 of this chapter for more on Citibank.

BANK REGULATORS...   ...AND THEIR TURFS

BANK REGULATORS...	...AND THEIR TURFS
Comptroller of the Currency	Nationally chartered banks
Federal Reserve Board	Bank holding companies Nationally chartered banks State-chartered banks that are members of the Federal Reserve
Federal Deposit Insurance Corp.	Nationally chartered banks FDIC-insured state banks and mutual savings banks
State banking supervisors	State-chartered banks

WHO SUPPLIES THE BANKS' SAFETY NET

THE BANKS

**Bank equity capital of
$37 billion**

**plus loan loss reserves of
$5.5 billion**

**cover total assets of
$888.6 billion**

THE FDIC

**Insurance funds totaling
$12.2 billion**

**cover deposits of
$988.9 billion**

THE FEDERAL RESERVE
Lender of last resort

Sources: Salomon Brothers, Federal Deposit Insurance Corp., and *Business Week* (Aug. 2, 1982).

consistently sided with the big banks, and because the Fed has more power and status than the Comptroller's office, Volcker's view has prevailed.[4]

Since the regulators are not doing their job, depositors need to know more about the institutions to which they entrust their money. In Penn Square's case, nobody—and certainly no depositors—thought to question a chain of supposed experts. Members of credit unions and savings and loan associations could hardly be blamed for assuming that the people in charge were law-abiding businessmen who knew what they were about. Not so: Seven institutions broke the law by depositing more than 10 percent of their net worth in Penn Square. (The aim of the 1981 law was to prevent a savings institution from putting too many eggs in one basket.) Several of them paid for flouting both law and common sense: According to the Federal Home Loan Bank Board, which regulates the thrifts, one was left insolvent, another was "severely impaired," and several others were "weakened" because of uninsured losses incurred from Penn Square.[5]

The investment committees of the credit unions and savings and loan institutions relied on money brokers to tell them where they could get the best return on their money, and in 1981 and the spring of 1982 the brokers were touting Penn Square, although the bank was hemorrhaging from the withdrawal of deposits by better-informed individuals. Money brokers are freelance salesmen who receive fees from banks for finding deposits of more than $100,000. Money brokerage is unregulated by the government, and while there are several respectable firms in the trade, such as Merrill Lynch and Salomon Brothers, there are also a host of fly-by-nights. All it takes to get into the business is a telephone. "Sometimes we get calls from brokers," said a savings and loan officer, "in which you can hear babies crying and televisions going in the background." Professional Asset Management, a large California money broker, warned clients in a letter that "a new crop of money finders has crawled out from the woodwork, operating from salesrooms, dealing with any obscure bank or savings and loan institutions who will deal with them, hawking certificates of deposit . . . with reckless abandon."[6]

But even the big, legitimate brokers make sad mistakes. PAM, a large Wall Street firm registered with the Securities and Exchange Commission, brought more deposits to Penn Square than did any other money broker. Its explanation was that the bank's year-end 1981 accounts looked excellent—even better than the Bank of America's. The accounts were signed by Peat, Marwick, Mitchell & Company, which audits more financial institutions than does any other accounting firm. "That's what scares me," said one money broker. "You used to think when a big auditing firm finished an audit, it was gospel."[7]

In congressional testimony Peat, Marwick representatives said that in auditing Penn Square they had followed procedures that are customary throughout the country.[8] If such is the case, the industry may indeed be in trouble. According to the Comptroller of the Currency, Peat, Marwick's audit was "unacceptable" because it inspected only 15 percent of Penn Square's loans when it should have looked at 80 percent. It also turned out that while the firm approved Penn Square's accounts for 1981, in a confidential letter to the bank's board it noted fourteen internal problems. A Peat, Marwick accountant gave the incredible excuse that his firm was prohibited by the accounting profession's standard of confidentiality from saying anything about these concerns to other banks or bank regulators.[9]

When Penn Square's directors were questioned as to why they had let the bank slide into a financial abyss, they pointed the finger at Peat, Marwick, which had told them, two months before the collapse, of the "truly remarkable and impressive" management changes that had taken place to improve the bank's prospects.[10] The directors said that Peat, Marwick's statements, as well as reassurances from the Comptroller of the Currency, had convinced them that the bank was in no real trouble. Since several of the directors had substantial financial dealings with the bank that were in violation of the law, their pose of naive trust looks a bit awkward. However, there was no doubt that the last link in the chain of "experts" was the Office of the Comptroller of the Currency, which knew of Penn Square's problems as early as April 1980 but "incredibly let the fire burn," in the words of the chairman of the House Subcommittee on Finance. To hear the regulators tell it, they had relied on the bank's directors and a new president, Eldon L. Beller, to douse the flames. But Beller, who was hired in 1981, later claimed that he had no authority over the bank's energy lending, which constituted 80 percent of Penn Square's loans and was the major source of its troubles. The Comptroller's office had viewed Beller's appointment as a satisfactory solution, an impression gained from the board of directors and Beller himself, who had originally assured the Comptroller's regional administrator that "he had the authority to clear up the problems." But Beller's views as to the extent of his authority are really beside the point, because as president he was legally responsible for the bank's activities.

Banks on the regulators' problem list are supposed to be closely monitored, but in Penn Square's case the Comptroller's office let sixteen months go by before it made a second audit, in April 1982, by which time it was too late. (How well the Comptroller's office is scrutinizing the other three hundred banks on its problem list can only be surmised.) Typical of the paper shuffling that prevails among government agencies, the Comptroller's office had informed the Justice Department in the late 1970s that one of Penn Square's officers might be liable for criminal prosecution. The Justice Department did nothing about it, the Comptroller's office forgot the matter, and the officer was still with the bank when it collapsed. (During the April 1982 audit the Comptroller's regulators found altered and falsified bank documents, as well as such other "substantial evidence of fraud" as three thousand missing, inadequate, or incorrect documents.)[11]*

The Comptroller also ignored Penn Square's change of auditors between 1980 and 1981, when it was on the problem list, although that should have been a red flag, according to the dean of the Graduate School of Business at Columbia University.[12] Unlike Peat, Marwick, the fired firm, Arthur Young & Company, had refused to give Penn Square a clean record because its reported reserves were inadequate for possible loan losses.

But perhaps the most revealing sign of weakness in the regulatory system was the fact that even in the last days before Penn Square's inevitable collapse the Comptroller of the Currency failed to warn other banks. According to the head of the Federal Home Loan Bank Board, the Comptroller instructed the board not to inform interested savings and loan institutions because

* See Chapter 12 for a discussion on ethics in accounting and auditing.

that "might precipitate the bank's closure."[13] The Oklahoma oil-
men who had benefited from Penn Square's largesse were better
informed. Robert Hefner III, whose G.H.K. Company had received sizable loans from the bank while Hefner was a Penn
Square stockholder, made a multimillion-dollar withdrawal from
the bank just days before the failure became official—on the advice, he said, of a "prominent New York financial institution."
Another oilman, who pulled out more than half a million dollars,
said he got "a tip from a friend of mine—a federal bank examiner."[14] Legal sources question such last-minute withdrawals by
people with inside knowledge, since no creditor has the right to
jump the line to the disadvantage of others.

Although the Comptroller of the Currency tried to shrug off
congressional criticism by claiming that Penn Square had been
an exceptional case, his office has a long history of ignoring obvious storm signals. The high regard for "secrecy," on the part of
auditors, regulators, and bankers, also contributed to Penn
Square's failure, said Fernand J. St. Germain, chairman of the
House Banking, Finance and Urban Affairs Committee. But such
hindsight is of little solace to the depositors, who lost at least $50
million. Nor has it had a salutary effect on the way bankers and
regulators operate.

***

Germain's opinion about bank secrecy is shared by other congressmen who have had dealings with bankers. Congressional
hearings reflect frustration and exasperation as bankers and bank
regulators repeatedly refuse to provide meaningful information.
While assuring the legislators that they are "on top" of the situation, bankers and regulators have shown that they either don't
know what they are talking about or are deliberately misleading
Congress and the public.[15]† "But," demanded an irate congressman, "why should the banks be given special treatment [on ac-

---

† In one case U.S. bankers refused to tell a Senate committee how much they
had on loan to the developing countries because of bank secrecy. It later turned
out that the real reason was that the bankers themselves lacked the figures
("International Debt, The Banks, and U.S. Foreign Policy," Committee on
Foreign Relations, U.S. Senate [Washington, D.C.: Government Printing Office,
1977]).

countability] when, as the bankers themselves state, they are a business like any other?"[16]

The bigger the bank, the less likely it is to be deterred by government overseers, mere gnats buzzing around an elephant. Small banks may be forced to pay dearly for their sins, but the big ones know that the most they need fear is a slap on the wrist, since the government will do nothing to jeopardize their solid reputations. "The Federal Reserve takes the position that it cannot make a judgment [on the big banks] because such a judgment might lead to a lack of confidence," explained a congressional source.[17]

Of the giants, Citibank is the recognized champion at running rings around the regulators. "Citibank's role," said a congressional critic, "is to defy the law."[18] As noted in a memorandum prepared by a Citibank vice president, the bank's management "feels it can defend all the tricks it is presently engaged in [and] receive no stronger than a sharp reprimand and a 'don't do it anymore' "—assuming, of course, that the regulators even discover the "tricks."[19]

The vice president's memo, which dealt with illegal foreign-currency transactions and loans, came to light when David Edwards, an officer in Citibank's international division, blew the whistle—and was fired for acting "in a manner that is detrimental to the best interests of Citibank." Edwards made the mistake of thinking he was doing Citibank a favor by bringing the matter to the attention of its board, not knowing that it accorded with a policy laid down in 1975 by Citibank's chairman, Walter B. Wriston.[20] After his dismissal, Edwards took a carton full of Citibank documents to the Securities and Exchange Commission (SEC), which opened a three-year investigation.

The results of the SEC probe were shocking. Not only had Citibank engaged in questionable foreign exchange practices to avoid taxes; its subsidiaries in Europe, Latin America, and Asia were employing "rinky-dink deals," in the words of a Citibank vice president, to evade legal requirements on bank reserves, liquidity (cash on hand), and lending limits. "Getting around tax and monetary regulations is bad enough," said Richard Dale, a specialist on international bank regulation who is affiliated with the Rockefeller

Foundation. "But getting around so-called prudential regulations, that is most dangerous." Karin M. Lissakers, an authority on international banking, added, "The overriding issue demonstrated by the documents [uncovered by the SEC] is the ability of banks like Citibank to deliberately subvert the rules and policies of sovereign governments. While banks and funds move freely across national borders, bank regulators and government authorities do not."[21]

Citibank's tax dodge was achieved through what in bank slang is called "parking." To reduce taxes in Western Europe on profits from foreign-currency sales, Citibank shifted the funds, by means of bogus transactions and a double set of accounting books, to its branches in the Bahamas, where such taxes on profits are much lower or nonexistent.[22] Parking, or booking, foreign-exchange transactions in the Bahamas is common among multinational institutions and is not illegal, provided that the paper transactions are not "contrived" and do not violate tax laws. (A "contrived" transaction is one for which there is no legitimate buyer or seller and where the price is inconsistent with prevailing markets.) According to the SEC investigation, Citibank covered up "contrived" transactions by using "thousands of false documents [to maintain an] appearance of legality." After Edwards said his piece in 1977, the bank "changed" documents and accounting procedures to mislead government authorities still further. For instance, parking was done by telephone so that "no record [of the transaction] ever appeared on the European branch's books." Internal memos show that Citibank's senior management was entirely aware that the bank was breaking the law. "Strictly confidential treatment is necessary," noted one such document, because "disclosure could mean instructions to discontinue, and might involve tax claims and penalties." Another memo admitted, "There is no doubt in anybody's mind that if all the facts were to emerge, we would not have a case."[23] Contrary to Wriston's denials, the SEC investigation indicated that he was informed of these illegal deals, which were detailed in a Citibank report prepared at his behest. Wriston told the SEC that he could not recall ever seeing the report, even though a copy, on record in Congress, bears Wriston's initials and a note from him to the bank's comptroller to "be sure and follow up on these points."[24]

Wriston's involvement in such wheeling-dealing reflects the

style of banking today. The lanky, athletic chairman is generally regarded as the most influential banker in the United States—the head of New York's biggest bank and the profession's most outspoken advocate of deregulation. Like Willard Butcher at Chase Manhattan, Wriston, sixty-four, made his career at the bank, but he did not have to contend with David Rockefeller or the political stigma attached to "David's Bank." The son of a successful academic, Wriston was brought up in a strict Methodist home where it was forbidden to smoke or drink or on Sunday to listen to the radio or go to the movies. But somewhere along the climb to power the values of that early religious upbringing were blurred, and by the time he became Citibank's president in 1970 Wriston had established a reputation as a ruthless, autocratic driver with a sharp tongue, who invested Citibank with a "Marine Corps spirit of real toughness," in the words of *Time* magazine. The toughest of the tough, Wriston consistently has taken a harder line than other New York City bankers vis-à-vis efforts by the financially beleaguered city to raise money, and New York officials charge that Citibank's tax evasion schemes have contributed to the city's plight. The city has hit the bank with $30 million in back taxes that it claims Citibank evaded by parking in the Bahamas financial transactions that were actually handled by the New York office and thus taxable. A Citibank senior vice president's attempts to dissuade city hall from taxing the bank got nowhere, because the authorities think Wriston has treated New York like a developing country.[25]‡

Under Wriston's management the bank began cutting corners in the 1970s in the drive for profits. A 406-page report by the Ralph Nader Study Group alleged, among other things, that Citibank invested trust funds in its parent holding company, Citicorp, to the bank's own advantage, and that it had failed to disclose interest-rate charges on certain checking accounts. While minor compared to the SEC's later revelations, such charges reflected the operating style at "Walter's Bank."[26]

Equally revealing of the man was his smear of Edwards after

‡ Citibank's inflexibility has made it the most unpopular American bank in Latin America. For example, it was the only U.S. bank to refuse local demands to enable Latin-American investors to purchase stock in foreign bank branches.

he blew the whistle on Citibank. Wriston told *Executive* magazine that Edwards' "famous accusations didn't arrive until after he was dismissed" and that Edwards was fired because he was incompetent. As amply proved by the SEC's chief investigative lawyer, Wriston's charges had no basis in fact. "This effort to portray Edwards simply as a disgruntled and incompetent employee is patently incorrect and unfair," wrote SEC lawyer Thompson von Stein. (Citibank's general counsel and senior vice president, Hans Angermueller, later acknowledged that Edwards' firing "wasn't fair.")[27] A brash young Texan with a flair for dreaming up new ideas for foreign-currency deals, Edwards was as ambitious as Wriston had been in his thirties. He was perfectly willing to exploit any legal loophole to earn money for the bank, but he balked at breaking the law because he considered it a bad business practice. "That's the bottom line," he told his Citibank superiors while trying to persuade them to end illegal parking activities. "We risk being tossed out on our ass from some of these countries."[28]

Citibank, which has earned a reputation for taking risks, apparently didn't care. An executive vice president warned Edwards that "you get along by going along," and that "anything that threatens the club from within must be expelled." "It's not a club!" Edwards retorted. "It's a bank." He began quoting from the bank's printed code of ethics, whereupon the vice president told him that he himself had written the code. "But who guards the guards?" wondered Edwards.[29]

In his public statements Wriston has made clear that whereas certain people need guards, bankers should enjoy unbridled freedom. Thus, while chastising the government for interfering with the banks, he has frequently complained of the lack of restraints on the American press, particularly on the issue of ethics. Yet lack of ethics was precisely what Citibank's "rinky-dink deals" entailed.

Unlike other wheeler-dealers, Wriston's behavior has never been influenced by a desire for great wealth. As his father once remarked, the family "never had any money in the house" when Wriston was growing up, and "if [Walter's] wife didn't take care of his own business, he'd be in the poorhouse."[30] While obviously an exaggeration—Wriston is the highest-paid bank executive in the United States—he has exhibited more interest in power than money. But power can be a dangerous weapon when not prudently used, and Citibank's evasion of laws designed to protect depositors could hardly be described as prudent.

After Edwards went to the SEC, Citibank attempted to put a good face on its illegal activities by employing a New York law firm, Shearman & Sterling, to make a report to the commission on his charges. But the objectivity of the 129-page report was called into question by *The Wall Street Journal,* which pointed out that Wriston was married to a former Shearman & Sterling associate, and that the bank's senior executive vice president was a former partner of the law firm. The SEC staff report was more blunt: It called the report "an elaborate, expensive, sophisticated whitewash, from start to finish."[31]

Citibank was willing to break the law because of the enormous profits involved. "To put this in perspective," explained the SEC staff, "Citibank foreign-exchange traders make thousands of transactions per day worldwide, many of which are of $5 million or more. Using just a one percent differential in 'selling' and 'repurchasing' a currency with Nassau . . . one $5 million trade can . . . transfer $50,000 of profits to a tax haven. . . ." By 1980 foreign-currency transactions accounted for 35 percent of Citibank's reported earnings. Although the bank was later forced to pay nearly $11 million in back taxes and penalties to the Swiss, West German, and French authorities, it clearly profited from breaking the law. What will probably never be known is the extent to which Citibank and other large banks benefited from driving down the value of the dollar—one of the allegations made at the time of the Edwards case. Since banks handle most foreign-exchange transactions, they are in a position to precipitate currency changes by selling or buying large quantities of a country's money. Although most nations enacted strict currency regulations in the 1970s to prevent such speculation, the SEC investigation showed that Citibank was able to get around them by "cooking the books."[32]

As foreseen by Citibank management, revelations of its illegal currency dealings provoked no more than a "don't do it anymore" letter from the Comptroller of the Currency. The attitude among bank regulators in Washington was that it was the

Europeans' lookout if an American bank broke their laws.[33] But the wisdom of so narrow a view can be questioned. For one thing, like most other big U.S. banks, Citibank pays practically no U.S. taxes. Citibank filings with the SEC, for example, indicate that its holding company paid no federal income tax in 1980.[34] One way to reduce U.S. taxes is to juggle foreign tax credits and investment tax credits (ITCs), the idea being to reduce the former in order to increase the latter. A complex interplay between the ITCs and foreign tax credits makes it advantageous for a bank to increase its U.S. taxable income and minimize its foreign taxable income in order to claim a higher ITC, which can then be "leased," or sold, to other banks or corporations for a profit. The result of this tax shell game is that the bank not only pays no U.S. taxes but also earns money by leasing its unused ITC credits to other banks and corporations.

In addition to the tax dodge, Citibank's behavior raised disturbing questions about the broader issues of policy and bank safety. For example, the SEC documents showed that Citibank subsidiaries, by temporarily transferring assets, had improved their balance sheets in anticipation of inspection. Since regulators in various countries use different fiscal years for examination purposes, the subsidiaries could easily mislead them by shifting high-quality assets from branch to branch as the days of reckoning came around. Citibank documents obtained by the SEC showed that in this way the bank's officials sought to circumvent regulations intended to ensure bank safety and to control the money supply.[35] Thus Citibank's West German subsidiary routed several billion dollars of loans and deposits through the Nassau branch in order to "evade" German reserve requirements. Such reserves —a form of insurance required by most Western countries—reduce the amount of money a bank can invest in loans. So the choice boils down to safety or profits à la Penn Square. Putting a bank's "goodies" briefly on a balance sheet to impress regulators is "dangerous," said the SEC report, because it touches on the "safety and soundness of the bank."[36]

Citibank, of course, claimed that it had done nothing wrong, a "pious public posture" that stood in "sharp contrast" to its real activities, said the SEC report. It also pointed out that, like other large banks, Citibank wanted to have its cake and eat it, too—

demanding that the U.S. Government (i.e., the taxpayer) bail out the banks when they get in trouble while at the same time opposing congressional efforts to give bank regulators greater access to bank records.* In Germany, for instance, Citibank officials, with the "approval" of the bank's head office in New York, used the excuse of "bank secrecy" to prevent examiners from the Comptroller of the Currency from seeing the books of Citibank's Nassau unit, which were kept in Frankfurt.[37]

With $119 billion in assets, Citibank is the United States' second largest financial institution, after the Bank of America; if it went under because of some foreign gamble, it might well throw the U.S. economy into a tailspin. Two thirds of Citibank's income comes from abroad, and a large chunk of that business is in financially unstable Latin America, where at least eight countries are in default. Citibank is believed to have between $8 and $10 billion on loan to Mexico, Argentina, and Brazil—all countries in economic straits. Yet Citibank makes no mention of its exposure in Latin America in its annual reports. Concerned stockholders may, however, read the fine print, which in the 1981 report was part of a footnote to the notes attached to the financial statements. It said that Citibank loans to Brazil totaled nearly $5 billion, an amount greater than Citibank's capital of $4.8 billion, or the total equity of the bank's shareholders.[38]

According to the House Subcommittee on General Oversight, Citibank has been disguising loans made to Latin-American countries in order to circumvent bank regulations.[39] The problem is all the more serious because some Latin countries (e.g., Brazil) deliberately underreport their foreign debt to avoid upsetting the international loan markets. The subcommittee estimated that at least $61 billion of the Latin-American foreign debt is owed to U.S. banks, but if other banks have been following Citibank's practice of hiding loans, as appears to be the case from evidence in the SEC documents, the true figure is probably much higher.

The House subcommittee also found that Citibank's numerous kinds of evasions had one thing in common: "They resulted in a mismatching of maturities of loans and deposits." In other words, Citibank held more money in deposits maturing early

* See Chapter 11, pp. 225, 235–36, 246–49, and Chapter 12, pp. 255–56.

(current liabilities) than it had in short-term loans (current assets). "The cumulative mismatching of deposits and loans placed the bank in an illiquid position [where] the bank's exposure relative to its capital was high," said a report by the subcommittee's staff. Mismatching deposits and loans has brought down many a bank in the past; as pointed out by the subcommittee report, the practice could cause Citibank a "loss of confidence" in the international marketplace, setting off "a cumulative chain reaction eroding the profits of the bank and its holding company."[40]

Compounding the financial risk, Citibank itself did not even know the extent of its own vulnerability. "Liquidity is not qualified to keep the numbers before management on an ongoing basis," a Citibank vice president had warned Wriston. Unaware of the extent of its own financial exposure, Citibank appeared oblivious to the damage it might inflict beyond its own balance sheets. In Germany, said the House staff report, Citibank's evasions "undermined [the] monetary prudential regulations" established by the government to ensure stable financial markets and safeguard local depositors. Similarly, Citibank's practice of evasion "undermines U.S. prudential regulations." Such "tricks" pose a serious threat to international financial stability. Banks rely on each other for the majority of their short-term funds, so "the problems of one bank can be transmitted to other banks through the interbank market." And Citibank is no ordinary bank. When it gambles, the entire financial system is in on the bet. "Since Citicorp is one of the largest banks worldwide and the largest player in the Eurodollar interbank market, it has the potential for creating a very systemic disturbance," the subcommittee staff concluded. Congressman John Dingell, chairman of the House subcommittee, summed up the problem: "The extent to which Citibank was able to circumvent and subvert local regulations raises the spectre of large multinational banks becoming a law unto themselves beyond the control of national governments. The present international financial crisis may simply be the most serious manifestation of this loss of control."[41]

**

The SEC revelations about Citibank were shocking for what they said about the United States' most aggressive bank, and equally shocking for what they revealed about the SEC itself. After proving conclusively that Citibank had been systematically breaking the law, the SEC's enforcement staff refused to take any action against the bank on the ground that its pursuit of unlawful profits accorded with "reasonable and standard business judgment." The SEC also concluded that Citibank's management had no duty to disclose improper actions since the bank had never claimed its top officers possessed "honesty and integrity."[42]

Citibank's chief defendants at the SEC were John S. R. Shad, chairman of the commission, and John M. Fedders, head of its enforcement division. Both are Reagan appointees. Fedders said that he did "not subscribe to the theory that a company that violates tax and exchange control regulations is a bad corporation." This view was upheld by Shad, a longtime supporter and fund-raiser for Reagan and a former vice chairman of the brokerage firm E. F. Hutton Group, Inc. Under Shad the SEC became a promoter of "capital formation" and was directed to reduce the amount of negative information about itself that a corporation must disclose to the commission. But SEC holdovers from the Carter administration disagreed and leaked the contents of the Citibank investigation to the New York *Times*. The dissidents charged that in contrast to the Carter period, when the SEC made headlines by exposing large-scale corporate bribery, Shad had turned the commission away from its statutory duty to protect investors in order to protect the corporations it regulates. The Citibank case was vital, they said, because it addressed the issue of management integrity.[43]

In the end—but no thanks to Shad and Fedders—Citibank paid the penalty of having its dirty laundry aired on the front pages of the New York press. Congress then took up the issue during hearings on the overseas lending practices of large U.S. financial institutions. "The SEC abdicated its responsibility under the law," said Congressman Albert Gore (D-Tenn.), a member of the subcommittee holding the hearings. "The SEC's decision to overrule its staff and drop the case told me that the new policy over there is to look the other way so long as the perpetrator is wearing a three-piece suit."[44]

Nevertheless, the publicity was not expected to hurt the bank's standing with investors. The episode "will not really have much effect in any future evaluation of Citibank," said a banking analyst at Paine Webber Mitchell Hutchins Inc. "We continue to like its aggressive management."[45]

But it was just such "aggressive management" that had caused Citibank so many problems, from bad bets on interest rates, credit cards, and mortgage loans to gambles on foreign countries that would never pay their debts. Even before the SEC revelations, America's two principal credit-rating agencies, Standard & Poor's and Moody's Investor Service, lowered the bank's debt rating because of its "reduced profitability levels." Standard & Poor's noted that Citibank had outstanding $22 billion in low, fixed-interest loans, and that in order to cover them it was borrowing funds at much higher rates—at a substantial loss to the bank.[46]

Back in the 1970s, when Citibank was aiming to be first among U.S. banks, Chairman Wriston rashly set a goal of 15 percent a year in earnings growth. For most of the decade Citibank met that goal, but in the process it endangered longer-term profits and stability. Citibank representatives in foreign countries were not asked to estimate the likelihood of repayment when they pushed loans, as long as they could demonstrate a 15 percent annual growth rate. But in the 1980s, when countries all over the world were announcing their inability to pay the interest—never mind the principal—these loans pulled down Citibank's earnings. The bank's "aggressive management" also blanketed the United States with twenty-six million unsolicited credit cards in a bid to corner that market. "Naturally," said one observer, "people with credit problems accepted the offer." Such consumer operations cost the bank $225 million in 1980 and 1981. "The reality," said *The New Republic*'s financial writer, William Quirk, "is that Citibank is bust. The true value of what it owns is less than what it owes."[47]

The market's response to Citibank's troubles has been harsh. The bank's stock is selling for half the price it fetched a decade ago. Since 1979 earnings have been dropping steadily, and investors who bought shares on the strength of Wriston's 15 percent promise have since dumped them because of the bank's increasingly poor performance. While the rise and fall of a bank's stock is purely a market judgment, it cannot be disassociated from the goals and values of the people who run the bank. As pointed out by the SEC investigators, Citibank's managers had shown themselves lacking in integrity, and while this may be "reasonable and standard business judgment," it may also go far to explain why so many U.S. banks and industries are in trouble today. "The public tolerates white-collar crime because it is presented to them as victimless," said a specialist in financial crimes. "They don't realize that someone always pays."[48]

If there is fraud in a bank, for example, an insurance company pays—and immediately hikes its rates to the bank, which passes on the extra cost to depositors in the form of higher service charges. If there is gross negligence, as in the Penn Square case, depositors pay. And if Citibank goes bust because it has broken laws that are meant to ensure a bank's safety, American taxpayers are going to pay.†

U.S. sociologists say that there is a difference, in the popular moral judgment, between a businessman or banker who may "trifle" with the law and street criminals who "really" break it. The difference arises, of course, because of the fear of physical violence, but in a lifetime of crime muggers will not steal what white-collar thieves take in a single year—more than $40 billion.‡

---

† See Chapter 11, pp. 225, 235–36, 246–49.
‡ Estimate of the U.S. Chamber of Commerce.

ROGUES' GALLERY—Chapter 3

MEYER LANSKY, financial genius of organized crime; headquartered in Miami; died in 1983.

SAM COHEN, a Lansky associate who previously controlled Miami National Bank.

IRVIN FREEDMAN, veteran real estate wheeler-dealer convicted in Outrigger condominium scandal in Miami, in which Miami National, Citibank, and Chase Manhattan were stung for $20.3 million in fraudulent loans.

LEO GREENFIELD, notorious Miami attorney and Freedman's partner in Outrigger, for which he was indicted but acquitted.

JOSEPH STEFAN, president of Miami National, who was convicted for his part in the Outrigger scandal; unindicted co-conspirator in New York bank-financed Nixon slush fund.

TRUMAN A. SKINNER, Miami National's lawyer and chairman of its loan committee; indicted in Outrigger case and pleaded guilty to misdemeanors; senior member of Helliwell, Melrose and DeWolf, a CIA-connected law firm in Miami.

MICHAEL CALANDRA, a Chase Manhattan vice president who loaned money to Freedman and was indicted in Outrigger case.

ROBERT MARLIN, Florida real estate wheeler-dealer; a partner in takeover of City National Bank; later formed part of a group attempting alleged takeover of Southeast Banking Corporation, Florida's largest bank; former member of board of directors of Miami National Bank and owner of now defunct L & C Construction Company involved in Outrigger scandal.

JOSEPH KOSOW, Boston moneylender with unsavory reputation in nursing home business; a onetime partner of Marlin in City National Bank takeover.

JOSEPH KLEIN, wheeler-dealer in Florida real estate; involved in mortgage deal with City National Bank.

ALBERTO DUQUE, Colombian entrepreneur and Marlin's partner in City National Bank takeover; charged by twenty-four banks with fraudulent misuse of loans.

DONALD BEAZLEY, named president of City National Bank in 1982; former president of the Nugan Hand banking group in Australia connected to Southeast Asian heroin trade and CIA (see Chapter 4).

Chapter 3

How lax management invites criminal infiltrators and bank robberies.

Much research and money have gone into the science of bank security, yet some of the biggest robberies are committed by men armed only with a smile. They get away with the money because slack management, greed for profits, and corner cutting encourage bank executives to deal with questionable customers. The bankers at first receive small, then increasingly larger, gifts in thinly disguised kickbacks; the kickbacks lead to questionable loans and eventually to bank fraud. That is the story of the Outrigger scandal in which Citibank and Chase Manhattan were stung for $20.3 million by con men connected to organized crime. Chase was robbed because it was so eager to drum up business that it failed to enforce internal regulations for loans, as in the Drysdale and Penn Square cases. For its part, Citibank did not inquire into the ethics or professional background of the people it employed—and paid through the nose for that omission.

Outrigger is the name of a luxurious condominium in North Miami begun in 1971 but never finished. Its promoters were Irvin Freedman, a veteran real estate wheeler-dealer; Leo Greenfield, a notorious Miami attorney; and Kenneth I. Wilpon, a New York City developer.[1] Wilpon had excellent contacts with Citibank, which suggested he seek financing for the Outrigger project from its wholly owned subsidiary, Miami National Bank. Miami National had previously been controlled by a henchman of Meyer Lansky, for many years the financial genius of organized crime, and thanks to these Mob connections the bank remained in excellent financial health. However, the bank's then holding company,

Data Lease Financial Corporation, ran into difficulties and had to forfeit Miami National to Citibank in 1975 as collateral for an unpaid loan.

Wilpon was introduced to Miami National's president, Joseph Stefan, a New York banker sent in by Citibank—and approved by the Federal Reserve—to clean up the smell lingering from the Lansky period. Stefan said later that he welcomed Wilpon because he was a "veteran customer of Citibank [which] introduced him as the best thing since apple pie."[2] Wilpon also met Truman A. Skinner, the bank's lawyer, chairman of its loan committee, and a member of one of Miami's most prestigious law firms, Helliwell, Melrose and DeWolf. As a result of these meetings, Miami National put together a $7.7 million mortgage package for the Outrigger project and directly invested $1.2 million. Wilpon's partners, Freedman and Greenfield, were themselves in no position to approach the bank, having already been sued by several Dade County banks for failure to repay loans, a detail overlooked by both Citibank and its Miami National.

The mortgage loans were only the first in a series to be obtained by Wilpon, Greenfield, and Freedman; bank records show that in 1977 and 1978 the trio got several personal loans from Citibank's Miami National, failed to repay them, and then got more loans.[3] Greenfield also helped his client, Philadelphia mobster Michael Grasso, Jr., to obtain a share of Outrigger's mortgage with Miami National funds. At the time Grasso was facing a charge of defrauding the Federal Housing Administration (he was later convicted).[4] Nor was Grasso the only questionable character involved. According to undercover police, the Outrigger Club was a meeting place for, among other crime figures, Santo Trafficante, syndicate boss for the southeastern United States.

Contacts with the Mob were not always felicitious for Outrigger's promoters, however. One such encounter was a conversation between Freedman and a representative of the Carlo Gambino crime family (who was known as "The Wop") that was taped by the Miami Organized Crime Bureau. "You got nice children," The Wop told Freedman. "You got a nice wife. Pay the fucking money. What the hell. You wanna get killed?"[5]

The upshot was that Freedman agreed to Mob rake-offs on the

Outrigger project for everything from carpets to construction contracts. Outrigger building subcontracts were given to organized-crime figures, and one was employed as the Outrigger's construction supervisor.

During the Miami National Bank's association with Outrigger, the Citibank subsidiary was stung for $2.8 million. A Justice Department Organized Crime Strike Force found that the bank had exceeded its legal lending limits by at least $600,000 in loans to Outrigger and its shareholders. Lawyer Truman Skinner and the bank's president, Joseph Stefan, also were charged with doctoring Miami National's annual report by underreporting losses, "thus grossly misstating the true financial condition" of the bank.[6] The Justice Department further charged that the pair had filed fake bank documents, made loans to "straw" representatives of Freedman and Greenfield, authorized unsecured loans to Wilpon, lied to the government bank examiners, and participated in a securities fraud.[7]

This hanky-panky by such ostensibly respectable figures as a veteran New York banker and a prominent Miami lawyer also says a good deal about the present state of banking. For, appearances notwithstanding, both Stefan and Skinner had a questionable past, and no one had bothered to check their credentials when they came to Miami National Bank. Before assuming the presidency of Miami National, Stefan was chief administrative officer of the Security National Bank of Hempstead, N.Y., which was declared insolvent in 1975 because of speculation in Long Island's real estate market. That same year a federal grand jury indicted several Security National officers for operating a secret, bank-financed slush fund for the 1972 Nixon campaign. Stefan was named as an unindicted co-conspirator.[8] For his part, Skinner was a ranking member of the Miami law firm of Paul Helliwell, a former CIA agent who used Florida banks for the benefit of organized crime figures.* Nor did Citibank make any inquiries about real estate developer Wilpon when he went to Miami National for Outrigger financing, although he had been involved with New York Congressman John M. Murphy, of Abscam fame,

* See Chapter 5.

in a questionable Long Island real estate deal that was the subject of a federal grand jury probe.[9]

If Citibank was lax, Chase Manhattan was even more so—and paid with a $17.5 million loan loss. Irvin Freedman took advantage of Chase's negligent lending procedures by applying to his old school chum, Chase Vice President Michael Calandra, for twenty-one unsecured loans, even though Freedman was already involved in two bankruptcy proceedings and had been sued by some three dozen creditors, including several banks. Calandra was in charge of commercial loans for the bank's Brooklyn division and had been with the bank for sixteen years. Consequently Chase's senior management did not challenge the loans made to Fredman by Calandra and his assistant, Jonathan Levine, who had been with Chase for fifteen years. Supposedly used to finance the Outrigger condominium and a Florida Keys hotel owned by Freedman, the money was diverted to Freedman's personal use through phony bank transactions and payments to dummy corporations.[10]

Freedman was not the only doubtful customer to benefit from Calandra's largesse. He also lent money to Freedman's associate, James J. Durkin, whose Pennsylvania coal mines were under investigation by the Pennsylvania Crime Commission because of "questionable . . . activities." A $4 million loan made by Calandra to a Durkin company was never repaid. Another borrower who enjoyed Calandra's favor was John P. Galanis, a former New York stock promoter charged with securities fraud in New York and Canada. In court testimony Galanis said that Calandra knew of his criminal convictions.[11]

Daniel Segal, president of a New York mortgage-brokerage firm that dealt with Calandra, said that he was able to get away with his "ingenious scenario of high finance [through] the basic principle of 'borrowing from Peter to pay Paul' "—or, in blunter terms, through a form of blackmail. Segal claimed his company was forced by Calandra to lend Freedman $375,000 in order to obtain Calandra's approval for a $900,000 loan. Chase wasn't blameless either, he said. "Where was Calandra's supervisor while all this was going on? How could [Chase] let a man like Calandra operate for so long and permit him to get involved in [such] situations?"[12]

When Calandra's house of cards collapsed in early 1980, Chase's senior management was forced to ask the same questions. While the bank's giant size obviously contributed to the latitude that Calandra was allowed, Chase's well-known eagerness for profits was also a factor. And though the bank had elaborate controls to prevent such lending practices, they were never put into effect. Thus a bank order stipulating detailed financial statements from new borrowers was not applied to Freedman. And while Chase had a credit-review policy when the Calandra loans were being made, individual loans were not reviewed unless the officer involved brought them to the attention of the credit-review committee—the equivalent of blowing the whistle on oneself.[13]

In 1982, eleven years after the Outrigger was started in Miami, a Florida federal grand jury indicted Freedman, Greenfield, Stefan, and Skinner (the latter two of Citibank) on charges ranging from racketeering to bank fraud. Freedman was found guilty of seventeen charges, including racketeering; Stefan of fifteen counts, from misuse of bank funds to mail fraud; and Skinner pleaded guilty to misdemeanors before the trial. Though acquitted, Greenfield could face retrial, according to the local prosecutor. Meanwhile, Chase Manhattan's Calandra and Levine were indicted in New York for their part in the scandal, along with Pennsylvania coal operator James Durkin.[14]

***

Among those involved in the Outrigger project was Florida real estate promoter Robert Marlin, whose now defunct L & C Construction Company was the general contractor for Outrigger. According to the Justice Department, Miami National agreed to underwrite a $2.03 million guarantee for L & C, thereby further exposing the bank to demands by Freedman and Greenfield, who could have claimed from Miami National had L & C failed to perform. (Because of the risk involved, banks normally do not provide such guarantees for construction companies.) At the time Marlin was a member of the bank's board of directors and its loan committee.[15] Although the Comptroller of the Currency ruled that Miami National did not have the authority to sign the underwriting agreement, Truman Skinner, the bank's lawyer, who was later indicted, ordered the then vice president to authorize it. Skinner did not disclose his potential conflict of interest when he became a director of Viking General, L & C's parent company, nor did anyone at the bank think to question why it was signing an agreement with a company owned by Marlin, a Miami National director.[16]

Although Marlin was not charged with any wrongdoing in the Outrigger affair, it became an issue when he set his sights on Florida's largest bank, the $6.4 billion Southeast Banking Corporation. Marlin's interest in banks was not misplaced: They offer a better source of speculative gain than almost any other business in Florida, including real estate. Thanks to Miami's emergence as the principal commercial bridge between Latin America and the United States, and to billions of dollars in "hot" money from Europe and Latin America, out-of-state and foreign banks have flocked to the area. In order to get a piece of the action, they are prepared to pay premium prices for local banks.

Marlin and his partner, Miami accountant Jack D. Burstein, cashed in on the bank bonanza in the early 1980s by acquiring stock in a medium-sized Miami bank, City National Bank (CNB),† at bargain prices from different shareholders. They then invited a young Colombian wheeler-dealer, Alberto Duque, to join them in a voting trust‡ to gain control of the $500-million-asset bank. (Another partner in the deal, Boston moneylender Joseph Kosow, dropped out, presumably to avoid unwanted attention from the Federal Reserve Board. Kosow, who was investigated by the Securities and Exchange Commission, has an unsa-

† Like Miami National, City National had a murky history. It was suspected of being used for the deposit of illegal "skim" money from casinos in the Bahamas during the late 1960s. One of the bank's directors, Max Orovitz, was a buddy of Mob financier Meyer Lansky and had been convicted of stock fraud in New York. ("Special Issue—Nixon and the Elections," *NACLA's Latin America & Empire Report* [Vol. VI, No. 8, October 1972].)

‡ In a voting trust the members agree to vote their stock as a single individual, thus giving them more power collectively

vory reputation in the nursing home business.[17]* Since at this point the number of stockholders had dropped to less than three hundred, CNB no longer had to report to the Securities and Exchange Commission or issue public reports on the state of the bank, making any takeover bid impossible to detect.

Marlin and Burstein subsequently sold their shares to Duque, who was so anxious to gain control of a Florida bank that he paid the pair two and a half times the market value for their CNB stock, giving them a $20 million profit on funds invested for little more than a year. In buying out the bank's majority shareholders, Duque sidestepped the interests of the two hundred minority shareholders, whose 12.5 percent interest in CNB was rendered virtually valueless. Not only did they have no say in running the bank, they had no means of selling their stock, since public trading of CNB shares had been suspended. Naturally this did not sit well with the minority stockholders, who filed a class-action suit against Marlin, Burstein, and Duque, in which they claimed that the trio had entered into a conspiracy "to defraud the minority shareholders of the true value of their shares."[18]

Undaunted by such complaints, Marlin and Burstein proceeded to buy up shares in Southeast. The idea, according to Southeast's lawyers, was to "turn a quick profit in a similar manner [to CNB] on the purchase and sale of Southeast securities."[19] Certainly Southeast would be a plum for any large out-of-state bank looking for an instant network of branches in Florida. However, to gain control an out-of-state bank would have to pay a premium price, as Duque had done to acquire the stock of Marlin and Burstein. And as in the CNB case, minority stockholders would be left in the cold.[20]

Southeast being considerably bigger than CNB, Marlin and Burstein brought in several partners. They included Samuel Adler, who was found guilty of breach of fiduciary duty in a Florida real estate case; Frank Tolin, a real estate developer in the CNB deal; and a mysterious group of Frenchmen, one of whom listed El Salvador as his address. They told the Securities and Exchange Commission that

---

* The Florida Secretary of State's office lists Kosow's company at the same address as Marlin's American Capital Corporation.

they intended to buy at least 24.9 percent of Southeast stock, and by the winter of 1982 they had acquired 14.4 percent.[21] A second block of stock, totaling 9.2 percent, was bought at the same time by a Florida physician, Dr. M. Lee Pearce, and the Pan American Hospital Corporation in Miami. Though alleging that they did not intend to take over the bank, the two groups accounted for more than 23 percent of Southeast shares, making them the largest stockholders in the bank. (Southeast's stock is widely dispersed, and the only other large block, 5.5 percent, is held by Morgan Guaranty Trust.) "If someone picks up a quarter of your stock, that's not a fish—it's a shark," commented a New York bank analyst.

Southeast did not help itself by engaging in a long and debilitating struggle with Chemical Bank of New York for control of Florida National Banks of Florida, Inc., a Jacksonville-based bank holding company. In pursuing Florida National, Southeast's management hoped to make their institution too big for even the largest New York bank to swallow when interstate banking is legalized. But the immediate effect was that the value of Southeast's stock dropped with each reverse in its fight with Chemical.[22] However unwise its pursuit of Florida National, Southeast had good reason to fear the consequences of a takeover.[23] Marlin was the main cause for concern because of his long history as a speculator in Florida real estate,† as well as his ties to CNB and his involvement in the Outrigger scandal at Miami National. Like Miami National, CNB engaged in questionable lending practices, such as some dubious mortgages that police said were picked up by CNB on Miami's Cricket Club condominium. There were several interesting coincidences about the mortgages. For one thing, the Cricket Club condominium was owned

---

†On several occasions in the 1970s Marlin's Viking General Corporation was charged by Florida state and county authorities with violating land-sale regulations and misusing mortgage funds. In one case investigated by the Florida state legislature's Select House Committee, Marlin was reported by the Miami Herald to have been unable to account for $424,000 missing from an escrow account for investors who had purchased land from his company. In a seventy-eight-page report on nearly $1 billion in rip-offs from the Florida mortgage business, the committee singled out Viking for fraudulent land sales. On

by Alvin Malnik, Meyer Lansky's alleged heir apparent, and Sam Cohen, a Lansky associate who had controlled the Miami National Bank. Among those with apartments in the condominium were Marlin, Alberto Duque, and Joseph Kosow, Marlin's one-time partner in the CNB voting trust.[24] Miami police also thought it interesting that the Cricket Club's annex was sold to Joseph Klein and his father Zola. The son has a record of fraudulent real estate dealings in Florida and is connected to organized-crime figures.[25] In one case studied by the Miami police, five units in the annex were resold four times in the same day, each time at a higher value. This was during the period when Duque and Marlin were buying stock in CNB. Court records show that the final player in the day's proceedings was CNB, which ended up with the mortgages on the five units.[26] (Often the purpose of such paper chases is to establish legally registered sales documents that set a value on the property for the purpose of financial transactions like bank mortgages. If the bank does not check the valuations or deliberately ignores them, it can end up lending many times more than the actual collateral for the loan.)

Duque's involvement with Marlin also raised questions since no one could explain the source of the Colombian's wealth. Contrary to the impression Duque gave in interviews with the Florida press, the thirty-four-year-old Colombian hardly merited the description of South American magnate. Although his father Luis had built a successful coffee business in Colombia, by 1981, when Alberto made his bid for CNB, Duque Industries was only seventh among Colombian coffee exporters. That in no way represented a fortune sufficient to support Alberto's financial specu-

---

another occasion the U.S. Department of Housing and Urban Development threatened to suspend Viking Corporation's license unless Marlin agreed to inform potential investors that the cow pasture he was peddling had no streets, drainage, or building permits. In 1976 the American Stock Exchange halted trading of Viking stock because of financial troubles arising from tax valuations and mortgage notes. Marlin later reorganized the company under the name American Capital Corporation. (Miami *Herald* [Jan. 17, 1971; Jan. 27, 1976; Jan. 29, 1976; June 1, 1976; June 18, 1976; Aug. 1, 1976; Feb. 25, 1977; and Nov. 2, 1981].)

lations, which by 1983 were reputed to have gone beyond $200 million.[27]

Soon after arriving in Miami in 1977, Duque started the General Coffee Corporation, a roaster, grinder, packer, and wholesaler of premium coffees. In 1981 he paid $45 million to acquire CNB, and in early 1982 he spent another $15 million to buy the Chase & Sanborn Division of Nabisco Brands. He also acquired Allsun, a producer of citrus and other fruit juice concentrates, with net sales of about $20 million, and a New Orleans coffee service company that supplies morning coffee to offices and industries. Other acquisitions included two private jets; a yacht; apartments and houses in Miami, New York, and Cancún; a one-hundred-acre estate in North Carolina; and four wives. Seen about Miami in a white suit and a white Rolls Royce, Duque acted the part of a rich playboy.[28]

But his multimillion-dollar acquisitions aroused suspicions in both Colombia and southern Florida. Duque himself admitted that there were rumors of Colombian drug connections but insisted that "when you're clean, you don't have to worry about what people say."[29]

A year later, in April 1983, bankers had plenty to say about how they had been taken for $122 million by Alberto and his General Coffee Corporation. Twenty-four banks, led by Shawmut Boston International Banking Corporation, filed suit against the Duque family on charges that funds advanced for coffee exports had been fraudulently misused. According to court documents in New York and investigations in Colombia, false bills of lading were filed for nonexistent coffee shipments from Luis Duque's company to his son's General Coffee Corporation. It was not the first time that U.S. banks had been so duped: Four years earlier Citibank had lost $42 million on fake Colombian coffee exports through the connivance of a Citibank vice president.[30]

Like his father, who rose from humble origins to become the political confidant of Colombian presidents, Albert knew the importance of well-placed connections. Though possessing the trappings of Florida wealth, including cars and homes, he reportedly did not get a "seal of legitimacy" until 1981, when he bought a North Carolina estate belonging to Mitchell Wolfson, a former mayor of Miami Beach and a pillar of southern Florida's financial and political establishment. Wolfson, who ran a conglomerate of entertainment industries until his death in 1983, was so taken with the charming young Colombian that he persuaded one of Miami's most prominent public relations firms to add Duque to its select list of clients. Articles soon appeared in the local press praising the "coffee baron," and Duque was introduced to real estate tycoons, Arab bankers, and Vice President Bush's son Jeff, who became involved with Duque in the construction of a downtown Miami high rise.[31]

But despite his aura of casual wealth, Duque was effectively playing Michael Calandra's game at Chase Manhattan‡ by borrowing from Peter to pay Paul. Thus, in order to gain control of City National Bank Duque used his Arab connections to borrow $22 million from Bahrain financiers and then used the bank to finance his acquisition of Chase & Sanborn. When finally taken to court, he left behind a stack of unpaid bills, including $17,000 owed the public relations firm. According to Duque, it was all very natural: "Fraud is routine in any kind of business operation in the United States," he told the Colombian press.[32]

The round-robin began unraveling in January 1983 when it was revealed that Alberto and his father Luis had received substantial loans from a government-owned bank in Colombia, Banco Popular, although they were not clients of the bank and did not qualify as small businessmen of the sort the bank was supposed to serve. The loans were made after Luis Duque's nephew became a director of the bank and Duque's friend, Julio César Turbay, was elected president of the nation. While not illegal, the loans smacked of political patronage; and after a local news agency pointed the finger, the Duque family came under pressure to repay. Almost immediately fake coffee manifestos began appearing, but Shawmut did not discover the ploy until mid-April.[33]

The credit crunch in Colombia appears to have forced Alberto to divert badly needed funds to Colombian banks. To hear Duque

‡ See p. 45.

tell it, however, he had no knowledge of his companies' affairs. "My hypochondria ruined me," he told the Miami *Herald,* stating that he washed his hands at least twenty times a day for fear of infections and that he took "many" pills daily. "I was so concerned with myself that I failed to keep a close eye on my businesses."[34]

Not a few of those who had dealt with Duque also felt sick. One business executive who entered into a multimillion-dollar joint venture with Duque said, "I feel like a fool." With hindsight bankers admitted they had not checked Duque's financial claims, which turned out to be "substantially inflated." "There were red flags all over the place," one banker who had lent money to Duque said of his financial statements, "but nobody investigated." That was not entirely true. While their colleagues were being impressed by Duque's jets, yacht, and fleet of expensive cars, some U.S. bankers took the precaution of checking Duque's Colombian credentials and decided against lending.[35]

After Duque filed for bankruptcy and the FBI opened an investigation into his affairs, the Colombian was forced to resign as chairman of City National Bank. But several of his associates survived, including the bank's president, Donald Beazley, who was hired by Duque to replace a Philadelphia banker who quit after only nine months because he did not like Duque's style of operating. Duque's was not the first scandal Beazley had the bad luck to become ensnared in, having earlier presided over the demise of Australia's notorious Nugan Hand Bank, with drug and CIA connections.* But Duque could not praise Beazley enough. "Experience is something that you can buy," said Duque a month before the roof fell in. "That's why we have Don Beazley. [He] gives me good advice."[36]

***

In their suit against Marlin and his partners, Southeast's lawyers insisted on the need for more information about the people who were snapping up the bank's stock. Other banks, such as

---

* See Chapter 4.

Florida's giant Flagship Banks, made a similar plea in attempting to fend off questionable suitors. While it can be argued that these were straightforward business deals, the issue hinges on whether banking is an industry, in which anyone can own a piece of the action, or a public trust, making ethical behavior at least as important as a quick buck. Because of the go-go atmosphere in banking, the issue has become confused. Bankers speak of their profession as an industry like any other, the only difference being that their "products" consist of money. They pretend to see no difference between the owner of an industry who speculates in stocks and a banker who speculates in loans. But there is a difference: The owner of an industry has every right to do what he likes with his money because it belongs to him; bankers do not have that right because the money in their vaults belongs to others.

Because of Marlin's questionable real estate dealings and his association with Outrigger and people like Kosow and Adler, Southeast's management worried about how he and his partners might use the bank if they obtained one quarter of the stock, effectively giving them control. As for Duque's bank, the Chase & Sanborn deal showed that CNB had followed the well-traveled path of insider lending responsible for most of the bank failures in the United States since World War II. Regulation O of the Federal Reserve System forbids banks to loan money to their officers in excess of $60,000 on a mortgage, $20,000 for education, or $10,000 for any other purpose. These limits were established to ensure that bank loans are granted on the basis of sound economic judgments, unclouded by considerations of employee relations. The law also aims to prevent bankers from involving their institutions in nonbanking activities, such as stock speculation—one of the principal causes of the bank crash of 1929.

One of the obvious lessons of the crash was that the U.S. economy is terribly vulnerable to wheeling-dealing by bankers, and thus people who own a bank must not only be financially solvent and experienced in banking but must also be able to prove good character. Theoretically these are the standards applied by the FDIC, the Federal Reserve, and the Comptroller of the Currency for approval of a bank acquisition. In fact, the only criteria for denying such approval is whether the buyer is in jail at the time the application is processed. A representative of the Federal Reserve Board admitted, "If there is no adverse information available against an investor's application [to buy or acquire substantial shares in a bank]—*and* if the adverse information is not in writing—the Federal Reserve's board of governors will approve the application."[37] In other words, if nobody blows the whistle, anyone can own a bank.

Part of the problem (in Miami and elsewhere) stems from a code of behavior called "bank reserve." Unlike other sectors of the economy, U.S. bankers can hide behind a legal screen of secrecy based on the confidentiality of their relationship with customers. Although the principle is generally agreed to be sound, bankers have misused the trust to hide questionable and/ or illegal activities like self-lending. Secrecy also discourages bankers from communicating their qualms to each other or to bank regulators. "I hate to play private eye," admitted a Texas banker, "but what else can I do when the regulators don't know what's going on? I have to protect myself and my institution." When asked why he did not inform bank regulators about the illegal activities of other banks, he admitted that "maybe there is a failure in the system. Whistle-blowing is frowned on in the banking community, and it would probably get back that I had done the informing." So bankers talk to regulators in code. "If I tell the Comptroller of the Currency that a bank is overdealing in foreign currency, that's my way of alerting the [regulators] that something funny is going on," he said. "And if a regulator asks me about a bank that I know is lousy, my way of saying so is, 'I have no opinion.' "[38]

A similar sense of "reserve" makes lawyers and auditors hesitate to expose erring clients, especially when they are also on the client's board of directors.† When a scandal erupts, few banks are prepared to confront the underlying causes, preferring to fire employees immediately responsible without questioning the policies that led to the problem. In the Outrigger case, for example, the growth-at-any-price policies of Chase Manhattan and Citibank

† A Florida study showed that twelve of the largest banks employed lawyers who were also directors of the bank. ("Business Monday," Miami *Herald* [Aug. 9, 1982].)

encouraged their officers to make risky loans to people of dubious probity. Although the bankers involved were dismissed, neither Chase nor Citibank altered its lending policies.

If bankers are negligent, bank regulators are worse. They will allow any kind of criminal to head a U.S. bank, including drug traffickers, thieves, and murderers.‡ "Before criminals owned bank officers; now they own banks," commented a Miami police official who specializes in financial fraud. "The truth is that the left hand doesn't know what the right is doing," admitted a Florida state bank regulator. "For example, when we call the Treasury and ask for information on some bank, the standard reply is that the Treasury will have to get a legal opinion on whether they can release the information to us. It takes them six months to reply, by which time the information is usually useless.

"Egos also get in the way," the bank regulator continued. "Every agency wants to take credit for cracking a crime. For example, there have been cases in which Florida bank regulators were told to suspend an investigation by another agency which claimed that it was responsible for the investigation!"[39] Wayne Dicky, chief of the Florida Department of Law Enforcement's Intelligence Center Bureau, agrees. "Law enforcement people don't want to share information, and no government agency has to inform another that it is working on an investigation."[40] In the case of one Miami bank, three different government agencies told me they were investigating the bank's South American owner, yet none was aware of the other two investigations.

Bank regulators have no central depository of information on people with criminal records; they must rely on the FBI's National Crime Information Center (NCIC) in Washington or organizations like Dicky's Intelligence Center. NCIC's input comes from only eight states that have agreed to participate; crimes committed in the other forty-two states, or abroad, are not on file. Though Dicky's operation is the most sophisticated of its kind in the United States, it too has huge information gaps (e.g., the center's computers do not include data on those who have committed federal crimes!).

While bank regulators' checks on U.S. citizens are at best per-

‡ See Chapters 7, 8, and 9.

functory, they at least have some sources of information if they want to use them. However, their investigations of bank buyers from abroad are simply a joke, though in that area most of the blame falls on the State Department, the Drug Enforcement Administration (DEA), and the FBI. In theory the local U.S. embassy will provide a background check on nationals applying to buy a U.S. bank. In reality all the embassy does is have its consulate authenticate notarized signatures. FBI checks on foreigners are limited to data provided by the NCIC, and that excludes just about everyone. Unless specifically consulted, the DEA never gets involved in a bank check, the theory being that banking has nothing to do with the drug trade. Sometimes the results are ludicrous, as in the case of a CIA bank in Miami that was sold to a Colombian with cocaine connections: Neither the seller nor the buyer was aware of the other's background.*

Nor do U.S. bank regulators make sure that the person applying to buy bank stock is the buyer and not a front. Such information becomes available only when there is an unfriendly takeover and the bank in question sues, as in the case of Florida's Flagship Banks, which was trying to fend off an unwanted Venezuelan suitor with links to a convicted bank swindler.† But even when bank regulators know of a person's disreputable past (e.g., Marlin's real estate dealings), their attitude is that if he isn't currently breaking the law, he is eligible to acquire a bank.[41]

On the state level there is also the issue of politics. Whether the state comptroller is elected or appointed, political considerations can influence how he runs the bank regulatory side of his office. In Florida, for example, Mary Weaver Repper, a former aide to State Comptroller Gerald Lewis, charged that she was ordered to shake down a Tampa banker for a $25,000 contribution to Lewis' 1982 reelection campaign. The banker, Gordon Campbell, president of Exchange Bank of Tampa, confirmed that he was approached by Lewis' people. They suggested that instead of the bank making contributions, individual directors do so in order that Lewis might honor a campaign pledge not to accept contributions from banks he regulated (in fact, he accepted $80,000 in

* See Chapter 5.
† See Chapter 8.

the first four months of the campaign). Exchange Bank apparently was approached because it needed the comptroller's approval for a sensitive merger. According to Mrs. Repper, Lewis' campaign managers also planned to collect $40,000 from NCNB Corporation, a North Carolina banking chain that was the other half of the Exchange merger. At the same time an attorney for the Barnett banking chain reported that Lewis' campaign manager had threatened a "scorched earth attitude" toward Barnett if Lewis was reelected because Barnett had been supporting Lewis' opponent in the race.[42] While all these charges and countercharges were being made, no one at the state level was keeping an effective eye on Florida's banks because most of the comptroller's top officials were out campaigning for Lewis.

The principal reason for these problems, according to many bankers, is that the industry has grown so fast that old guidelines have gone by the board. "Faith and confidence used to be the key to banking and bank regulating," said Alexander McW. Wolfe, Jr., the vice chairman of Florida's Southeast Bank. "Unfortunately banks are now being used for ego trips, illegal activities, or speculation." Oakley Chaney, a veteran banker with Southeast's international division, agrees. "Banking isn't what it used to be. Before, if a banker introduced you to someone, that automatically was an endorsement, but not anymore. This has become a dog-eat-dog industry."[43]

Banks are under "tremendous pressure," according to McW. Wolfe, to show substantial gains in quarterly earnings. In this respect they have become like any other industry. But such pressures can lead to unwise lending and speculation as banks try to grow too fast. "At Southeast," said McW. Wolfe, "our priorities are, in order: liquidity, quality of assets, consistency of earnings, growth of earnings, and, lastly, growth of the balance sheets."[44] Because of those priorities Southeast is considered stodgy and sluggish by other Florida bankers, and its stock price has been depressed, making it an attractive quarry for Marlin and others. With every quarter bank-stock analysts seize on the percentage change in earnings as the sole indicator of a bank's health; at the end of the first quarter of 1982 Southeast was beseiged by a chorus of doomsayers because its earnings dropped by 36 percent. Yet the true state of a bank, which depends on such fundamentals as liquidity and quality of assets, may be much better on a long-term basis than is shown by quarterly reports. In other words, security may be more important to depositors and stockholders than short-term profits.

Bankers spend a great deal of money on publicity to convince the local community that "you can trust in us," yet they themselves do not think of banking as a trust. Ethical considerations that formerly served as operational guidelines have become anachronistic, and naturally the changed atmosphere has attracted gamblers and con men. A bank's style is set by top management; and if a chairman or president tolerates corner cutting, as Walter Wriston did at Citibank,‡ that is reflected in the ranks, in the employment of people with questionable backgrounds (e.g., Miami National's president, Joseph Stefan), and the type of people with whom they do business (e.g., the con artists who promoted Outrigger). And behind the con men may well be organized crime.

‡ See previous chapter

Part II

ROGUES' GALLERY—Chapter 4

FRANK NUGAN, Australian-born promoter and co-owner of Nugan Hand Bank in Sydney, which was used to launder funds for the CIA and Southeast Asian heroin traffickers and for the illegal arms trade; died in 1980, an apparent suicide.

MICHAEL HAND, Bronx-born co-owner of Nugan Hand Bank, former Green Beret who claimed he worked for the CIA; fled to United States in 1980 after bank's collapse; whereabouts unknown.

BERNIE HOUGHTON, former undercover agent with U.S. Naval Intelligence; Saudi Arabian representative of Nugan Hand; whereabouts unknown.

WILLIAM COLBY, former director of the CIA and lawyer for the Nugan Hand Bank.

EARL P. "BUDDY" YATES, retired rear admiral and former chief of staff for strategic planning with U.S. forces in Asia and the Pacific; president of the Nugan Hand Bank.

EDWIN F. BLACK, retired general and former commander of U.S. troops in Thailand during the Vietnam War and later assistant army chief of staff for the Pacific; president of the Nugan Hand Bank's Hawaiian operations.

EDWIN WILSON, former CIA agent under indictment in the United States on charges of selling explosives in Libya and supplying trained men, arms, and technology to Libya and other military buyers; used Nugan Hand Bank to finance arms-smuggling operations.

DONALD BEAZLEY, a New York banker who became president of the Nugan Hand group of companies, and after its collapse joined Alberto Duque's bank in Miami (see Chapter 3).

Chapter 4

Nugan Hand: murder and the good old boys of the CIA.

Early on a Sunday morning in 1980 two patrolmen, driving along a lonely stretch of highway near the Australian port of Sydney, came upon a Mercedes sedan with its lights on. Inside the car, slumped across the front seat in a puddle of blood, was the body of a middle-aged man. Searching his pockets, the patrolmen found the business card of William Colby, former director of the CIA. On the back of the card was the itincrary of a trip Colby intended to make to Asia. Beside the body were a new rifle and a Bible with a meat-pie wrapper as a place mark. On the wrapper were scrawled the names of Colby and Congressman Bob Wilson of California, then the ranking Republican on the House Armed Services Committee.[1]

The dead man turned out to be a Sydney merchant banker named Frank Nugan, co-owner of the Nugan Hand Bank. His apparent suicide set off an international scandal involving heroin and arms traffickers, the CIA, and enough high-ranking U.S. military officers to launch a small war. The Nugan Hand saga is revealing as much for what it says about banks as about the CIA, for the bank was the fulcrum of a multitude of illegal and lucrative activities, from heroin running to investment swindles, as well as paymaster for CIA covert actions against Australia's Labor Party.[2]

While banks have been used for similar operations in the past, only recently have they been established solely for such purposes. One obvious reason is the huge sums of money criminal enterprises now generate, amounts that can be handled only by a bank. Drug traffickers and other criminals still tote suitcases of money across borders, but it is a risky business and nowadays represents only a small fraction of the cash volume. Gold, jewelry, and other valuables also present transport problems. Banks, on the other hand, can instantly telex billions of dollars to any city in the world, and criminal investigators say that when a bank wants to hide the trail it is almost impossible to follow. Banks have the added advantage of being the least-regulated sector of international business because of bank reserve. Unlike the producer of manufactured goods or a commodities trader, a banker needs no license to export and is not required to provide detailed data on foreign dealings. Thus there are no physical barriers and almost no legal ones to recycling dirty money. Given the opportunities for large, quick—though illegal—profits, the only surprising thing is that more crooks have not joined the game.

***

Frank Nugan was a fast learner. A thickset man with a flair for self-promotion, Nugan had an ingratiating manner that could "charm the pants off anybody," as one colleague recalled.[3] The son of a Spanish migrant who had done well in the food-packing business, Nugan took a law degree at the University of California and returned to Sydney, ambitious for the "open combat" of the business world. The young Australian was a natural partner for Michael Hand, a tough-talking Green Beret with the Special Forces in Vietnam who visited Australia when it was a rest and recreation center for American troops. Hand left Vietnam in 1968 to settle in Sydney, where he joined forces with Nugan to promote Australian tourism, mining, and real estate through an outfit called Australiasian and Pacific Holdings, Ltd. The company may well have been a CIA front, since four of the original shareholders listed Air America, the CIA airline, as their address and two other investors were from a CIA-related institution.[4]

In 1973, the pair formed the Nugan Hand Bank. It attracted depositors with offers of private-banking services, the highest interest rates in the region, tax-free deposits, and complete secrecy. Within six years it had twenty-two branches around the world. But Nugan Hand's biggest business came from laundering money for Asian and Australian heroin dealers; not coincidentally, the bank's officers read like a Who's Who of the CIA. Despite CIA denials of involvement, there is strong historical evidence to support the suspicion that the bank was founded to help finance the CIA's role in Southeast Asia's heroin traffic.

As noted by scholar Alfred W. McCoy in *The Politics of Heroin in Southeast Asia,* after World War II Washington believed that the United States was the rightful heir to Europe's Asian colonial empires. To legitimize their "foreign adventures," America's cold warriors embraced a militant ideology that regarded all Asian nationalist struggles as pawns of "international communism." The CIA became the vanguard of the anti-Communist crusade; any ally was welcome and any means justified. During the early 1950s, for example, the CIA backed the formation in Burma of a guerrilla army of Nationalist Chinese, who were responsible for almost a third of the world's illicit opium supply. In Laos the CIA created a Meo mercenary army whose commander manufactured heroin for sale to American GIs in South Vietnam. And in late 1969 new heroin laboratories sprang up in the Golden Triangle, where Burma, Thailand, and Laos converge. "The State Department," wrote McCoy, "provides unconditional support for corrupt governments openly engaged in the drug traffic."[5]

In view of such activities, a drug bank set up by the CIA has a certain logic, particularly since a bank was obviously necessary to recycle the huge sums of money involved in the heroin traffic. Evidence uncovered by detectives and journalists, particularly *The Wall Street Journal*'s Jonathan Kwitny, also shows that Nugan Hand arranged arms deals in South America, Africa, and the Middle East, and served as financial intermediary for former CIA agent and notorious arms dealer Edwin P. Wilson.[6] Records seized by the Australian authorities show further that the bank received lengthy reports about military and political activities, mostly in Cambodia but also in Laos, Vietnam, and Thailand. They were prepared by Nugan Hand's Bangkok representative, a former career British naval officer, and seemed to have no connection with the bank's normal business.[7]

Equally suspicious, the CIA, FBI, and U.S. Customs refused, on grounds of national security, to release information that they held on the bank's activities. When the Australian weekly *The National Times* petitioned, under the U.S. Freedom of Information Act, for FBI records, it received only 71 of 151 pages requested. Of these, most had been blacked out in heavy ink with the notation "B–1," meaning that disclosure would endanger U.S. "national defense or foreign policy." Observed Nugan Hand liquidator John O'Brien, "It has obvious overtones that somebody is covering something up."[8]

The question is whether the people who ran the bank were in it for the money or because they thought they were serving a political cause. McCoy, whose observations were made in the late 1960s, did not think the CIA was in the drug traffic to finance its clandestine operations or because of a few corrupt agents. Rather, its role was the "inadvertent [and] inevitable consequence of its Cold War tactics."[9] But by the mid-1970s the cold war hysteria had passed, and political reasons for dealing with drug traffickers seemed less compelling. So either the CIA was carrying on its own private cold war or Nugan Hand was an intelligence cover for crime. Frank Nugan's activities suggest the latter.

For an agent with a cause, Nugan engaged in some funny sidelines—such as defrauding several large insurance companies of their interest in a Nugan family fruit and vegetable business—in addition to fraudulent dealings at the bank. He also lived high (literally: He had a bottle-a-day scotch habit) in a lavish Sydney home that he had remodeled at a cost of $500,000. The day he died Nugan was completing negotiations for the purchase of a $2.2 million country estate[10]—a venture that does not suggest a man about to commit suicide. Indeed, there is as much mystery surrounding Nugan's death as there is about his checkered career in banking. Though Nugan was facing criminal charges over the family food business, he seemed his charming, chipper self to the very end. In the last six months of his life he had gone on the wagon, lost nearly fifty pounds on a crash diet, and taken to attending church almost daily. If the sudden changes were signs of unraveling, Nugan's associates seemed unaware of them; Hand and the other directors were taken by surprise when Nugan's body was found, as shown by an impromptu cover-up that failed to conceal the bank's illegal dealings. And when an official inquest was held, the coroner's suicide verdict was challenged on the ground that Nugan would have to have been a "contortionist" to have shot himself in the head with a rifle from the position in which he was sitting. Nor were the dead man's fingerprints found on the rifle. Even after the inquest was closed, some were still unconvinced that the body in Nugan's Mercedes was really his, and in 1982 the New South Wales attorney general ordered an exhumation of the corpse after witnesses claimed to have seen him in a bar in Atlanta, Georgia. The remains were positively identified as Nugan's by means of teeth and a webbed foot.[11]

Much of the evidence detailing Nugan's operations was destroyed by Nugan's partner, Green Beret Michael Hand, who had often boasted of working for the CIA.[12] When he learned of Nugan's death, Hand rushed back to Sydney from a business trip in London. He was joined by the bank's president, Earl P. "Buddy" Yates, retired rear admiral and former chief of staff for strategic planning with U.S. forces in Asia and the Pacific. Hand and Yates called the bank's other directors to an emergency meeting at the bank. Among those present was Bernie Houghton, a former undercover agent who had worked with U.S. Naval Intelligence in the Pacific and was the bank's Saudi Arabian representative. According to Stephen K. A. Hill, one of the directors present at the meeting, the group shredded enough records to fill a small room. What they could not destroy they packed in cartons and carried that night to the back room of a butcher shop owned by a former army sergeant in Vietnam who was an associate of Houghton. Hill said that Houghton brought along his lawyer, Michael Maloney, to oversee the ransacking, and that Maloney warned them, "I am fully aware of what has been going on. You all face jail terms of up to 16 years." Hand then broke in to say that if Maloney's orders were not obeyed, "terrible things" would happen. "Your wives will be cut up and returned to you in bits and pieces."[13]

Meanwhile, in Manila three-star General LeRoy J. Manor, the recently retired chief of staff for all U.S. forces in Asia and the Pacific, was trying to persuade Nugan Hand's public relations officer to stop the wire services from reporting Nugan's death. On a secret assignment for the Air Force in the Philippines, Manor was also helping to run Nugan Hand's Manila office.[14]

Nor were Manor and Yates the only high-ranking former U.S. military and intelligence officials working for the bank. General

Edwin F. Black, commander of U.S. troops in Thailand during the Vietnam War and later assistant army chief of staff for the Pacific, was president of Nugan Hand's Hawaiian operations. The consulting offices of General Erle Cocke, Jr., a retired general with the U.S. National Guard, served as Nugan Hand's Washington headquarters. On the intelligence side Nugan Hand associates included: William Colby, director of the CIA between 1973 and 1976, who served as a lawyer for the bank; Walter McDonald, a former deputy director of the CIA, who worked as a consultant; Guy Pauker, a CIA adviser, also a consultant; and Dale Holmgren, flight-service manager for a CIA-run airline in the Far East known as Civil Air Transport, who opened Nugan Hand's Taipei branch. The bank's man in Manila was Roy Manor, a CIA consultant involved in the aborted rescue mission of American hostages in Iran. Robert "Red" Jansen, former CIA station chief in Bangkok, represented Nugan Hand in Thailand. Also linked to the bank were the CIA station chief of Australia and two CIA case officers.[15]

The beginnings of this star-studded assembly can be traced to the Vietnam War, which had brought together such people as Houghton and Hand. Like Hand, Houghton took up residence in Sydney, where he opened a chain of restaurants that would later play host to U.S. congressmen, CIA officials, and military brass, including Representative Wilson's Armed Services Committee. Hand had had some experience in real estate promotion as a salesman for a development project promoted by the singer Pat Boone and financed by the American shipping magnate D. K. Ludwig. According to confidential reports obtained by the Australian Federal Bureau of Narcotics, Hand later used the landing strip constructed on the real estate development for heroin flights made from Asia to Australia by an Air America pilot. As acknowledged by U.S. drug enforcement officials, Air America figured prominently in the CIA's heroin traffic from Southeast Asia's Golden Triangle.[16]

The bank was also actively engaged in the drug trade. One of its principal branches was in Chiang Mai, in the heart of Thailand's poppy-growing fields. Australia's biggest drug pushers operated out of this region; they also banked with Nugan Hand. Among the bank's clients was the $100 million "Mr. Asia" heroin syndicate, which also arranged for the contract murders of at least three persons in Australia. Neil Evans, former head of the Chiang Mai branch, testified that during six months at the bank he saw millions of drug dollars pass through the branch. He also said that Hand had told him that he had arranged for Nugan Hand to become the CIA's paymaster "for disbursement of funds anywhere in the world on behalf of the CIA and also for the taking of money on behalf of the CIA."[17]

Evans' charges confirm those of Peter Wilcox, an American energy consultant who said he met Hand in Singapore on the recommendation of General Black, himself a graduate of the CIA's wartime predecessor, the Office of Strategic Services (OSS). Wilcox said that Hand and Nugan tried to recruit him for the bank with the story that he was needed for "deep-cover" work as part of an unidentified intelligence operation. Wilcox declined the offer. Later his military friends told him that the bank was moving "unbelievable" amounts of money covertly out of Australia, Indonesia, and Thailand.[18]

The bank apparently was able to carry on such operations because of highly placed contacts at the Australian Federal Bureau of Narcotics. One of the bureau's informants worked for the bank, and he tipped off investigators. "They are bigger than anything you have ever seen here in the heroin game and are said to be part of an American security organization. If you caught these blokes, all hell would break loose."[19] The day after these allegations the informant found himself being tailed instead of Nugan or Hand. Within a year it had become apparent to the investigators that Frank Nugan had direct access to bureau information, which he often obtained within hours of its internal appearance. According to a former bureau officer, "Nugan was getting to hear about our inquiries literally before we could even update our holdings on them." In 1978 the bureau's director placed on file a memo suspending any further investigation into Nugan Hand. A year later the bureau was disbanded.[20]

The bank also had fruitful contacts with the Australian Security Intelligence Organization (ASIO), a secret counterspy group that worked closely with the CIA and may have been responsible for the narcotics bureau's strange behavior in the Nugan Hand case. Statements by two FBI agents sent to Australia in 1982 and an ultrasecret wiretap of Frank Nugan's phone suggest that ASIO was involved in the affair.[21]

The Pentagon operates a vital base at Pine Gap, in central Australia, which monitors U.S. satellites watching the U.S.S.R. and China and directs the United States' nuclear submarines. When the Labor Party was voted into power in 1972, Prime Minister Gough Whitlam quickly antagonized Washington by pulling Australian troops out of Vietnam and condemning President Nixon for the bombing of Hanoi. But nothing so enraged the CIA and ASIO as Whitlam's repreated criticisms of the Pine Gap installation. Ray Cline, former CIA deputy director of intelligence, later confirmed a joint CIA-ASIO plan to destablize the Whitlam government through misinformation and contributions to opposition politicians. The Nugan Hand Bank played an important role in the fall of Whitlam's government, in November 1975, by financing bugging and forgery operations.* A former executive of the bank also told *Inquiry* magazine that under William Colby the CIA laundered millions of dollars through Nugan Hand to support pro-U.S. political parties in Europe, allegedly including Italy's Christian Democrats.† The bank was founded while Colby was director of the CIA, and he continued to play a part in its affairs after he left the agency, including Nugan Hand's mysterious Panama branch and an attempt to take over a Florida bank.[22]

In addition to drugs, Nugan Hand was involved in various arms deals with Indonesia, Thailand, Malaysia, Brazil, and the white Rhodesian Government of Ian Smith. The bank also did business with Edwin Wilson, the former CIA agent convicted in the United States of selling explosives to Libya and charged with supplying trained men, arms, and technology to Libya and other military buyers. Memos and testimony by Nugan Hand employees show that Hand met with Wilson in Bangkok, and that Houghton held discussions with him in Switzerland. Intelligence sources also claimed that Houghton used Nugan Hand's Saudi Arabian branch to finance Wilson's arms-smuggling operations.

In view of such activities, one might ask why so many high-

---

* The Labor Party was returned to power in the March 1983 elections.
† For further CIA Italian connections, see Chapter 9, pp. 187–88.

ranking U.S. military men lent their names and prestige to the bank. Part of the answer may lie in the U.S. intelligence community's obvious ties to Nugan Hand. While Colby and Admiral Yates denied any connection between the CIA and the bank, General Black was not so sure. "I'm not saying it's not possible," he allowed, "but I certainly wasn't aware of it." Walter McDonald, a Nugan Hand consultant and former CIA deputy director, was also uncertain. "I really don't see it happening, but I can't vouch for it."[23]

Technically they may have been correct, since the bank apparently was originally part of a deep-cover intelligence operation known as Task Force 157, which worked with the CIA but was controlled by the U.S. Office of Naval Intelligence and was directly responsible to strong-willed Secretary of State Henry Kissinger. The task force gained notoriety when twenty-one of its former agents took the Navy to court to demand civil service benefits after the group was abruptly disbanded in 1977 because of some unknown internal scandal. Ed Wilson had a desk and his own staff at the task force's Washington headquarters and is credited with supplying the operation's front name, "Pierce Morgan." Informed sources said that Task Force 157 used the Nugan Hand Bank for covert naval intelligence money, just as the CIA used it to undermine Australia's Labor government. According to *The National Times* of Australia, General Black figured prominently in the bank's operations, having previously been "in charge of various paramilitary operations in Asia involving a number of unorthodox financing arrangements."[24]

Another, simpler, explanation for such involvement is greed: The bank was a marvelous moneymaking machine for its directors. The Saudi Arabian branch, for example, hauled in upwards of $10 million from unsuspecting Americans working there. Aramco, Bechtel, and other large U.S. concerns in Saudi Arabia not only allowed Nugan Hand to solicit their employees for savings and investments but also permitted bank salesmen to hold meetings on company property and use company bulletin boards. Henry C. Beck Company of Dallas even went so far as to sponsor Houghton's entry into Saudi Arabia. Houghton carried off "bags of cash" from U.S. Air Force personnel stationed in Saudi Arabia.[25]

Nugan Hand earned hefty fees, usually 22 percent, for money laundering and for tax avoidance purposes, from 194 companies as well as show business celebrities. After the bank's collapse in April 1980, none of the latter came forth to claim their money for fear that such illegal activities would be exposed. There wasn't much to claim in any case. Although many of the documents detailing Nugan Hand's activities were destroyed by the bank's directors, there was enough evidence to show that large amounts of money had been siphoned off by Nugan and others, leaving a shortfall of more than $50 million when the roof fell in after Nugan's death. Although thousands of smaller investors in the United States and Australia clamored for the return of their life savings, the bank's directors appeared unconcerned. "I don't feel guilty because some guy got swindled," General Black, the bank's Hawaii representative, told The Wall Street Journal.[26]

Smart people, on the other hand, got out in time. They included the generals, as well as Hand, who fled to the United States on a false passport after the paper-shredding operation. Houghton also disappeared from Sydney after transferring $150,000 from the bank's Hong Kong branch to a personal account in the United States.[27]

Another who abandoned ship was Donald Beazley, who had been brought in as president of the entire Nugan Hand group of companies and later became president of a Miami bank owned by a mysterious Colombian entrepreneur.‡ A former Federal Reserve bank examiner, Beazley was billed as Nugan Hand's "first real banker." Although he later claimed that he was "just there on an interim basis [to] see if I liked what I would find," that isn't the way he talked when he was presented to the bank's directors as Nugan Hand's new boss. After being introduced by Admiral Yates as "the finest banker in the United States under the age of 35," Beazley said, "It is a privilege and an honor for me to be president [of] this company." He added that he had "had the opportunity to see it grow" during a close two and a half year relationship with "Mike and Frank and Buddy," and concluded by boasting that "the decision that I would want to be associated with this group [was] one of the best ones I've ever made, decision-wise." He told the group, "You're fortunate to

‡ See Chapter 3, pp. 51–53.

have probably one of the best money-market operators that I've ever seen and certainly one of the highest-qualified tax desk departments . . . that I've ever seen." This, even though Nugan Hand's money market operations were consistent and intentional money losers, as the bank built up deposits by offering investors much higher interest rates than it could command by reinvesting the money for its own benefit. And many of Nugan's tax schemes later proved to be thinly veiled frauds.[28]

When confronted by *The Wall Street Journal* with tape recordings of his statements, Beazley admitted that he might have said such things but that he couldn't remember. He conceded the possible accuracy of reports that as late as March 1980 he was assuring clients that the bank was solid and would continue.* Beazley also suffered a memory loss as to the transfer of $200,000 from Nugan Hand to his account in Florida. He said he could not recall what the money was for, nor has he provided proof that he repaid it, as he claimed.[29]

Nugan Hand's part in the heroin and arms traffic underscores the increasing importance of the financial sector for criminal elements. Investigations by the Australian Royal Commission showed that the bank regularly transferred funds from Sydney to Southeast Asia for payment of heroin shipments to Australia, which were sent in containers to the West Coast of the United States. The bank also appears to have been a financial conduit for an Australian mobster in his business dealings with Santo Trafficante, Jr., the underworld's boss in Florida and the heir to Lucky Luciano's heroin network.[30]† In addition to drugs, both Nugan and Hand were personally involved in the illegal arms traffic. The CIA prefers such "bankers" because they have no qualms about financing the agency's political causes, and association with the CIA provides the bankers with a cover for criminal activities.

But Nugan Hand's directors were not satisfied with the laun-

---

* Just before the bank collapsed, Beazley and Houghton entered into negotiations with former CIA contract agent Ricardo Chavez to buy a British bank, London Capital Securities. *(Parapolitics/USA* [March 1, 1983], citing *The National Times* of Australia [Sept. 12, 1982].)

† See Chapter 5, pp. 79–82, and Chapter 6, pp. 105–7.

dering business or the CIA's covert projects. They also swindled $50 million from investors, like the Americans working in Saudi Arabia, many of whom believed the bank legitimate because of the high-ranking generals associated with it. General Black's explanation that it was not his lookout if such people were duped parallels the CIA's indifference to the consequences of backing political organizations that use anticommunism as a cover for crime. As observed by McCoy in *The Politics of Heroin in Southeast Asia,* heroin addiction in the United States was nearly eliminated during World War II because heroin supplies were cut off and the international criminal syndicates were in disarray. Within a few years of the war's end addiction was again on the rise due to reorganization of the drug syndicates and expansion of Asia's opium industry, in which the CIA played a major role for political reasons. As documented by McCoy, the CIA helped "inflict a heroin plague on ourselves," because it thought that any means justified the end, though in this case the end was as dubious as the means.[31]

One must also ask why the CIA is still in the drug business (as evidenced by its involvement with Nugan Hand), particularly after Vietnam proved the futility of such methods, and why it was connected to an organization that swindled American citizens.

The author gratefully acknowledges the work of Jonathan Kwitny, whose investigations of Nugan-Hand in *The Wall Street Journal*, August 24–26, 1982, provided much of the factual information for this chapter.

ROGUES' GALLERY—Chapter 5

PAUL HELLIWELL, a Miami lawyer-banker; head of special intelligence in China during World War II for the Office of Strategic Services (OSS), forerunner of the CIA; CIA paymaster in Florida during the 1961 Bay of Pigs invasion; co-owner of Castle and other Caribbean banks used by the CIA and crime figures to launder money and evade taxes; head of the prestigious Miami law firm of Helliwell, Melrose and DeWolf.

CHARLES "LUCKY" LUCIANO, famous mafioso who set up Asian network for import of heroin into the United States; key figure in OSS/CIA alliance with underworld; died in Naples in 1962.

LOUIS CHESLER, Florida real estate promoter associated with Luciano's heir, Meyer Lansky; partner with Helliwell and Wallace Groves in a Bahamian gambling casino.

WALLACE GROVES, onetime Wall Street financier who served a two-year prison term for fraudulent use of the mails to sell stocks; a partner with Chesler and Helliwell in Bahamian gambling; also a partner with Chesler of Resorts International, a controversial U.S. gambling concern, in a Bahamian casino; an alleged undercover agent in the CIA's clandestine section; connected to Miami National Bank when it was run by Sam Cohen for alleged Lansky casino skims.

BURTON W. KANTER, a Chicago tax lawyer who worked with Helliwell in setting up tax shelters through Castle Bank; involved in California real estate racket; indicted but not convicted in a Castle tax evasion scheme; lawyer to the Pritzker family, owners of the Hyatt hotel chain; lawyer and financial promoter for Cablevision Systems Development Company, the United States' largest privately held cable television company.

MORRIS KLEINMAN, an old bootlegger and Mob associate who was allegedly a co-owner of Castle Bank.

TRUMAN SKINNER, senior member of Helliwell's law firm, also involved in Outrigger scam (see Chapter 3).

FELIX CORREA, a Colombian wheeler-dealer connected to the narcotics traffic who bought Helliwell's Bank of Perrine in Miami; jailed by Colombian authorities in 1982 on charges of massive bank fraud.

DONALD ALEXANDER, former head of the Internal Revenue Service (IRS), who helped torpedo Operation Tradewinds, an IRS probe of Caribbean tax evasion schemes.

Chapter 5

Florida's bent bankers, the CIA, mobsters, and offshore havens.

Like Frank Nugan, Miami lawyer Paul E. Helliwell used banks to serve his CIA drug connections in Southeast Asia.* But Helliwell was far more experienced in the politics of drugs, with a sharply honed intellect and instinct for survival the younger man lacked. In a long career that embraced the opium trade in China, CIA covert work in Florida, and Mob-connected schemes in the Caribbean, Helliwell faltered only once, when one of his CIA banks ran afoul of the Internal Revenue Service. Until its demise in 1977, his Castle Bank in the Bahamas formed a Caribbean bridge between the poppy fields of Thailand and organized crime in the United States. A spook's spook, Helliwell also proved a master manipulator of Caribbean bank havens and Panamanian shell companies in his dual role as CIA paymaster and mobsters' counselor. Too nimble an operator ever to get caught, he died a natural death at the age of sixty-four, a wealthy and respected member of the Miami business community.

Helliwell's career in intelligence and drugs dated to World War II, when he served as chief of special intelligence in China for the Office of Strategic Services (OSS). When the latter was reorganized as the CIA, he was in on the ground floor (he was Colonel Helliwell in those days, and Howard Hunt, of Watergate fame, was one of his agents). CIA sources claimed that in Asia Helliwell frequently bought information with five-pound shipments of opium ("three sticky brown bars," according to one source.)[1] After the war he returned to his native Florida, where he helped set up and run Sea Supply Inc., a CIA front in Miami. Until

* See previous chapter.

1961, when the CIA's Cuban operations diverted Helliwell's attention, Sea Supply sent huge amounts of weapons and equipment to opium-smuggling Nationalist Chinese troops in Burma and to Thailand's police, who were also involved in the opium trade.[2]

In those years Helliwell was also the Thai consul in Miami. The consulate operated out of his offices; its registered foreign lobbyist was Washington lawyer James Rowe. And Rowe's partner was the more powerful lobbyist Tommy "The Cork" Corcoran, who at United Fruit's behest had helped trigger the CIA's overthrow of the Arbenz government in Guatemala. Corcoran also represented Chiang Kai-shek's relatives and the Civil Air Transport, a CIA front that, like Sea Supply, was involved in the Asian opium trade. At the time Helliwell employed Rowe, he and Corcoran were two of the closest advisers to Lyndon Baines Johnson, the rapidly rising Senate majority leader.[3]

Narcotics have often been used as a political weapon, one of the best known examples being General Chiang Kai-shek's regime in China before World War II. Thailand's government in the 1950s also depended on the opium trade to finance political and intelligence activities. It came to power through the arms provided by Helliwell's Sea Supply.[4] An "old China hand," Helliwell met many of the principals in the notorious "China lobby." Back in Florida, he arranged a secret account for Chiang Kai-shek's relatives at one of his Caribbean shell banks, and rich Thais and other Asians invested in Florida land-development companies associated with Helliwell. These banks and real estate schemes represented the other part of the heroin puzzle described in the previous chapter.

During World War II heroin addiction dropped dramatically not only because supplies were cut off but also because the crime syndicates were in disarray. Five years before the United States entered the war, organized crime was dealt a serious blow with the arrest and conviction of the legendary Salvatore Lucania, known to the world as Charles "Lucky" Luciano. Charming and strikingly handsome, Luciano ranks as one of the most brilliant criminal executives of the century: It was due to his efforts that the old Mafia was reorganized and modernized as twenty-four family cartels. Luciano also forged an alliance between the Mafia and the Jewish gangs of Meyer Lansky, who became Luciano's lieutenant and later the financial genius of organized crime. With the end of Prohibition in sight, Luciano turned to heroin, which offered an attractive substitute for liquor. His agents developed an efficient supply network in China, where Chiang Kai-shek had come to power with the help of the Shanghai heroin cartel.[5]

But in 1936 Thomas Dewey's organized-crime investigators put Luciano behind bars, removing the underworld's most influential mediator from active leadership. At the same time that Dewey was "racket-busting," Benito Mussolini was waging a vicious vendetta against the Mafia, which had insulted him during a state visit to western Sicily. The outraged dictator responded by unleashing a reign of terror that nearly destroyed the Mafia. But World War II gave American and Italian mobsters a new lease on life, thanks to a cynical alliance between the U.S. Government and organized crime that involved the intelligence community in the politics of drugs.

Apprehensive that Nazi saboteurs might be infiltrating the docks and shipyards of the East Coast, U.S. Naval Intelligence officials struck a bargain whereby Lansky, then Luciano's lieutenant, would provide Mafia henchmen to patrol the waterfront in exchange for the promise of Luciano's release from prison at the end of the war. Shortly after V-E Day, New York's Governor Dewey, who had made his reputation by putting Luciano behind bars, signed the parole papers.[6] The Mafia had also made a deal, known as Operation Underworld, with the OSS to provide gangland assistance for the Allied armies when they landed in Sicily. Later, when he was deported to Sicily, leaving Lansky to look after the shop in the United States, Luciano expanded the syndicate's overseas connections, with more than a little help from his friends in the OSS, now called the CIA. When Communist waterfront strikers shut down Marseilles in 1947, thus closing a major French port to American shipping, the CIA called on Luciano. He furnished hit men; the CIA supplied money and weapons. After several murders the docks were reopened for American shippers—and the syndicate's heroin smugglers.[7] To prevent further strikes, the CIA provided support and money for former Nazi collaborators in the postwar unions of France.[8]

When the syndicate later moved into Southeast Asia's Golden

Triangle, the CIA was again accommodating. Ever zealous to fight communism, the agency shipped cash and munitions to Laotian, Nationalist Chinese, and Thai mercenaries, who were also opium growers employed in the syndicate's heroin trade. CIA planes provided safe passage for the first leg of the drug's journey to the ghettos of the United States.[9] In later years the CIA was to employ Cuban exiles in the South American cocaine and marijuana trade as informants and hit men for covert operations in Latin America.† The end result of such activities was that the CIA became a crucial middleman for drug producers and organized crime.

***

Paul Helliwell moved briskly among such alliances. A banker-lawyer, he frequently shifted directions, using the same banks to launder funds for the CIA and hide phony tax schemes for politically prominent Asians and wealthy American gangsters. He also promoted land rackets and Caribbean gambling schemes associated with Meyer Lansky. Taken together, these seemingly disparate interests form the three parts of the heroin story: Southeast Asian suppliers, the CIA, and the Mafia. By bringing them together in the same bank or business deals, Helliwell proved himself the consummate spy, a man whose career mirrored the CIA's own history of involvement with drugs and organized crime.

Among the Florida real estate companies that benefited from Helliwell's sleight of hand was General Development Corporation, controlled by Louis Chesler, a Florida real estate developer and associate of Lansky, and "Trigger Mike" Coppola, a Lansky crony.[10] Chesler was the partner of Wallace Groves, a onetime Wall Street financier who had served two years in prison for using the mails to sell fraudulent stocks. Groves, too, had Lansky connections through a Bahamian gambling casino at Lucayan Beach that was controlled by Intercontinental Diversified Corporation, a Panamanian holding company. Helliwell was Intercontinental's lawyer; his partner, Mary Jane Melrose, was its vice president.

Intercontinental, which was listed on the New York Stock Exchange, came to the attention of the Securities and Exchange

† See Chapters 6 and 8.

Commission in the late 1970s, when an audit disclosed $3 million in missing funds. According to CIA sources, the elusive money was part of a $5 million CIA fund that was funneled to another Helliwell bank, Castle Bank, located in the Bahamas. CIA documents obtained by *The Wall Street Journal* further showed that from 1965 to 1972 Groves had worked for the agency in its clandestine section, charged with such operations as funding political parties and organizing coups. In the early 1970s IRS agents reported evidence, gleaned from taped conversations, that Intercontinental, operating through Castle Bank, had paid Bahamas Prime Minister Lynden O. Pindling $100,000 to grant the holding company a two-year extension of its gambling casino license. Although Helliwell denied the charges, it is public record that his Castle Bank did loan Pindling $50,000 toward the purchase of a $450,000 home.[11]

To complicate the picture even more, Chesler and Groves were partners in a gambling venture with Resorts International, through a Grand Bahamian company whose counsel was the law firm of Helliwell, Melrose and DeWolf. A controversial gambling concern with casinos in the Bahamas and Atlantic City, Resorts was linked to a squadron of notorious people, from Eddie Cellini, brother of a top Lansky lieutenant, to Robert Vesco, Howard Hughes, Bebe Rebozo, and Richard Nixon.[12]‡

Helliwell was a busy man. In addition to his CIA fronts and Caribbean projects, he secretly purchased twenty-seven thousand acres of central Florida real estate for Walt Disney as the future site of Disney World. Other clients were more questionable, one of them being a group of insurance companies run by C. V. Starr, a former subordinate of Helliwell in the OSS China section. Senate hearings found that the insurance companies received con-

‡ Resorts' management has denied allegations that the corporation had CIA links in its earlier incarnation as the Mary Carter Paint Company. However, Gigi Mahon, an associate editor at *Barron's* financial weekly and the author of a book about Resorts International, said that the CIA had not responded to her two-year-old request for information on Resorts under the Freedom of Information Act. "They admit they have the files on Mary Carter/Resorts, but to date have found excuses not to produce them." (Gigi Mahon, *The Company That Bought the Boardwalk* [New York: Random House, 1980], p. 42; *Rolling Stone* [April 28, 1983], p. 6.)

tracts from the Teamsters' leader, Jimmy Hoffa, and employed agents from the underworld. Helliwell was also counsel to the Miami National Bank, an institution controlled by Lansky's buddies Lou Poller and Sam Cohen* and used to launder casino skims and other Lansky business through a Swiss bank. Miami National, in turn, was connected to a Florida real estate development company owned by Groves through interlocking directorates.[13]

It was a cozy club in Miami, and nothing better demonstrated the congeniality of political and criminal interests than Helliwell's Castle & Trust, a Bahamian shell bank that specialized in tax shelters for America's famous and infamous. A brilliant tax lawyer, Helliwell set up Castle to handle a quarter of a billion dollars in foreign trusts for more than three hundred prominent Americans and corporations. He acted as counsel to the bank, along with another tax lawyer of controversial repute, Burton W. Kanter, of Chicago. Helliwell's Bank of Perrine served as Castle's correspondent bank in Miami, and Castle was a conduit for money from Intercontinental Diversified Corporation.

While there is nothing unlawful about trusts that are designed to avoid taxes, trusts that evade taxes are another matter. According to the IRS, the Castle Bank trusts fell into the latter category. Essentially the investigators charged that the Bahamian bank served as a fake depository for money that never left the United States. But Castle kept the accounts, out of reach of the IRS. A consideration in determining whether a trust is legal or not for tax purposes is whether it is managed by a trustee not related to or closely associated with the owner, since the price for the tax advantages is surrendering all control of the trust. That did not appear to be the case with the Castle accounts. Moreover, many of those holding accounts with Castle declared on their U.S. income tax returns that they had no foreign bank accounts.[14]

Castle Bank and Helliwell would never have come to the government's attention had it not been for an IRS probe, code-named Operation Tradewinds. Started in the late 1960s, Tradewinds was undertaken primarily to trace the illegal profits of U.S. mobsters, particularly Lansky, to such Caribbean bank havens as

* See Chapter 3, pp. 42–43, 50.

the Bahamas and the Cayman Islands. Relying on a strict code of banking secrecy that makes the Swiss look like blabbermouths, hundreds of banks have set up operations in the Caribbean. Some are legitimate, but most are what is known as "brass plate" operations: They consist of a name on the door, a telex number, and a part-time secretary. About 15,000 companies are chartered in the Bahamas, and there is one bank for every 600 residents—twenty times the U.S. ratio. In the Caymans, once known mainly to skin divers and stamp collectors, companies have set up more than 14,000 telex numbers (there are only about 13,500 people in the area) to serve as "domiciliary companies."

The Caribbean banks are used by organized crime and Latin-American drug merchants to launder money; they are also ideal instruments to evade taxes. Often the money is used to buy stateside real estate; in one twelve-month period, for example, offshore firms bought more than $130 million worth of Florida real estate, almost all of it in Dade County. Gangsters win both ways: Not only is their dirty money now invested in clean enterprises but their offshore firms can claim nonresident tax benefits. IRS findings show that at least $150 billion are involved in tax haven operations, and the amount is steadily growing.

The man in charge of the IRS Bahamian investigation was Richard Jaffe, whose mild manners hide a formidable intelligence and tenacity. In the course of his investigations Jaffee met a Miami private investigator, Norman Casper, whom friends describe as "just like the friendly ghost." Casper had a peculiar talent for getting people to tell him their secrets. "I had a big, big shoulder, I found out, and there was a lot of crying done on it and I did a lot of listening," he later told Congress. Jaffe employed Casper as a part-time undercover informant, and one of the people who cried on his shoulder was Michael Wolstencroft, the manager of Castle Bank. From conversations with Wolstencroft and other employees at the Nassau bank, Casper learned that a number of prominent Americans, including gangsters, kept trusts with Castle. Naturally enough, Jaffe and his superiors were eager to learn their identity. Early in 1973 Wolstencroft told Casper that he was stopping in Miami on his way to Chicago, allegedly to deliver bank accounts to lawyer Kanter,[15] and asked Casper to set him up with a date for the evening. Knowing from his informants in Castle that Wolstencroft would be carrying a list of the accounts, Casper asked Sybil Kennedy, a former police trainee, to help him by having dinner with Wolstencroft. The banker called for Ms. Kennedy and foolishly left his briefcase at her apartment when they went out. Casper and Jaffe photographed its entire contents. Kennedy later visited Wolstencroft at his Castle Bank offices and swiped a Rolodex file that would confirm the names found in the briefcase. Wolstencroft didn't find out what had happened until two years later.

There were some catches in the caper, however, one of which was the sort of people who had Castle trusts. "As soon as I saw the names," Jaffe recalled, "I knew there would be a cover-up."[16] There was no problem with depositors like Moe Dalitz, Morris Kleinman, and Samuel A. Tucker, who had been identified by the Justice Department as organized-crime figures and were among seven Castle depositors connected to the Cleveland syndicate. But some of the other people with Castle trusts raised eyebrows: actor Tony Curtis; *Playboy* publisher Hugh Hefner; Robert Guccione's *Penthouse;* Chiang Kai-shek's daughter and her husband; a now defunct rock group called Creedence Clearwater Revival; and Chicago's wealthy Pritzker family, owners of the Hyatt hotel chain. Helliwell and his law partner Melrose had several accounts, as did Chicago lawyer Burton Kanter.[17]

Although Helliwell held the largest number of accounts in Castle, the Pritzker family accounted for its main business, according to investigations by Pulitzer Prize–winning reporter Knut Royce. Kanter was a tax lawyer for Pritzker interests and sat on the board of directors of the Hyatt International Corporation. Other Pritzker associates in Castle included Hefner, who planned to join with a Pritzker company in an Atlantic City casino venture, and Cayman Assurance, a Cayman Island self-insurance company created by Helliwell and owned by the Pritzkers. In tax-related cases the government charged that Cayman Assurance was a tax fraud vehicle to divert money from the United States to Castle Bank.[18]

Also on the Castle list was Stanford Clinton, senior counsel of the Teamsters' scandal-scarred pension fund and a former associate of the Pritzker law firm. Clinton helped the Pritzkers obtain from the pension fund loans of $54.4 million for their hotels, and it was through him that the family came in contact with Jimmy Hoffa. But Jay Pritzker, a lawyer and the driving force behind Hyatt, told the New Jersey Division of Gaming Enforcement that the source of the loans was irrelevant. "You are [i.e., "We were"] making a legitimate borrowing at a legitimate rate of interest, and you are going to pay it back," he was quoted as saying. "What difference does it [i.e., the lender's reputation] really make, other than the risk of unfair accusations? Morally, I see nothing wrong with it."[19]

According to a former Castle president who asked not to be identified because he is still a banker, Helliwell established Castle in partnership with Morris Kleinman, a former bootlegger and Mob associate. Kleinman's interest was controlled by a Panamanian trust directed by his nephew, Albert Morrison, who was Helliwell's accountant.[20] IRS sources alleged that another owner was Burton Kanter.[21] The presence of hard-core gangsters in Castle affairs would help explain Helliwell's seeming double cross of Brigadier General George Olmsted, who had known Helliwell when he ran the OSS China section. Olmsted headed the International Bank in Washington and got stuck with the worthless assets of Castle's sister Bahamian bank, Mercantile Bank and Trust Ltd. Mercantile had most of the same directors and shareholders as Castle, including the ubiquitous Helliwell. In the early 1970s Mercantile found itself in trouble because of large loans to unidentified "American investors" for stock market speculation. To hide the problem Mercantile's officials created shell companies to "buy" the loans; five trusts and a number of loan portfolios were transferred to Castle, which at the time was in a stronger position. The former president of Castle Bank said that he had objected strenuously to the transfer but that the bank's directors nevertheless had "rammed them down my throat." When he asked Helliwell why Castle had to absorb the trusts, the lawyer replied that the transfers were made at the behest of Kanter, who, said Helliwell, had fretted that if the trusts were not transferred, "he'll [i.e., Kanter] end up with his face down in the Chicago River."[22]

Meanwhile a two-thirds interest in Mercantile was palmed off on the International Bank in Washington, which apparently thought the bank a good buy on the basis of a Price Waterhouse audit that declared Mercantile sound. In fact, most of its assets were sham loans, and in 1977 Mercantile was closed by the Bahamian Government, costing International $9 million. International is suing Price Waterhouse over the audit, but the accounting firm argues that it cannot be held responsible for the actions of a Bahamian affiliate. Like Castle, Mercantile was a conduit for CIA money, and Price Waterhouse accountants were "under orders" to make sure "outsiders" did not have access to the books. If they probed around, said a CIA source, they "could unravel a trail to the intelligence community."[23] Of course, the trail might as readily have led to U.S. gangsters.

***

One of the issues that arose from the Castle affair was the advisability of trusting "brass plate" operations in Caribbean bank havens: While some of Castle's clients were in a position to twist arms to preserve their investments, others were badly hurt. Among the latter were owners of desert plots in California's Antelope Valley who had purchased a mirage on the installment plan from a Castle company called International Computerized Land and Research Company. Most of the land was peddled to customers from Europe and Asia who had little opportunity to compare the company's glowing brochures with the bleak reality. The land company's affairs were "serviced" in California by an organization called Central Pacific & Associates, whose incorporation in Illinois had been handled by Kanter's law firm. Kanter and several associates also were listed as directors. Two other Castle subsidiaries also hawked desert land from Central Pacific's offices.

Although Kanter was able to sidestep suits arising from the Antelope Valley sales, he and three lawyer associates were indicted in 1976 by a federal grand jury in Reno on a tax fraud conspiracy to use a Castle Bank trust account to evade $700,000 of the purchase price of a Reno apartment complex. Kanter was acquitted, but his law partner, Roger Baskes, was convicted.[24]

Meanwhile two members of Creedence Clearwater Revival, the defunct rock group with a Castle Bank trust, are suing Kanter, Baskes, their law firm, Castle, and others for professional malpractice and fraud over losses sustained from Castle's liquidation

HOW CREEDENCE CLEARWATER TAX EVASION
SCHEME WORKED, 1969-77

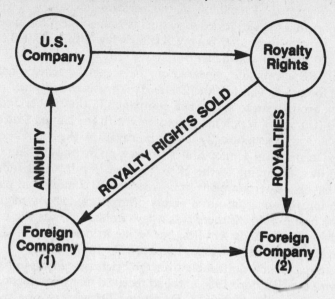

(1) Foreign Tax Haven
(2) Foreign Tax Haven (Different Country)

Clearwater royalties went through a Castle Bank trust (foreign tax haven no. 1, or the Bahamas) to a company in the Netherlands Antilles (foreign tax haven no. 2), where the rock group supposedly paid taxes, thus offsetting U.S. tax liabilities. In fact, an IRS investigation showed that no taxes were paid. The Bahamian trust paid the rock group an annuity through the performers' wives.

Source: "Oversight Hearings into the Operations of the IRS (Operation Tradewinds, Project Haven, and Narcotics Traffickers Tax Program)," Hearings before a Subcommittee of the Committee on Government Operations, House of Representatives, 94th Cong., 1st sess., Oct. 6, Nov. 4 and 11, 1975 (Washington, D.C.: Government Printing Office, 1976).

in 1977. The pair claims Kanter and the others misled them about the tax advantages that accrued from a Castle trust and "misappropriated" $3 million of the performers' money. They also report that the IRS levied assessments against them for unreported income—this, after paying Kanter's law firm $300,000 to set up a watertight tax shelter![25]

Until IRS agent Jaffe appeared on the scene the scheme had seemed foolproof. Through the Castle Bank trusts the royalties of the rock group went to some shell companies in the Netherlands Antilles (Curaçao), which has a tax treaty with the United States. Since the Antilles supposedly taxed the royalties, they could not be taxed again in the United States. In fact, no taxes were paid in the Antilles, according to the IRS. "The net result," said Jaffe, "was that this entertainment group received $2.5 million in one year in income and paid not a penny of taxes. Somebody might take the position that if there was a law violated, it was the tax law of the Netherlands Antilles, but to me it looked like a $2.5 million rip-off of the American taxpayer."[26]

Jaffe himself ran into trouble over the briefcase caper. He had been with the IRS since 1956 and had received many commendations for his intelligence work. Displaying the wisdom of a seasoned bureaucrat, he never made a move without the approval of his superiors, and he kept a record of everything he did. So he was stunned when, during a Washington press conference, his chief, IRS Commissioner Donald Alexander, denounced the methods whereby Jaffe had obtained copies of papers in the Castle Bank manager's briefcase—methods that the Justice Department had ruled to be perfectly legal. Alexander also blew Casper's cover at the press conference, alerting people like Helliwell and Kanter to what was afoot.

Alexander was a Nixon appointee, and one of his first acts as IRS chief had been to review the President's tax returns, declaring that there was no evidence of fraud. He subsequently removed from IRS Form 1040 the question about foreign bank accounts, although it was considered essential by many IRS investigators in Operation Tradewinds. Alexander then canceled Tradewinds even though it had recovered $52.5 million in unpaid taxes, nearly one third from drug traffickers. Jaffe was suspended and served notice that he was liable to criminal indictment for his part in the briefcase affair, despite the fact that his superiors had encouraged and approved his actions.

In the beginning Alexander played the part of the righteous citizen appalled by such methods as photographing the contents of a man's briefcase. But there were too many inconsistencies in his performance. For one thing, he misled Congress by stating to the House Government Operations Committee that he had had no part in canceling Tradewinds. He also claimed not to have seen all the names of the Castle depositors and vehemently denied allegations that his former Cincinnati law firm, Dinsmore, Shohl, Coates and Deupree, had any connection with the bank. It was later learned that the firm had dealt with Castle when Alexander was a senior member.[27]

Sensing a cover-up, Congressman Charles Vanik (D-Ohio), head of the House Ways and Means Committee, investigated the matter and found that Alexander had been deliberately feeding the press partial or out-of-context statements from internal government memos that were bound to prejudice IRS tax cases. The crowning blow came when the IRS gave 90 percent of its Castle Bank file to Kanter after he had been indicted for his part in the affair. The reports were released, without prior consultation with Justice Department lawyers, in response to a Freedom of Information request filed by Kanter. His application for the IRS documents was acted on in a mere three weeks—unprecedented bureaucratic haste for a process that normally takes months or even years. The IRS's directors claimed it had all been a "clerical error," but Congressman Vanik observed that the reports "provided those under investigation with a blueprint on how to elude prosecution." He said that the behavior of Alexander and his underlings had been "absolutely disgraceful" and demanded "severe disciplinary action."[28] The Attorney General's office joined the chorus of complaints by telling Congress that if Alexander continued his cutback activities the "IRS will be destroyed as an effective force."[29]

Although Alexander was later absolved by the Justice Department of any wrongdoing, Jaffe had the last word: "Don't get mad, get even!" Not only was he cleared of any crime by a grand jury in Miami, but the Supreme Court also vindicated him by approving court use of the evidence obtained from the famous briefcase.[30] After quitting the IRS, Alexander went into private practice—as an expert on offshore tax havens!

By dismantling and smearing the IRS intelligence service, Alexander did grave harm to a number of government cases, including an extensive probe of the Teamsters' pension fund that was halted in the fall of 1974 and never reopened. Although the Justice Department carried on with the Castle Bank case, IRS morale was shattered, and to this day, says Jaffe, agency policy is to deemphasize criminal enforcement of tax laws. The international office of the IRS is essentially inoperative insofar as criminal investigations are concerned, although it should be a major participant in any government attack on the narcotics traffic.[31] Most of the successful prosecutions of gangsters and crooked politicians were made possible by IRS investigators. Al Capone, Frank Costello, Huey Long, Bobby Baker, and Spiro Agnew were but a few of their quarry. But since Alexander's brief reign, many in the intelligence division have followed Jaffe's example by retiring or resigning, or have ended up pushing papers in some district tax office.

**

After Castle Bank's demise, Kanter went on to new adventures in cable television, which has turned out to be another good tax dodge. He disbanded his old firm in the wake of the Castle affair, put a new one together (Kanter and Eisenberg), and started another career as legal adviser and financial promoter for the spectacular cable TV operator Charles Dolan. Since the late 1970s, when the two men linked forces, Dolan's Cablevision System Development Company has become the nation's largest privately held cable television company.

Unlike the usual corporation, Cablevision is composed of a series of separate companies, each set up within its franchise area as a limited partnership. The advantage of buying a unit in a partnership rather than purchasing a share of a corporation—or lending money to one—is that any losses may be offset directly against the individual partners' income from other sources. The other feature of such tax shelters is that they allow partners to show that they are "at risk" for a lot of money. By signing notes saying they will be responsible for future losses in the venture, investors can take deductions not only for the actual cash they have put up but also for any money they could be called upon to provide in the future.[32]

Much of Cablevision's seed money came from Chicago investors through Kanter; at least two of the reported investors, Hefner and the Pritzker family, had held trusts in Castle.[33] But while proclaiming an undying admiration for Kanter, Dolan found that association with the lawyer was causing his company too much adverse publicity, and in August 1982 he announced that he was buying out 52 percent of the Kanter law firm's holdings. Dolan added that Kanter and Eisenberg would no longer participate in Cablevision's management and would not be involved in any future limited partnerships. Although the tie was not completely cut, it appeared that Kanter would have to find other fields for his talents. That he would succeed seemed highly probable: Even IRS agents admit that he is one of the smartest lawyers in the business.[34]

As for Helliwell, he died on Christmas Eve 1976 at the age of sixty-four. As brilliant in his way as Kanter, Helliwell went the Chicago lawyer one better: Despite all the controversy surrounding him, he was never charged with a crime.

***

The intriguing thing about such tales is that they have a way of reemerging. There were three postscripts to the Castle story that kept the scandal alive long after Helliwell's death: the CIA, the famous Outrigger real estate scandal in Miami,† and a Colombian banker with drug connections.

The first was Helliwell's CIA connections. While there was no doubt that he had worked with the agency in the 1950s and early 1960s, and that the CIA had at one time used his Caribbean banks to launder money, it is not at all certain that he represented the "Company" in his other ventures. According to *The Wall Street Journal,* the Justice Department dropped its pursuit of Castle Bank under pressure from the CIA. But if Helliwell was not a CIA agent at the time—and Jaffe seems convinced that he was not—then that calls into question a whole series of other

† See Chapter 3.

claims. For instance, it would suggest that the Castle Bank loan and alleged bribe to Bahamas Prime Minister Pindling had nothing to do with CIA covert operations but was a straightforward exchange for a gambling license. It is at least suggestive that the CIA story appeared in *The Wall Street Journal* just before the Supreme Court handed down its decision upholding Jaffe's briefcase evidence. (Jaffe believes it could have been a plant to give the Justice Department an excuse for not pressing forward with the Castle Bank investigation, and it is true that most of the cases withered away.) What does not seem in doubt was Kanter's eagerness to promote *The Wall Street Journal*'s interest in the CIA. He sent Jim Drinkhall, who was writing his paper's stories about Castle, a memo that cited an unidentified informant who claimed to have talked to Edward Ord, a former attorney with the tax division of the Justice Department. According to the informant, Ord had "indicated" that Casper, the Miami private eye, was a CIA agent and that he "ran across the Castle Bank operation while working on one of his CIA projects." But when Drinkhall got in touch with him Ord said he had never heard of Casper and that he "absolutely did not" say there was a connection between Castle and the CIA.[35]

Banker William Losner, Helliwell's assistant for many years, may have supplied a partial answer to this mystery when he said that the CIA knew all about Helliwell's Mob connections and used his banks for that very reason.[36] "Paul loved intrigue," said Losner. "He lived on the knife's edge. He was an extremely intelligent man . . . but you wouldn't believe the payoffs . . . the celebrities I saw with crime figures when I worked for him . . . you wouldn't believe!"[37]

Maybe the point is not to believe. The Nugan Hand and Castle Bank cases both show that "national security" is used as a cover for criminal activities. If the CIA does not choose to expose or discipline its former associates, then we can be reasonably sure that the work they did for the CIA was also criminal. It goes without saying that unless there is a Jaffe to screw up the works, the Helliwells of this world will go on spinning their webs.

Of course the intriguer can be too clever, and that proved to be the case with the second joker in the Castle deck of cards—Truman Skinner. He was the senior member in Helliwell's firm after the latter died, and apparently he thought he could emulate the old man. So he too became involved in a bank scam, the Outrigger case described in Chapter 3.‡ When the authorities began to look into Outrigger's accounts with Miami National Bank, they found Skinner smack in the middle of the scandal: He was a member of the bank's board of directors, on the loan committee, and was connected to one of the companies involved in the affair. After his indictment in the case, Skinner was forced out of the law firm; Helliwell's law office, once the biggest in Miami, was never the same.

The sign on the door still says Helliwell, Melrose and DeWolf, as if to defy time and death. Inside, the offices are furnished with overstuffed couches, old-fashioned prints, and dusty law books—not at all like the modern fixtures of other firms on Miami's glass-and-chrome Brickell Avenue. A fading Mary Jane Melrose talks of retirement, wistfully recalling the good old days in Florida.

Whatever may be said of Helliwell, he had more ability than the current crop of wheeler-dealer bankers who have converged on southern Florida. Had the old man been alive, he would have instantly spotted Felix Correa as an amateur, but Helliwell had been dead for five years when Losner and Melrose sold his Bank of Perrine to the Colombian, who provided the third, and most ironic, postscript: Despite his drug connections,[38] Correa was unaware that Perrine had a shady past of its own, with links to the CIA and organized crime. Nor did Perrine's sellers know who Correa was until he landed in a Colombian jail for a $150 million bank fraud. Needless to say, bank regulators in Florida had no line on either man.

A self-made millionaire, Correa began his career as a gas station operator in the coffee hills of western Colombia. The gas station had to be abandoned, however, when the authorities discovered that it was selling stolen fuel. Ever enterprising, Correa set up a small real estate agency in 1973 in the regional capital of Medellín. The business was apparently a phenomenal success: Within nine years Correa had amassed an empire of fifty-six com-

‡ See pp. 43–47.

panies, including banks and a string of investment houses, and the country's second largest textile manufacturer.

Aged forty-five, Correa appears much older because of his mane of white hair and the sunglasses he wears to hide a glass eye —a memento of some unknown act of violence in his past. A pleasant man of surprisingly simple tastes, Correa was well liked in the Medellín business community, and yet there were always rumors about the source of his fortune. Medellín is the center of the South American cocaine traffic and the home of most of Colombia's major drug dealers. Files of the Drug Enforcement Administration (DEA) indicate that Correa did business with the biggest of them, including high-level money launderers.[39] One of his early financial backers, Juan Evangelista Olarte, was involved with a drug ring in Miami. Correa himself admitted that his banks and financial institutions might have laundered drug money but argued that "these people [i.e., drug traffickers] have done good things for the country."[40]

Like other ambitious Latin Americans, Correa thought that owning a bank in the United States would cap his entrepreneurial career, so he asked Fabio Hurtado, a Colombian who had worked in U.S. banks, to shop around in Miami. Hurtado came up with the Bank of Perrine, which the Helliwell estate had put on the market. After his application was approved by Florida bank regulators and the Federal Deposit Insurance Corporation (FDIC) in 1981, Correa bought Perrine for $6 million, renaming it Florida International Bank.

But Correa had a problem: He had built his financial empire by offering the highest interest rates in Colombia, upwards of 50 percent a year. By June 1982 it had become apparent that he could no longer prop up the house of cards by borrowing from one of his institutions to pay another. Since 1979 the Colombian banking authorities had been urging Correa to clean up his financial mess, but even they did not know the extent of his illegal dealings, which included cooking the books, fraud, accepting deposits without a license, and massive insider loans through fictitious or dead persons. Altogether $150 million had disappeared into the personal coffers of Correa and his associates by mid-1982, when the Colombian bank superintendency at last intervened by seizing his assets. Twenty-one foreign banks were stuck with $26 million in bad loans to Correa's Banco Nacional.[41] Correa and four of his executives were arrested, including Hurtado, who had been the front man for Correa's purchase of the Bank of Perrine. Some said they were jailed for their own safety (a death squad was formed in Medellín to eliminate them). Eight of Correa's associates fled the country, among them Olarte; a ninth was murdered in Bogotá.

When Losner and Melrose heard the news, they were open-mouthed. Why, they wanted to know, hadn't the Florida state regulators done a better job in checking Correa's credentials? Coming from two Helliwell associates, the question might seem ironic, but they had a legitimate complaint. Anyone applying to buy a U.S. bank must provide evidence of solvency, good character, and the ability to run a bank. Correa's Colombian references maintained that he had these essential qualities. The trouble was that U.S. regulators did not check the validity of the references, merely sending them to the U.S. consulate in Bogotá to be notarized. For example, Correa's file in the state regulators' offices in Tallahassee includes a police document from Medellín stating that he had no criminal record, which conveniently overlooked Correa's earlier role in the theft of gasoline from Esso. The file also contains statements claiming that Hurtado, who posed as a partner in the bank's purchase, was the owner of a large financial company called Furatena in Medellín. In fact, Correa was the owner; Hurtado had no connection with the company. Then there were statements from the Colombian banking authorities that they had no reason to veto the acquisition, though they knew Correa to be in trouble at the time. As for personal references, one came from an economic adviser to Correa, while another came from a politician who had received loans from Correa's bank.

The Florida regulators were particularly impressed by Christian Mosquera, Correa's representative in the Perrine negotiations, because he had been a bank superintendent in Colombia, but the former superintendent was an employee of Correa (and later joined the board of Correa's Florida bank). In November 1982 Mosquera was detained for questioning about his part in the affair. And, unbeknown to Florida regulators, the Colombian Planning Department, which must approve all Colombian investments abroad, had denied Correa's application to buy the Bank of Perrine. By going ahead with the purchase Correa was liable to a $12 million fine.[42] As to the FBI check on Correa, it relied on partial files on U.S. citizens in Washington* and therefore was useless.

The regulators also relied on sources in the United States: Citibank gave Correa a letter of reference; the well-known accounting firm of Deloitte, Haskins and Sells told the Perrine lawyers that Correa's financial condition was sound. Ken Meyers, a lawyer and former Florida senator, handled the U.S. side of the negotiations. "U.S. bank approval was given on the basis that [Correa's] Banco Nacional was acting as intermediary for Correa," Meyers explained. But that was not what Correa's lawyers told the Colombian Planning Department, which knew of Banco Nacional's troubles and for that reason denied permission for the acquisition. Handling the FDIC part of the Correa application was the Washington lawyer Adam Yarmolinsky, who relied on Meyers, who relied on Hurtado, who was paid by Correa. Even after Correa went to jail, Meyers found it difficult to believe that he could have been capable of such wrongdoing. "We had absolutely no adverse information in any shape or form."[43]

The Bank of Perrine is not the only U.S. bank that, thanks to the failure of bank regulators to check the applicants' backgrounds, has been acquired in recent years by questionable or crooked foreign interests.† As shown in Chapter 3, "bank reserve" is an excuse for shoddy work—or worse. Even when a background check turns up evidence of criminal connections, the regulators usually ignore it. The reasons can only be surmised, but one may be political influence. Another is bureaucratic sloth. Under the current system, applications are automatically approved (usually in ninety days) unless some outsider steps forward to denounce the applicant to the regulators—and even then the acquisition will go through if the applicant is not actually in jail when the application is filed!

***

---

* See Chapter 3, p. 56.
† See Chapters 7, 8, and 9.

When I first told William Losner of Correa's downfall, he groaned, "Not again!" Losner had gone through all the Castle Bank troubles with Helliwell, and the news about Correa seemed like the return of the albatross: He would never get rid of the taint that seemed to trail Helliwell's bank. But toward the end of the interview he grew more cheerful. "Am I glad I resigned from the board of Perrine after Correa bought the bank." When I asked him why he had resigned, he said that "at the very first board meeting they started talking about making a loan through the Bahamas!"

ROGUES' GALLERY—Chapter 6

RICARDO "MONKEY" MORALES, Cuban exile informant who worked with the CIA, FBI, and Venezuelan secret police; supplied the explosives to blow up an Air Cubana airplane in 1976, killing all seventy-three people aboard; cocaine trafficker; killed in Miami bar brawl in 1982.

SANTO TRAFFICANTE, JR., Meyer Lansky's lieutenant in prerevolutionary Cuba; Mafia boss of Florida and one of U.S.'s. most effective organized-crime leaders; worked with CIA in attempted assassination of Fidel Castro.

ISAAC KATTAN, a Colombian drug-money launderer who dealt in cocaine; his operation was the biggest uncovered in Miami to date.

Chapter 6

Miami—port of entry for cocaine and marijuana; U.S. headquarters of Latin-American terrorists and Cuban-Colombian drug merchants—the country's most fear-haunted city.

Ricardo "Monkey" Morales' favorite movie was *Casablanca*. He saw it again and again, always crying when Ingrid Bergman flew off to safety, leaving Bogie to deal with the Nazis in Africa. His passion for the film reflected his own life in Miami: In a twisted way the ubiquitous spy saw himself as the hero in a real-life thriller of international intrigue and murder. "I don't play to win or lose," he said. "I just play to stay in the game."[1]

A self-admitted assassin and drug trafficker, the forty-two-year-old Cuban exile worked briefly as a secret agent under Fidel Castro before defecting to Miami, where he was employed by both the CIA and the FBI. While still in the FBI's pay, Morales went to Caracas, where he joined the Venezuelan secret police, known as DISIP, serving as chief of Venezuelan airport security. According to the Monkey, the head of DISIP was a CIA recruit and privy to a plot to bomb an Air Cubana plane on its weekly flight from Caracas. In court testimony and published interviews Morales boasted of his part in organizing the October 1976 bombing that cost the lives of all seventy-three people aboard, including the entire Cuban national fencing team, returning from a match in Venezuela. Morales was unrepentant about the operation, which he and Miami police insisted had been a CIA job.[2] "If I had to, I would do it over again," he told the Miami *Herald*.[3] Nor did he regret his other escapades, including murder, assassination attempts, some twenty-five bomb attacks in the Miami area, and a highly publicized career in drug trafficking. But then

the Monkey could afford such bravado since he knew his intelligence connections would protect him from prosecution.[4] When
he finally met his end during a shooting brawl in a Miami bar in
1982, the smooth-talking Cuban died by the only law he knew.*

The stocky, silver-haired mercenary might have seemed an ab-
erration in Boston or Bakersfield, but in Maimi he blended well
into the milieu of international intrigue and crime. Like Casablanca and Saigon, Miami, for geopolitical reasons, has become a
meeting place for intelligence operatives, drug traffickers, terrorists, mobsters—and bankers, who have flocked to southern
Florida because of the deluge of "hot" money. In the atmosphere
of violence, espionage, and quick bucks, adventurers like Paul
Helliwell† and "Monkey" Morales thrive. Some wear three-piece
pin-striped suits, others the dark glasses and gold chains of the
Hispanic tough. Yet each forms an essential part of a city where
Asian heroin and Colombian cocaine have been brought together
in the violent right-wing politics of drugs.

Though not always a mecca for spies, Miami has attracted
schemers of one sort or another almost since its founding. Long
before the narcotics boom made it the drug capital of the United
States, southern Florida was a rendezvous for Caribbean pirates
and slave traders. In the early days much of the city's income
came from looting vessels wrecked along the treacherous coast;
and during Prohibition, when rumrunners made Miami "the
leakiest spot in America," bootlegger fines were carried as a substantial asset in the city's budget. Visitors to the Florida Keys
can still buy a drink at the ramshackle bar where Hunphrey
Bogart fought Edward G. Robinson in *Key Largo*. A similar cel-
luloid atmosphere pervades the hotels along the "Gold Coast" of
Miami Beach; half the properties are owned by notorious mobsters.‡

---

* The bar was owned by a former business associate of Enrique "Kaki"
Argomániz, who worked for Miami's giant drug laundromat, World Finance
Corporation (see Chapter 8). *(Parapolitics/USA* [March 1, 1983], p. 25, citing
the Miami *Herald* [Dec. 22, 1982] and the Washington *Post* [Feb. 6, 1983].)
† See Chapter 5.
‡ Organized crime is also heavily involved in Florida trucking, the garment
business, produce and citrus, warehousing, cold storage, and fishing. (James
Cook, "The Invisible Enterprise," *Forbes* [Sept. 29, 1980].)

After Castro's revolution in 1959, Miami took on a new texture with the arrival of several hundred thousand Cuban refugees. Recently they have been joined by impoverished blacks fleeing the tyranny of the Duvalier family in Haiti, wealthy refugees from the political turmoil of Central America, and middle-class Colombians in search of economic opportunities. (Altogether about seven hundred thousand Latins, or 40 percent of the population, live in Dade County.) They give the city its special flavor, making it more lively and cosmopolitan, providing a cultural mix that has helped to make Miami the United States' principal bridge to Latin America.

Floridians agree that Hispanics contribute significantly to southern Florida's progress. At the same time it is evident that elements within the Spanish-speaking community are responsible for much of the city's drug-related notoriety and soaring crime rate.* While the Anglos blame the Latins for this disorder, the Latins blame one another, according to a pecking order based on time of arrival (i.e., the Cubans look down on the Colombians, who sneer at the Haitians; there are also class distinctions, reflecting the immigrants' former status in Latin America). Serious differences divide the Hispanic and black communities; both suffer from the scarcely disguised racial prejudice of older Anglo Floridians, whose votes assured the approval of a 1980 referendum that denied public funds to promote bilingualism. "I wonder who really upsets whites more," observed Monsignor Bryan Walsh, who once ran a resettlement program for Cuban children, "the poor Cuban on welfare or the rich Cuban with three Cadillacs and a Mercedes out buying the county."[5]

While most of the Cuban exile community is honest and hardworking, some have continued careers in crime begun in prerevolutionary Cuba; others have resorted to violence for political motives or because it seemed an easy way to make money. Whatever their trade, all have been marked by a single event—the 1961 Bay of Pigs invasion, which brought the CIA to Miami

* A study by a Florida grand jury found that Latin Americans account for the largest number of felony arrests in Dade County. (Final Report of the Grand Jury, in the Circuit Court of the Eleventh Judicial Circuit of Florida in and for the County of Dade [May 11, 1982].)

in force. Some two thousand Cuban exiles were hired by the agency, which trained them in the arts of bomb construction, demolition, and efficient murder. But, as one historian has observed, "With the failure of the Bay of Pigs, Cuba became to America what Algeria had been to France."[6] Like the right-wing Organisation de l'Armée Secrète (OAS), which rebelled against Charles de Gaulle's accommodation with Algeria, the CIA's Cuban agents were left in political limbo when the invasion failed. Some continued to work with the CIA in its secret war against Cuba, while others served as CIA mercenaries abroad, as "Monkey" Morales did in the Congo.[7] But patriotism soon degenerated into thuggery, with anticommunism as a cover for blackmail and drug running. "These people came out knowing how you do it," said a former commando leader who trained Cubans for the invasion. "They found it absolute child's play when they started in [with drug smuggling] over here, because we [i.e., U.S. law enforcement] didn't have that type of defense. They didn't even need most of their expertise."[8]

Washington's first inkling of a "Cuban Connection" came in 1970, when the Bureau of Narcotics and Dangerous Drugs, the Drug Enforcement Administration's predecessor, cracked a major heroin and cocaine ring run by Cuban exiles. By the mid-1970s law enforcement agencies were inundated by an exile-directed drug flood. Other criminal activities flourished, again with political cover. Miami police said that many instances of crime in the Cuban exile community alleged to have been politically motivated, such as the kidnapping and fleecing of supposed Castroite sympathizers, were actually straightforward shakedowns. "Ninety percent of the people in exile terrorist organizations like Alpha 66 and Omega 7 are extortionists," said a former member of the Dade County Organized Crime Bureau. "They have no intention of going back to Cuba—that's just a cover for the same old Mob rackets. But people are afraid to challenge them because they're killers."[9]

The record of these Cubans is impressive: It far surpasses the terrorist acts of Italy's Red Brigades or Libya's assassin squads. Many of those responsible for such terrorism (e.g., Morales) are also in the narcotics big time. As noted by crime historian Hank Messick, the original excuse for expanding the Miami cocaine market was to fight communism. "Just as [Meyer] Lansky excused some of his crimes in the name of protecting Jews and then Israel, so did some Cubans hide their appetite for quick money behind the flag."[10]

It was an amazingly successful ruse. Because of their alleged hatred of Castro, these Cubans were literally allowed to get away with murder. Today they are "comfortably into their third decade as America's first and only home-grown international terrorist group."[11] Despite their bloody careers, they move about freely, hold press conferences, and rarely go to jail; when they do, they stay but briefly. Of eight Cuban terrorists serving jail sentences at the end of 1980, one was out on bail, two more were expected to be out on bail shortly, one was to be paroled, and four others were awaiting early release.[12]

The ruse worked for the same reason that it did in Southeast Asia, where the politics of drugs drew the CIA into the heroin traffic.† Morales, for example, was involved in several marijuana and cocaine rings—he once was caught red-handed with a ten-ton marijuana pickup—yet he was never convicted because of his role as an "undercover agent." In one cocaine case in Miami Morales admitted to the defense lawyer that he had murdered an anti-Castro activist and tried to execute another. "He told me about the murder," said the lawyer, "as cavalierly as if he were talking about a new pair of shoes." Morales apparently thought nothing of publicizing such deeds since he told the same story to the Miami *Herald*. His employers must have known, too. During the attempted execution of an anti-Castro Cuban in 1968 (the target survived seventeen machine-gun bullet wounds), Morales was a contract agent for the CIA; he was working for the FBI when he murdered Eladio Ruíz in broad daylight outside an apartment building in downtown Miami. After the execution Morales casually climbed into a waiting car and drove away. Witnesses reported that the car was followed by another car, with two well-dressed Anglos riding shotgun.[13]

Though Morales always claimed to disdain heroin, some of his partners allegedly dealt in the drug, and several of his former colleagues in the CIA were deeply involved in the traffic.[14] Their

† See Chapters 4 and 5.

heroin connections came to light during the 1970 bust that uncovered the "Cuban Connection": A large number of those arrested were CIA-trained veterans of the Bay of Pigs invasion,
including Mario Escandar, an alleged leader of the narcotics network with powerful friends in the Miami community.[15]‡

The links among Miami, the CIA, and the heroin traffic were
not accidental. Under the corrupt dictator Fulgencio Batista,
Cuba became the principal U.S. entry point for heroin shipments
from Lucky Luciano's China network.* Meyer Lansky,
Luciano's lieutenant, controlled the Cuban traffic as well as most
of Havana's gambling casinos. But Lansky's main base was Florida, where he met a Sicilian-born Tampa gangster called Santo
Trafficante. The latter had earned his reputation as an effective
organizer in the Tampa gambling rackets, and in 1940 he assumed responsibility for Lansky's interests in Havana. By the
early 1950s Trafficante had become such an important figure that
he delegated his Havana concessions to Santo Trafficante, Jr., the
most talented of his six sons. When his father died in 1954, Trafficante Junior succeeded him as Mafia boss of Florida and fell
heir to his relationship with Lansky. Unostentatious and self-
effacing, he proved one of the most effective organized-crime
leaders in the United States.[16]

After Luciano's death in 1962, the logical successors to his
leadership in the narcotics trade were his two subordinates,
Lansky and Vito Genovese. But Genovese was serving a fifteen-
year sentence on a heroin-trafficking charge; and Lansky, then in
his sixties, was too old and too carefully watched to become
actively involved. Thus, by death and default the responsibility
fell to Trafficante.[17]

Castro's revolution not only upset policymakers in Washington
but also cost Trafficante and Lansky their lucrative Cuban base.
The loss was partially offset by Trafficante's control of the Florida *bolita* lottery, a Cuban numbers game that became enormously profitable when the refugees started pouring into Florida.
Trafficante's organization recruited Cuban gangsters to run the
lottery and serve as narcotics couriers and distributors; and when

‡ See Chapter 8.
* See Chapter 5.

the CIA called for volunteers for the Bay of Pigs invasion, Trafficante supplied his quota.[18]

As in Southeast Asia, right-wing politics forged an alliance in southern Florida between the CIA and organized crime. In 1960, when the CIA was devising plots to eliminate Castro, it used a contract agent, Robert Maheu, to contact the mobster John Roselli, who in turn introduced Maheu to Trafficante and Sam Giancana, the Chicago capo. During a 1961 meeting at Miami's Hotel Fontainebleau, Maheu gave Trafficante and Roselli poison capsules to be smuggled into Cuba to kill Castro, but the attempt failed. Two years later Trafficante was again involved with the CIA in a bizarre boat raid against Cuba co-sponsored by William Pawley, a former assistant secretary of state and wealthy financier who had been a colleague of Paul Helliwell's in China and was co-founder of the Flying Tigers, later a CIA airline known as Civil Air Transport, involved in arms smuggling in the Far East. Pawley also participated in the CIA coup against the Arbenz government in Guatemala in 1954, along with another Helliwell associate, lobbyist "Tommy the Cork" Corcoran; prior to Castro's takeover Pawley had owned the Havana bus system and sugar refineries.[19]†

There were other links between southern Florida and Southeast Asia. After the Bay of Pigs disaster, the Miami CIA station worked with the Trafficante organization on new assassination plots against Castro. The head of the station, Theodore Shackley, was later transferred to Laos, where he helped organize the CIA's secret Meo tribesmen army, which was deeply involved in the heroin traffic. And when William Colby became the director of the CIA in 1973, Shackley took over his job as chief of covert operations in the Far East.‡ To complete the picture, Trafficante himself showed up in Saigon in 1968 during an Asian tour aimed at replacing Luciano's old China network with one based on the opium production of Southeast Asia.[20]

***

The foundations for Miami's emergence as an international crime center were laid in the 1930s and 1940s, when gangsters

† See Chapter 5.
‡ See Chapter 4.

like Lansky and Trafficante settled there, but it was not until after the CIA organized hundreds of trained killers in the early 1960s that Miami began to fulfill its promise of notoriety. Protected by their CIA ties and frustrated in their political ambitions, these agents turned to the drug trade for a living. When America's drug boom took off in the mid-1970s, they became the pioneers of a criminal-industrial complex in southern Florida that now ranks as the state's biggest business, with annual revenues of at least $10 billion.[21]

The irony is that while the U.S. Government allows such thugs as "Monkey" Morales to operate freely for reasons of "national security," it ignores the genuine weakness they expose in the nation's physical safety. Cuban and Colombian drug traffickers have proved that the country's air defenses are a joke. Dozens of drug planes penetrate U.S. air space daily, undetected by radar. If they can fly in and out with impunity, a hostile plane or some mercenary terrorist could do the same. "The Air Defense radar coverage of the approaches to Florida is a disgrace," wrote John L. Warr, a Customs air officer in Tampa. "This situation must be corrected for the purpose of national security, if for no other reason."[22]

Presumably that was one reason why the Reagan administration announced, in early 1982, a cabinet-level task force, headed by Vice President George Bush, to deal with Florida's narcotics problems. Although the task force did make a temporary dent in the drug flow, its principal activity seemed to be the issuance of glowing press releases to encourage a large Florida turnout for the Republicans in the November elections. Most of the narcotics seizures and arrests for which the task force took credit were actually the work of local agents who had been on the cases long before Bush's publicists arrived on the scene. And while the task force did beef up local agencies with three hundred additional men, most were temporary personnel who lacked the street knowledge of Miami needed to penetrate the city's two hundred or so drug rings.

Five months after the task force's much-heralded arrival— time enough for the drug traffickers to figure out new ways to avoid detection—cocaine smuggling and homicide were again on the rise in Miami. True, the Colombian marijuana industry remained depressed, but that was due less to the task force than to competition from homegrown pot, now believed to be the United States' third most valuable cash crop.[23]

The Army and the Air Force agreed to cooperate with the task force by lending Customs some helicopters and radar-equipped Hawkeyes, which were intended to drive smugglers from southern Florida skies. But as Ed Lowry, a retired Customs pilot, pointed out in a blistering nine-page letter to the U.S. Commissioner of Customs, all that happened was that the smugglers switched from small to big airplanes capable of outflying pursuers. Contrary to official propaganda, said Lowry, "these large aircraft are seldom caught or even disturbed in their smuggling." He also criticized the Customs Air Patrol's flight schedules, which frequently leave south Florida open territory for smugglers between midnight and dawn. "Schedules are made two weeks in advance. Everybody in the country knows when Customs is going to be working." Many Miami police and federal agents privately agreed with Lowry. "Ninety percent of the agents I know would like to write a letter like that," said an agent with the Drug Enforcement Administration (DEA). Nor were Lowry's criticisms directed only at Customs. "The military has long smiled [at the drug traffic]," he wrote, when in reality they ought to be worried about the implications for national security.[24]

***

As in the days of Prohibition, Miami has both gained and lost from the drug trade: Narcotics fuel southern Florida's economy but are also responsible for making Miami the most dangerous city in the United States. "We bankers are always saying how Miami has become an international banking center like London or New York," observed the chairman of a Florida bank. "But that's a lot of hogwash. The reason so many banks have opened offices here is because of the hot money, particularly drug money." A prominent Miami lawyer agreed. "There is no real interest here in preserving or creating a quality of life. I don't think there is any real community outrage about the drug trade. I push the junior lawyers here to join civic groups instead of playing racquetball. They're not interested."[25]

Legitimate trade between Latin America and Florida amounts

to more than $18 billion a year, but that is less than a quarter of the earnings generated by the narcotics traffic, 80 percent of which flows through southern Florida. Charles Kimball, a real estate economist who keeps close watch on foreign purchases of southern Florida property, estimates that nearly half the $1.5 billion invested yearly by foreign companies in Miami real estate comes from illegal sources—drug dealers, organized-crime syndicates, foreign criminals, and international swindlers.[26] In other words, the construction industry in Miami would be on the rocks were it not for shady investors. The same can be said of the retailers of such luxury items as yachts and airplanes, and of accountants, lawyers, and other professionals who have fattened on the narcotics traffic. "You know what would happen if we really did our job here?" asked a spokesman for U.S. Customs, one of five federal agencies trying to stop the drug traffic. "If we were 100 percent effective, we would so drastically affect the economy that *we* would become the villains."[27]

Of course, in their public pronouncements the Miamians speak quite differently, reflecting the nationwide hypocrisy that blames Latin Americans for the drug traffic but refuses to recognize that there would be none without a U.S. market of fifty-two million consumers. The Cuban and Colombian mafias that direct the drug flow out of Miami are no different in their violent ways from the Italian, Irish, and Jewish mafias that organized during Prohibition; they have since been absorbed into the American mainstream. And while a high percentage of the criminals in Miami speak Spanish, crooks from all over the world have been attracted to the city because of the drug trade. Like the bankers, they go where the action is. In that sense Miami has indeed become an international center—for crime.

Crime is very much on the minds of Miami's citizens. Instead of talking about the weather or last night's TV program, neighbors discuss the latest robbery or murder on their street. Everyone has a personal horror story, such as getting caught in the crossfire of a gangland shooting at the local shopping center, or watching in terror as the occupants of two cars spatter each other with machine-gun fire at a stoplight. Perhaps the most bitter reaction was that of a Colombian banker who swore that if one more thing happened to him and his family, they would pack up and return to Bogotá, once considered the most dangerous city in the hemisphere. During his very first week in Miami the banker's briefcase was stolen—from under his legs while he was paying his bill at the desk of the luxurious Omni Hotel. Then the hubcaps on his car were stolen. One night he and his wife went out to dinner, leaving their newborn son with their Colombian maid, who had been with the family for years. Their house had two different alarm systems, one of which was connected to the local police station. Returning home, the couple found the maid floating lifelessly in the swimming pool; their infant was safe in his crib, but his clothing and body were drenched with water, as if he had been in the pool.[28]

The Miami *Herald* is full of such stories from people who want to know why "the city of my dreams" has become "Dodge City South." Since the drug boom began, the homicide rate in southern Florida has jumped more than 400 percent. In 1981 Dade County recorded 1.6 homicides a day, putting Miami at the top of the FBI's list of the most dangerous cities in the United States. Six other cities among the FBI's top eleven were also in Florida. "When you see a helicopter, you know they've found another body," said a university professor, whose backyard was used to dump one of them. The dead man was a Colombian who had been attending the birthday party of a neighbor's young daughter. Like most crimes in Miami, the murder was never solved, and to this day the professor and his neighbors have no idea why the man was killed, "except that he was a Colombian."[29]

The Miami police force has been enlarged by the addition of new recruits, and there are more judges on the criminal circuit, but even so the city cannot cope. "In an average month we file 2,705 felony cases after screening," said Lieutenant George Ray Havens, head of Miami's Criminal Investigative Division. "If every individual charged was granted a jury trial, we wouldn't be able to file another case for at least three years. The U.S. attorney's office has sixty-three full-time lawyers, but even if they didn't take any more cases it would take nine years to finish the ones already filed." The Criminal Investigative Division has twenty-seven agents and receives 476 requests for investigations every month. "If the case is complicated—say, a financial racket —we just can't handle it," said the lieutenant.[30]

The Miami police refuse to accept drug cases because they have no more room to store the seized drugs, even after burning tons of marijuana in the Florida Power and Light Company's furnaces. At any given moment the sheriff's office in Key West is sitting on a $4 million stash of evidence—a target so inviting that the sheriff's men do little except guard it. Paroles jumped 50 percent between 1978 and 1980—convicted drug dealers have so crammed Florida prisons that burglars, armed robbers, and the like are being turned loose to make room.[31] Even so, most drug traffickers, and especially the biggest of them, serve only a short time; the average sentence is less than two years, with parole in a year. About all the hard-pressed authorities can do is keep a body count, and even that is a challenge: So many bodies have piled up at the Miami morgue that the Dade County medical examiner has rented a refrigerated hamburger van to house the overflow. "If you stay here, you arm yourself to the teeth, put bars on the windows, and stay at home at all times," said Arthur Patten, a Miami insurance executive. "I've been through two wars and no combat zone is as dangerous as Dade County."[32]

As residents go shopping for protection, the area is beginning to resemble an armed camp. Sales of security equipment, including alarms, locks, floodlights, guard dogs, surveillance systems— all the paraphernalia of fear, are rising exponentially. Gun sales are also soaring; in 1981 they rose 46 percent over the previous year to a record 66,198. "Most customers are people like your mother," said one gun shop owner. "They're just average, everyday folk who want to continue to live."[33] Even those who favor gun controls are skeptical of their success in southern Florida. "If you take guns away, they'll use knives," said a police captain. "If you take away knives, they'll use a hammer. Hammer, saw. Saw, machete. Pretty soon we'll be back to hands."[34]

For people who live, as I do, in a notorious Latin-American danger zone, this siege mentality is all too familiar: Never wear jewelry on the streets; don't go out at night or attend large public events (at the Orange Bowl, for example); put bolts, locks, and alarms on the doors; and keep a large attack dog. Many Latin Americans came to Miami in search of security. But because of the drug trade and political intrigue* not a few are beginning to agree with the Colombian banker who said it was "safer in Latin America."

Nobody is immune. The regional commissioner for the Customs Service was mugged and robbed outside a Miami discotheque. The life of a federal judge was threatened by drug defendants, and a Florida drug gang paid $200,000 for hit men to kill the state's entire list of witnesses in a case against the gang's members. After Florida's Governor Robert Graham visited Colombia to seek greater cooperation from local authorities in the struggle to stop the cocaine trade, the Colombian mafias sent a hired assassin to Tallahassee in an attempt to kill him.[35]

Of all the ethnic mafias, the Colombians are most like the Sicilians, with tightly knit organizations based on blood ties. The penalty for family betrayal is death; it is usually carried out by a shuttle assassin, who takes the morning flight from Bogotá to Miami and returns that night. Long the world's leaders in counterfeiting dollars, the Colombians have become more sophisticated in recent years, combining drugs, stolen securities, and counterfeit money in giant money-cycling operations that span three continents. Since the mid-1970s, when their role was primarily that of supplier, they have taken over most of the U.S. distribution of cocaine. The Cubans still dominate marijuana distribution. Police say that the traffic's rationalization closely resembles the organizational changes brought about by Prohibition, when a network of cooperative syndicates developed throughout the United States. The older syndicates continue to deal in drugs, but they function mostly as wholesalers dependent on the Colombian and Cuban networks for their supplies. The Latin mafias operate like any multinational corporation, with separate divisions for imports, transport, distribution, and finance. Each smuggling operation has one hundred to two hundred employees in Miami, usually illegal aliens on false passports. The Florida organizations are supported by larger ones in the

---

* One of the spillovers from the Central American wars has been an increase in kidnapping threats against wealthy refugees in Miami. Colombian drug traffickers occasionally resort to kidnappings, but a more common method of dealing with rivals is assassination.

producing countries, where complacent politicians are often paid to look the other way. Some two hundred thousand peasant families in four countries depend on the traffic for their livelihood.

Given the international scope of the traffic and the huge sums of money involved, it seems unbelievable that any U.S. task force, even Mr. Bush's, can "interdict" the flow: No matter how many tons of narcotics are seized or how many people are arrested, there will always be more where they came from. Alcee Hastings, southern Florida's most lenient federal judge, has often been criticized for the light sentences he gives drug traffickers, but Hastings has a point when he complains that most of the people who come before him are low-level traffickers. "Drugs are tearing the hell out of the social fabric of America, but we're not catching the right people," he said. "They're arresting a mule† a minute, an offender an hour. When they start catching bankers, judges, senators and newspaper editors, you'll see who's tough. The ringleaders are in a lot of trouble if they come before me."[36]

A four-month study of the Drug Enforcement Administration (DEA) made by the Miami *Herald* in 1981 went a long way toward explaining the basis of Hasting's complaint. In addition to finding the usual bureaucratic infighting, the study showed that the administration's principal weakness is its obsession with statistics. To make the DEA look good, agents are directed to concentrate on quick seizures and arrests. The result is that they are often tied up for days on relatively small buy-busts that yield no new information and no important indictments. "All of us in law enforcement have got to get away from this attitude that our sterling successes involve the number of tons of marijuana and cocaine we can seize," James York, commissioner of the Florida Department of Law Enforcement, told the Miami *Herald.* "A ton of cocaine isn't worth a damn. You've got to penetrate the organizations." Assistant U.S. Attorney Robert Perry added, "Street operations are dangerous, disruptive, labor-intensive, expensive, and frequently unsuccessful." Although street work is essential to gathering intelligence and cultivating informants, he said, arrests stemming from buy-busts usually produce low-level defendants, low bails, and light sentences.[37]

† A mule is a low-level drug courier.

Getting the ringleaders involves long, tedious investigations for which few DEA agents are trained and on which they receive little support. Example: A two-month investigation by an inter-agency task force called Operation Greenback led to the imprisonment of Isaac Kattan, a Colombian and the biggest drug-money launderer ever caught in Florida. But while an impressive catch, Kattan was still only a middleman. Other members of the task force, such as the IRS agents, wanted to delay his arrest in order to identify his bosses, but the DEA, itching for a catch, insisted on arresting him when he was seen dealing in cocaine. "They got twenty kilos of coke but not much else," said a member of the task force. "We found that chopping off Kattan's head didn't kill off the organization; another head popped up to do the same things. If the DEA hadn't been in such a hurry to make an arrest, maybe we would have gotten the organization."

The Government Accounting Office (GAO) has also objected to the eagerness for action, blaming the Justice Department, which oversees the DEA, for not "taking the profit out of" drug trafficking. In a 1981 report GAO pointed out that although Congress had passed a law in 1970 enabling the government to seize the financial assets of criminals, the DEA "simply has not exercised the kind of leadership and management necessary to make asset forfeiture a widely used law enforcement technique." In the ten years following the law's enactment, the Justice Department obtained a mere $2 million in forfeited criminal assets, GAO found, and even then most of the assets were items like planes and boats that drug traffickers consider expendable.[38]

If caught, the most a trafficker need expect is a year in jail, and that deterrent is trivial in view of the enormous profits. As for the State Department's idea that the traffic can be halted by dumping the herbicide paraquat all over the Third World, it is about as realistic as the DEA's infatuation with statistics. As in Turkey, the peasants just move their crops elsewhere. Moreover, there is no known herbicide for the coca leaf bush, which is the source of cocaine and the biggest item in the South American drug trade. If any deterrent is to be found, it has to be at the money end. The law of supply and demand has already been at work in the marijuana market. Marijuana is a declining crop in such producer nations as Colombia and Jamaica because it can no longer compete with U.S. production. The DEA didn't stop Colombia's marijuana shipments; economics did.

When Congress passed the forfeiture laws, the idea was to make drug trafficking unprofitable by seizing every U.S. and foreign bank account of the offender. But that approach to the problem implies a whole new strategy on the part of drug agents, who have always seen narcotics in the simplistic terms of cops and robbers. According to GAO, the Justice Department's poor record in seizing financial assets can be attributed to the failure of DEA and department prosecutors to press such cases in court. As revealed by the Miami *Herald* study, such cases have not been pursued, primarily because they are more time-consuming and complex than the quick buy-busts. According to Lieutenant Havens, "The attitude of the average bureaucrat is: big cases, big problems; little cases, little problems; no cases, no problems. People don't want problems."[39]

It is also unhappily true that most people have a price, and with so many "narcobucks" floating around Miami, the corruption of some police agents, judges, and others is inevitable. Half of an entire division of the Dade County police force has been indicted for payoffs and drug trafficking. Two individuals were charged with working with a known drug racketeer. John Scharlatt, a former group supervisor of the DEA's Miami offices who was assigned to Vice President Bush's task force, skipped town in the summer of 1982 after being indicted by a federal grand jury on smuggling and corruption charges.[40] Admitted Florida's Attorney General Jim Smith, "Frankly, I lie in bed sometimes at night and it . . . just scares me, the level of corruption we may have in Florida."[41]

Outspoken Miamians like insurance executive Arthur Patten have been vilified by their fellows for speaking their minds about the city's "combat zone." Municipal leaders called Patten a coward and told him to shut up. He also lost business from hotel clients who were angered by the bad publicity. But playing ostrich won't solve the problem. As the Miami *Herald* has repeatedly said, "Reality, not image, is South Florida's problem."[42]

A Florida grand jury that studied Miami's crime problems agreed with the Miami *Herald:* "We recommend that the hard issues begin to be addressed. We find that we have not fully com-

mitted ourselves as a society to eradicate narcotics, and probably
we never will. Our local economy apparently has benefited enormously and our culture has become tolerant of marijuana and
even of cocaine. Yet we ask the small numbers of law enforcement personnel assigned to narcotics interdiction to stop a supply
for which we create a demand. That is clearly a costly hypocrisy."[43]

ROGUES' GALLERY—Chapter 7

ISAAC KATTAN, a major Colombian launderer of drug money, with headquarters in Miami, who dealt with four Florida banks; sentenced to thirty years in prison in 1981.

LIONEL PAYTUBY, vice president of the Great American Bank in Miami, who was implicated in Kattan's laundering operation; arrested in 1982 on charges of running large drug money–laundering ring and a Quaalude lab.

MARLENE NAVARRO, Colombia's "queen of cocaine"; involved in Paytuby's operation; a fugitive from U.S. and Colombian justice.

FELIX CORREA, a Colombian banker alleged to be the "brains" behind Paytuby's laundering operation between the United States and Switzerland; purchased Miami's Bank of Perrine from CIA paymaster Paul Helliwell; jailed in Colombia in 1982 on charges of massive bank fraud (see Chapter 5).

ARTURO FERNANDEZ, well-known Colombian launderer who used eight Miami banks; worked with Kattan.

ORLANDO ARREBOLA, vice president of Miami's Continental National Bank, charged with laundering conspiracy led by Fernández; acquitted in 1982.

JAIME MICHELSEN, head of Colombian financial conglomerate and Bank of Colombia, which owns the Eagle National Bank in Miami; charged with stock manipulation in Colombia.

ABDULLAH DARWAISH, member of a group of Arab investors that purchased a multistate bank holding company on the East Coast; charged with embezzlement by New York State senator.

JAMES THERRIEN, Chase Manhattan's man in Bogotá; allegedly involved in self-lending and other wheeling-dealing.

Chapter 7

The banking industry booms in Florida, as dope smugglers and related villains need laundries for their cartons of cash. How easy it is for a crook, particularly an alien crook, to buy a bank, and why U.S. law enforcement agencies cannot stop them.

Miami, the Wall Street of the $79 billion narcotics traffic, has attracted more than one hundred banks from two dozen countries. The most prestigious address is Brickell Avenue, a block from the bay, where gold-and-black skyscrapers rise incongruously above the palm trees. Coral Gables, the Latin-American headquarters of some one hundred multinational corporations, is also considered a chic bank location. Architecture tends to reflect management style: Citibank's Miami headquarters is housed in a sleek glass building embellished with ultramodern chandeliers; Credit Suisse's Brickell offices gleam with chrome and mirrors. By contrast, the Cuban exiles' Republic National Bank operates out of an old-fashioned structure decorated with middle-class Latin-American art. Then there are the fly-by-nights, some of which look like converted hamburger stands. It takes only $2 million to start a southern Florida bank (compared to $6 million in, say, Ohio), and a lot of people have discovered that with an initial investment of $100,000 to $200,000, they can join Florida's bank rush.

If a bank attracts even a small fraction of the $4 billion deposited by foreigners each year, the profits can be enormous. Much of the money is "hot" and therefore accepted only in non–interest-bearing accounts, or changed into cashier's checks, which can take several months to return to the bank for collection, giving it another source of interest-free funds. If the bank is willing to launder drug money on a regular basis, it can collect 2 percent commission, in addition to having interest-free money to lend out at daily rates as high as 20 percent. And if a bank should prove unprofitable, its owners can sell it to a foreigner for two or three times its real value just because it has a Florida charter.

The smaller the bank, the more dubious the buyers it is likely to attract. "In Miami they have a saying in Spanish: 'The sharks are on the streets, not in the sea,'" said Richard H. Dailey, president of the small Dadeland Bank, controlled by Panamanian and other Latin interests. "You wouldn't believe how many people come in here to ask if the bank is for sale. This would never happen in San Francisco," added Dailey, who started his banking career in California. "We used to have the same problem," agreed Aristides Sastre, president of Republic National Bank, "but it's become less prevalent because we've grown so much. I don't know anywhere else in the United States where people just walk in off the street and offer to buy the bank."[1]

In addition to foreign and locally controlled banks, Miami has thirty-seven Edge Act corporations (i.e., foreign and out-of-state bank subsidiaries that deal exclusively in overseas transactions) and another fifty or so foreign bank agencies and representative offices. Indeed, there are so many banks in southern Florida that they resemble the supermarkets—one to a block. The out-of-state and foreign buyers claim that their institutions have been attracted to southern Florida by the area's explosive growth, its Latin-American trade, or the need to service customers, like the multinational corporations in Coral Gables. But according to the Treasury Department there is an additional attraction for at least one third of the banks in Miami: the huge profits to be made from laundering drug money.[2] As many as forty banks have neglected to report cash deposits of $10,000 or more, as required by law. The majority are small banks, known to both cops and crooks as Coin-O-Washers, and set up primarily as laundries. At least four such banks are controlled by drug dealers, according to law enforcement officials.[3]

Because the ultimate sales of marijuana, heroin, and cocaine are made on the streets, the dealers amass huge amounts of small bills. These are fed into high-speed money counters; if that becomes too cumbersome, the money is weighed (e.g., three hundred pounds of $20 bills total $3.6 million). A common sight in Miami banks is an unshaven Latin lugging several shopping bags crammed with cash to a teller's window. More professional middlemen prefer to deliver cardboard boxes of cash to the bank's back door. If there is any problem, the courier will usually abandon the money. Thus, when a Miami teller questioned a woman about where she had obtained the money in her shopping bag, because it smelled of fish, she dropped the bag and fled, leaving $200,000 behind.

While the government has tightened bank reporting regulations for large cash transactions and has arrested half a dozen Miami bankers, the laundering business still flourishes. Since the drug boom began, the Florida banking system has consistently registered staggering surpluses of cash each year—$8 billion in 1982—or more than twice the surplus cash in all the rest of the country. Financial experts calculate that more than half the surplus is hot money.[4]

Customs officials acknowledge that the banks have been more cooperative in recent years, but, even so, William Von Raab, U.S. Commissioner of Customs, said that in 1981 Florida banks failed to report $3.2 billion in cash transactions, evidence of "flagrant violations by some of the employees of many of the institutions and even by some of the institutions themselves."[5] Such "sleazy" practices declined briefly after Senator William Proxmire (D-Wis.) came down hard on Florida banks during hearings on drug-money laundering in the summer of 1980. "But now we're back to pre-Proxmire levels," claimed an undercover agent who worked on a Miami FBI sting in which the agents posed as middlemen in a laundering operation. "The bankers were delighted to deal with me when I was 'dirty,'" she continued. "Bank guards were always willing to carry crates of money into a back room with counting machines. Cash reporting requirements never hindered banks, since they could afford to pay the fines if caught."[6]

While there isn't a Florida banker who won't swear his bank is clean, the fact is that some people must be laundering the billions of dollars in drug money flowing into the state; and because the traffic is so huge, these people must be bankers. "Without banks, I feel that it would be almost impossible that these [drug-money] transactions would continue to happen," Miami banker Anthony Infante told Proxmire's committee. Infante said that "it is extremely difficult for a professional banker not to be aware of the way in which drug traffickers try to use our institutions to facilitate their illegal transactions. In 20 years as a bank officer in Florida, I have seen very few cases in which cash deposits of any substantial amount are necessary in the normal transactions of a customer."[7]

Infante feels that bankers must "go beyond the letter of the law" to solicit information about customers, but other Miami bankers take the attitude that it's none of their business where the money comes from. "It's not really up to bankers" to police drug-cash transactions, said the vice chairman of Miami's Continental Bank, which has been involved in a major drug-related laundering operation.[8]* But lawyer Rudolph Giuliani, a former New York deputy attorney general who helped Chemical Bank stop drug-money laundering at its branches,† disagreed. "I've heard some bankers complain that it's not their role to act as detectives, that they shouldn't be put in that position. It is my view that they are wrong as a matter of law and as a matter of sound business judgment. As a matter of law, the law places the responsibility on banks to obtain and report [information] concerning domestic and foreign transactions. And similarly, irrespective of legal ramifications, any bank that allows itself to be used as a conduit for drug money is in danger of severely damaging its image and its reputation for prudence and integrity. At the same time, it is exposing its employees, who have to deal with many sensitive situations, to being tempted to involve themselves in crime."[9]

Giuliani said he found that many bank employees were ignorant of cash reporting regulations and that ignorance led to negligence—or worse. He also urged better customer checks. "Among

---

* See pp. 131–34.

† Chemical cleaned up its act in a hurry after pleading guilty to 445 misdemeanor counts arising from failure to report transactions that were made to wash dope money. A felony charge was dismissed. ("Banks and Narcotics Money Flow in South Florida," Hearings before the Committee on Banking, Housing and Urban Affairs, U.S. Senate, 96th Cong., June 5 and 6, 1980 [Washington, D.C.: Government Printing Office, 1980], p. 201.)

the problems that I've seen is that there were accounts maintained for drug traffickers and for others who were engaged in illegal activities under phony corporate names, and a simple visit to the business entity, the address that was given when the account was opened, would have revealed the fact that there was no such business in that location or that they were not conducting the business they purported to be conducting." By verifying customers' claims, he said, Chemical "was able to rid itself of a number of very questionable situations where people were engaged in either drug trafficking or illegal gambling activities."[10]

Partly because of Chemical's experience, the bank regulatory system in New York leads the nation in controlling drug-related cash transactions. To a large degree this is so because the New York banks realize how seriously such connections can damage their position as an international banking center. In Florida either the money is too tempting or Miami bankers do not realize how unprofessional their laundering activities appear to other world money centers. "A bank, as any other business, can be as good as the community which it serves," said Infante. "There is no doubt in our minds that if the drug situation continues, the decent and respectable members of our community will eventually leave the area, thereby damaging the image that Miami has been for so long trying to build as an international banking center." Alexander McW. Wolfe, Jr., vice chairman of Florida's giant Southeast Bank, added, "People will not take this place seriously as an international banking center until this hankypanky stops."[11]

Southeast ought to know. When confronted by the Proxmire committee with evidence that a major Colombian drug-money launderer kept large deposits in his bank, President David A. Wollard sheepishly admitted that he had no information on the man. "I honestly read more about it in the paper than anyplace else," he explained. He was equally frank in prescribing a solution to the problem of bank laundering. When asked whether putting some bankers behind bars would encourage their brethren to obey the law, he replied, "I can see where that would greatly stiffen the resolve of all banking officials to comply. Something needs to happen in the Miami community to raise our awareness that this kind of activity is not good for the community and will not be tolerated and will be severely punished with some long prison sentences."[12]

But no Florida banker has received a prison sentence, despite numerous indictments, possibly because, as one frustrated bank regulator observed, juries "always seem to think that if the guy wears a three-piece suit, he can't be guilty of any serious crime." The Proxmire hearings and studies by the Government Accounting Office (GAO) have shown that most bankers believe they risk, at worst, a slap on the wrist. Senator George J. Mitchell, a member of the Proxmire committee, summed it up as follows: "One of the principles of law enforcement is that if persons subject to laws have a widespread belief that they will not be prosecuted, violations of the law are invited. And just as we seek to make examples of those who commit murder and rape and arson, by prosecuting them vigorously and imposing substantial punishment, the theory of general deterrence [should apply] to bankers as well. There isn't a bank in this country that wouldn't know about [a banker's imprisonment] within 24 hours if that happened."[13]

One reason it has not happened is that the regulatory agencies cannot, or will not, stop bank laundering. The Bank Secrecy Act of 1970 gave regulators a powerful tool for uncovering illegal bank transactions, but according to GAO they have not used it.[14] The act requires banks to identify the depositor and source of money for cash transactions of $10,000 or more, except in the case of customers, like big retail operations, that have large cash flows. The information is supposed to be filed with the Treasury within fifteen days of the money's receipt. Transfers of $10,000 or more to foreign banks must also be reported. However, GAO found that a significant number of banks ignore the requirements. Some that do comply delay the reports so that they arrive in Washington as much as two months after the transaction has occurred, by which time it is too late to take action. Few of the banks surveyed by GAO claimed that the reporting requirements were onerous, so excessive paperwork cannot be claimed for failure to obey the law. In any case, said lawyer Giuliani, the banks have no right to complain about being overregulated if they do not regulate themselves.

According to one Florida state regulator, most of the bank reports that are filed gather dust in Treasury offices since "nobody knows what to do with them." GAO confirmed that few law enforcement agencies use the reports and blamed the Treasury for failing to encourage their distribution. As for the bank regulators, "they displayed a reluctance" to make the banks toe the line. Moreover, they had no idea which banks were in violation, or how many violations there had been at a given bank. One reason for the regulators' ignorance, GAO discovered, was that they took the bankers' word that they were observing the law, without auditing their books to verify that this was so. Neither the Federal Reserve nor the Comptroller of the Currency thought to match large cash surpluses deposited with the Federal Reserve by Florida banks against the information they provided in cash transaction reports to the Treasury. The Proxmire committee had to do the regulators' work for them by presenting evidence that four southern Florida banks had made cash deposits of $284 million with the Miami Federal Reserve Bank which they had not reported to Treasury. The Comptroller of the Currency's explanation to the committee was that the regulators had never considered adding two and two.[15]

The Proxmire hearings also showed that the Treasury's own divisions, including the IRS and the Comptroller of the Currency, hide information from one another and—needless to say— from such other agencies as the state bank regulators, Customs, or the DEA. According to Robert Serrino, director of the enforcement division of the Comptroller of the Currency, "bank secrecy" prevents regulators from disclosing suspicious information, no matter how general, to any other agency. Given the regulators' "dismal" record on the reporting of cash transactions, said Senator Proxmire, it looked very much as though the regulators were using bank secrecy to protect bank violators.[16] Paul Homan, deputy controller of the Office of the Comptroller of the Currency, explaining why the regulators are not keen to prevent bank laundering, told the Proxmire committee that drug-money deposits have no effect on a bank's "financial safety and soundness." According to Homan, "So long as the bank invests those [drug] deposits in overnight money and is able to cover when the deposits are withdrawn, there is no financial threat to the bank other than the peripheral one of perhaps affecting the confidence that people have in it because of known associations with criminals."[17] In other words, the fact that a bank does business with criminals, or is even owned by them, is of minor importance to the overseers of the nation's banks. It is not surprising, then, as Senator Proxmire said, that "many banks are addicted to drug money, just as millions of Americans are addicted to drugs."

Unable to prod bank regulators into action, in 1980 the enforcement division of the Treasury initiated a joint task force with the Justice Department, called Operation Greenback, which uses Bank Secrecy Act reports to identify individuals and organizations involved in laundering drug money. Modest in scope and relatively new, Operation Greenback is the first successful attempt to "take the profits" out of drug trafficking. It has also proved a useful exercise in exploring the various methods used in money laundering.

Isaac Kattan, a Colombian who ran a sizable money laundering operation in Miami, was caught in the Operation Greenback net in 1981 and was given thirty years in prison, one of the few harsh sentences received by a Florida drug trafficker. Though he dealt in hundreds of millions of dollars, Kattan's methods were crude by the standards of more sophisticated money dealers.‡ As go-between for Colombian drug suppliers and U.S. buyers, Kattan received instructions, usually by telephone, to pick up payment for the drugs in Miami parking lots, restaurants, alleys, and even on busy Biscayne Boulevard. He and his Latin helpers then lugged the cash to Kattan's apartment, where four money-counting machines, a computer, and a telex were installed. When the money was sorted and neatly stacked in cardboard boxes, Kattan took it to one of his friendly Miami banks for deposit, using as a cover a currency-exchange business run by his Miami travel agency. The money was either telexed from the bank to a Colombian currency exchange house or was sent a more roundabout route through a stock firm or real estate operation. When the dollars arrived in Colombia, the exchange house converted them to pesos, usually on the black market. For such services middlemen in the drug trade collect a stiff fee. Operation Greenback agents estimated that Kattan had stashed in Swiss bank accounts

‡ See Chapter 8.

more than $100 million from his profits in the laundering business.

Since it is the source of three quarters of the cocaine and marijuana entering the United States, Colombia plays a key role in laundering. The principal exchange houses for drug laundering are located in Barranquilla on the Caribbean coast (marijuana) and Medellín (cocaine). The more sophisticated operations include a network of offshore bank havens in Panama, the Bahamas, and the Cayman Islands, as well as shell companies incorporated in Panama and the Netherlands Antilles. The idea is to create so many zigs and zags of intermediary money stops that it becomes virtually impossible to trace the paper trail out of, and often back into, the United States. Kattan got caught because he made little attempt to hide the trail. He often personally carried boxes of cash from his home to the bank, and he broke a cardinal rule of money launderers by dealing in dope. But his biggest mistake was to rely on the discretion of a Miami brokerage firm, Donaldson, Lufkin, and Jenrette, which alerted the DEA that Kattan was moving suspiciously large amounts of money through one of its accounts.

The firm's scruples contrasted sharply with those of four Miami banks with which Kattan did business: Great American Bank, the Bank of Miami, Northside Bank of Miami, and the Popular Bank and Trust Company.[18] When federal agents raided the Bank of Miami, they found that bank employees were switching money from one Kattan account to another. According to the investigators, Kattan and members of his organization hauled huge sums of money to the Bank of Miami and the Great American Bank, the latter alone taking $60 million. In a court affidavit one agent said that he heard Kattan apologize to Great American Bank official Carlos Nuñez for a suspicious-looking transaction. "Don't worry—the main thing now is to count the money," Nuñez assured him.[19]

Agents found a number of irregularities at the Great American Bank, according to court documents. Large cash deposits were sometimes accepted by the bank's installment-loan department, the depositor being given a cashier's check in return. The cash was then logged in as the bank's own money. Pages of the cash-deposit log and some cashier's checks were missing. When questioned about the practice, Nuñez said that a bank vice president, Lionel Paytuby, had approved the procedure as a favor to special customers. One bank employee told authorities that Latins bearing cardboard boxes arrived almost daily at the bank. Agents said that bank employees assigned to count the money sometimes complained that the bills were wet or smelly—as if they had been buried.[20]

While bank officials complained that the Operation Greenback raiders "descended on the banks en masse like storm troopers," there was a certain hollowness to the complaint. At least one of the four—the Bank of Miami—had earlier been identified by a Treasury report as an institution frequently used by drug financiers to launder their cash.[21] As for the Great American Bank, its name again hit the headlines in late 1982 when Paytuby and three other bankers were arrested by the DEA on charges of operating a giant drug-laundering operation, with forty-one domestic and five foreign bank accounts. The bank was also charged on twenty-one counts for sanctioning the laundering of $94 million in dope profits over a fourteen-month period. The indictment carried possible fines of $7 million and marked the first time that a southern Florida bank had been charged with a drug-laundering conspiracy. John Walker, the Treasury's chief of enforcement, said that the Great American Bank had been indicted because it had consistently failed to fulfill currency-reporting requirements, and that this failure "wasn't due to the actions of an isolated employee [but] was, in fact, a bank practice."[22]

Among the accounts seized was one belonging to Juvenal Betancur, brother of Colombian President Belisario Betancur. Paytuby also was charged with running a laboratory that produced Quaaludes, another popular drug. His associates read like an honor roll of the Colombian underworld, including Marlene Navarro, the "queen of cocaine," and Jader Alvarez Moreno, whose two small children were murdered in Colombia by a rival drug gang. Also cited in the laundering operation was the Colombian banker Felix Correa, who bought the Bank of Perrine in Miami from CIA paymaster Paul Helliwell.* According to U.S. authorities, Correa was the brains behind a laundering operation

* See Chapter 5.

POSSIBLE FLOW OF MONEY
FROM NARCOTICS SMUGGLING IN MIAMI

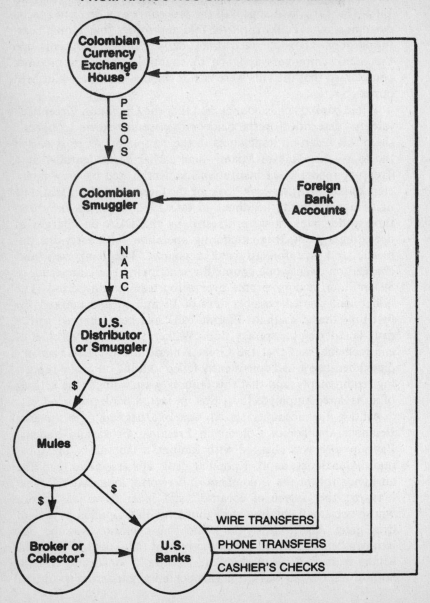

*Possible roles of "finance and investment companies" and/or "exchange houses."

between the United States and Switzerland.[23] The money-cycling operation came to the attention of Operation Greenback agents through a bizarre arms-for-drugs trade involving Colombian narcotics traffickers, the Colombian Castroite guerrilla movement M-19, Cuban exiles in Miami, and members of Fidel Castro's government.†

Probably the most common method of laundering money is through cashier's checks, which are safer and more portable than cash and less easy to trace than ordinary checks because they do not have to bear the recipient's name and address. The checks usually change hands eight or nine times before returning to the bank, and they are common currency in the black markets of the drug-producing countries. According to bankers, any bank that has more than 3 percent of its deposits in such checks is likely to be engaged in a laundering operation. The Proxmire committee reported that quite a few Miami banks were over that percentage.

Additional profits are made in money-cycling operations, of which several of the most sophisticated are located in Medellín and Panama. As dirty money is moved through a series of currency transactions in Europe, the Middle East, and Latin America, sizable profits can be made by taking advantage of exchange differences. The money can then go through the black market, to be loaned out at interest rates of up to 55 percent, and returned to the United States with tax advantages through an offshore haven. By that time it is completely clean. These money machines also deal in stolen securities, illegal commodity trades, the black arms traffic, and shady real estate operations, so the potential for profits is limitless. As one Operation Greenback agent pointed out, "We have no sophisticated regulatory system to catch up with such sophisticated schemes. The most we can do is follow up large-scale patterns of cash transactions."[24]

Not coincidentally, many of the Florida banks implicated in the drug traffic are controlled by Latins. While some have unblemished reputations, an unusually high proportion of the twenty-one Latin banks in southern Florida have been cited by U.S. authorities for suspected laundering operations. One such is Continental National Bank, founded in 1974, the first Miami

† For more details, see Chapter 8.

bank to be owned and managed entirely by Cuban exiles. Over the years it has generated considerable political controversy because Bernardo Benes, the bank's vice chairman, has angered many Cubans by advocating a dialogue with the Castro government. In 1978 the bank's president resigned in protest against Benes' position on Cuba.

The first indications that Continental was accepting large dope deposits came in 1978, when Customs and the Treasury uncovered a Miami laundering operation run by a well-known Colombian narcotics financier, Arturo Fernández, who worked with fellow launderer Isaac Kattan. Eight banks‡ were involved, but the overwhelming portion of the money—$95 million—was deposited in Continental. Most of Fernández's early transactions had been with the Canadian Royal Trust Bank of Miami and the Bank of Miami. But when Orlando Arrebola, a Bank of Miami official who knew Fernández, moved to Continental to become a vice president, Fernández switched most of his accounts to that bank, where government investigators said he usually dealt with Arrebola. The banker was charged with laundering drug money, but he was acquitted in 1982 when a Miami jury ruled that taped evidence of Arrebola's conversations with undercover FBI agents was insufficient proof of his involvement in a conspiracy. The undercover agents had set up a money laundromat and claimed that Arrebola had helped them open an account at Continental and had counseled them on how to launder money. According to his attorney, Arrebola may have had reason to suspect that drugs were the source of the money pouring into Continental, but, he said, the government's case fell far short of proving anything more than that. "H:s intent was merely to do his job well at his bank. His intent was to further the business of the bank," claimed the lawyer, although he admitted that Arrebola's actions might have "helped the [laundering] conspiracy along."[25]

There appeared to be some truth in the lawyer's contention

‡ Continental, Bank of Miami, the Canadian Royal Trust Bank of Miami, Central National Bank (renamed Eagle National Bank), Southeast, Biscayne Bank, Pan American Bank (later merged with Caribank), and Manufacturers National Bank (Miami *Herald,* June 5, 1980).

Southern Florida banks that handled suspected drug money and/ or systematically underreported cash transactions to the Treasury, according to the Treasury, the Comptroller of the Currency, the DEA, and the U.S. Customs Service.

Bank of America (international branch)
Bank of Miami (Latin)
Biscayne Bank (Latin)
Capital Bank
Central National Bank; renamed Eagle National Bank (Latin)
Continental National Bank (Latin)
Flagship National Bank
Great American Bank (in process of merger with Barnett Banks)
Intercontinental Bank (Latin)
Landmark National Bank
Manufacturers National Bank
Metropolitan General Savings and Loan Association (Latin)
Northside Bank of Miami
Palm State Bank
Pan American Bank; absorbed by Caribank (Latin)
People's Downtown National
Popular Bank and Trust Company (Latin)
Republic National Bank (Latin)
Royal Trust Bank of Miami (Canadian)
Second National Bank of North Miami
Southeast Bank

Sources: "Banks and Narcotics Money Flow in South Florida," Hearings before the Committee on Banking, Housing and Urban Affairs, U.S. Senate, 96th Cong., June 5 and 6, 1980 (Washington, D.C.: Government Printing Office, 1980); Latin America Weekly Report, May 29, 1981; Miami Herald, June 5 and 6, 1980, and Dec. 14, 1982; "Business/Monday," Miami Herald, July 5, 1982; United Press International, Oct. 16, 1982; St. Petersburg Times, Aug. 14, 1982; El Espectador [Bogotá], Feb. 13, 1981.

that Arrebola was just doing his job. In a report to the Comptroller of the Currency, the local bank examiner said he had told

Continental's management that even if the bank "is in compliance with the reporting regulations, some of the transactions may involve the laundering of illicit monies," and he went on to cite thirty-four such cases. But, said the examiner, Continental's management "does not intend to discourage" such transactions "since a fee is levied for the handling of these deposits."[26]

As any banker will point out, it is up to senior management to make sure that its institution does not break the law. Bankers also agree that compliance involves more than filling out forms— it means that the bank does not engage in activities that the law was intended to prevent. But Continental's vice chairman, Benes, told NBC News that it was enough to fulfill the letter of the law. "It's not really up to bankers to become investigators of customers."[27]

That attitude poses serious questions about the ethics of bankers, and the issue is the more complex when the banker is a foreigner, whether a Latin in Miami or an American in Bogotá. Bank regulators say that the 134 U.S. banks controlled by foreign investors are in general neither worse nor better than their American counterparts, but they also admit that there are exceptions in which the foreigner uses the bank for his own shady purposes. Federal Reserve figures show that foreign-owned banks make close to 20 percent of all business loans in the United States and account for 40 percent of the banking business in New York. Since 1978 foreign banks have acquired the twelfth and thirteenth largest U.S. banks, as well as two others that rank among the top fifty.[28]

While foreign banks in other parts of the United States have flouted the law, Comptroller of the Currency reports disclose that most of the shady operations occur in southern Florida, especially among Latin-controlled banks. (A 1982 study by the Comptroller reported that Latin banks accounted for 204 of the 367 violations committed by all foreign-owned banks throughout the country.[29]) In view of the regulators' poor record in checking the credentials of foreign buyers,* it is more than likely that questionable individuals and institutions are continuing to invade U.S. banking.

---

* See Chapters 3, pp. 47–53; 5, pp. 95–99; 8, pp. 159–60; and 9, pp. 180–85.

Two cases illustrate the problem: a Miami bank acquired by a Colombian financial group that faced penal charges for alleged stock manipulation; and a multistate bank holding company bought by Arab investors, one of whom had been accused of embezzlement. Both underscore the bank regulators' determination to play dumb.

The first caper involves Jaime Michelsen, head of a Colombian financial conglomerate called the Grancolombiano Group, which owns the Bank of Colombia, the largest private bank in that country. In 1980 Michelsen took over the Central National Bank in Miami through a Netherlands Antilles corporation. The bank's name was changed to Eagle National, the eagle being the symbol of Grancolombiano. The following year Michelsen shifted control of Eagle to the Bank of Colombia's Panamanian subsidiary. No one doubts that Michelsen is an experienced banker with plenty of money. The question is how he makes it. Investigations by Colombia's equivalent of the Securities and Exchange Commission and of a Senate commission revealed that two Grancolombiano investment funds had engaged in stock manipulation to the benefit of the conglomerate but at a $33 million loss to thirty-seven thousand small investors.† The Exchange Commission brought criminal charges against Michelsen and several of his executives, and when the case came before Bogotá's superior court, Michelsen's lawyers allegedly tried to bribe one judge and to disqualify another by planting false evidence against him. The authorities subsequently ordered the arrest of two Grancolombiano executives, including a vice president of the Bank of Colombia; Michelsen was told that he could not leave the country.[30]

The stock scandal occurred between 1978 and 1980, when the Federal Reserve was processing Michelsen's application to buy Central National. Because the charges against Grancolombiano were so serious, the economic attaché of the U.S. embassy in Bogotá sent three communications to the Federal Reserve's Board of Governors in Washington detailing the evidence against Michelsen and urging them to deny his application. Nevertheless

† About half the investors eventually recuperated their money (*El Espectador,* Dec. 30, 1982).

the Federal Reserve approved the application, and officials of its Atlanta office, which has jurisdiction over Florida bank applications, later denied that any negative information had been received from the embassy, though copies of the communications are on file in Bogotá.[31] The regulators' attitude was the more irresponsible because Central National was one of the banks that had been cited by the Treasury for laundering drug money.[32]

In the second case a group of Arabs used holding companies in the Netherlands and the Netherlands Antilles to take over Financial General Bankshares (FGB), a holding company with banks in Washington, D.C., Maryland, New York, Tennessee, and Virginia. The investors included wealthy individuals from Saudi Arabia, the United Arab Emirates, and four smaller Arab states. At first they tried to secretly buy control of FGB through the good offices of their advisor, Bert Lance. When the stockholders and the Securities and Exchange Commission got wind of this scheme, they filed suit against the Arabs, forcing them to make an offer at nearly three times the original stock price. However, state regulators were still unhappy, and representatives of Virginia, Tennessee, and Maryland filed with the Federal Reserve formal objections to the purchase on the ground that the Arabs' interests were in conflict with the needs of the communities the banks served. The Federal Reserve overruled them.[33]

Alan R. Cohen, New York's acting superintendent of banks, was upset by the decision, since his office was forced to abandon its investigation of the Arabs when the Federal Reserve approved their acquisition of FGB. Similar complaints have been voiced by other state regulators. Under the United States' dual banking system, a state's control over a bank with a national charter is dictated by the Federal Reserve, which has final authority for national banks. The system also puts U.S. investors at a disadvantage in a state such as Florida, where the law permits foreign banks to buy local ones with national charters but forbids out-of-state banks to do so. Foreigners also get tax breaks that are denied U.S. banks when, like the Arabs who bought FGB, they use offshore holding companies for their transactions.[34]

New York State Senator Carol Berman strongly protested the FGB takeover during congressional hearings in the fall of 1982. Like the state regulators, she feared the Arabs would neglect the needs of the banks' local communities. She also charged that one of the principal investors, Abdullah Darwaish, had embezzled $100 million from the ruling family of Abu Dhabi. The Arabs' "advisers have made a point of telling us that Middle Eastern culture, economic practices, and political institutions are different from ours, and we should not judge them by our standards," she observed. Apparently U.S. bank regulators swallowed that alibi. But even had they known of the charges against Darwaish, said Berman, "I am not convinced that . . . they would have thought it relevant that a controlling partner of an important bank holding company is an embezzler."[35]

***

The shady practices of foreigners in U.S. banking are matched by the shenanigans of American bankers in foreign countries. The principal difference is that American offenders take it for granted that because they are abroad they can get away with stunts they would never dare try at home. While such activities may break the laws of the host country, many nations—particularly the developing ones—are incapable of controlling the convoluted maneuvers of multinational banks. In nations where corruption is rife, U.S. bankers are often glad to play the game: At least one large U.S. bank reportedly has a policy of paying bribes in Latin America to attract lucrative accounts of local corporations and government agencies.[36] But, as with laundering drug money, such policies tend to corrupt the bank's overseas representatives, who may fall into evil ways for their own profit and at a cost to the bank. At the very least, that sort of permissiveness breeds a negligence that can be equally expensive in the long run. That is what happened to Chase Manhattan's operations in Colombia.

Chase owns 34 percent of a local bank called Banco de Comercio, and Comercio advertises itself as a Chase bank. James Therrien, the U.S. bank's representative on Comercio's board, is an American who has been with Comercio for many years and is Chase's key man in Bogotá. New York court documents and statements on file with the Colombian Superintendencies of Banks and Corporations show that Comercio's board of directors, including Therrien, used the bank to promote its own interests in some very questionable deals.

These activities came to light in the summer of 1982 when Colombia's banking system was reeling from a series of shocks, starting with the collapse of Felix Correa's drug-connected financial empire.‡ Like other banks that went under when the scandal broke, Comercio had engaged in lending to members of its board of directors and their companies, placing the bank in a difficult position. If one or more of those companies were to go broke— not an impossibility in view of the country's poor economic condition—Comercio would be left holding the bag.

As with Citibank,* an honest but naive Chase employee named John Marcilla brought these matters to the attention of senior management in New York and was fired for his efforts. An expert in electronic data processing, Marcilla had been assigned to Comercio in 1975. Shortly after beginning his two-year stint, he and his assistant, Ed Hurley, examined loan records and discovered irregularities. According to Marcilla, 87 percent of Comercio's loans went to members of the bank's board of directors or their companies. Many were unsecured (as much as $74 million was unrecoverable), and some had been overdue for as long as thirty-three months. Loans were made to Therrien, his wife, and daughter at 4 percent interest, when the then going rate in Colombia was between 18 and 36 percent. Marcilla also charged that Comercio officers sometimes accepted kickbacks when loans were granted, and that Therrien had "offered to split 50–50 with me" when confronted with the irregularities.[37]

Marcilla found that insider loans had jeopardized Comercio's stability. At one point, he said, the bank was on the verge of bankruptcy, unable even to pay salaries, and Marcilla was asked by Comercio's senior management to list assets that the bank could sell quickly to raise cash. But when Marcilla blew the whistle on Therrien, he and Hurley were transferred out of Colombia. Marcilla was told to take a vacation, then learned that he had been fired for "not performing his job in the manner expected or desired by his Chase superiors."[38]

‡ See Chapter 5.
* See Chapter 2, pp. 29–39.

Like David Edwards of Citibank, Marcilla took his case to court and lost: Under New York State law employees who are not covered by a contract or collective bargaining agreement have no legal recourse if dismissed. His charges against Therrien and Comercio never even entered into the case as evidence. "The best that can be said is that the plaintiff was terminated from Chase because Chase was displeased to have these accusations of irregularities, and for the sake of this motion I have to assume that that is the fact," explained the judge. "But Chase can do that. If Chase does not like somebody coming in with accusations of irregularities they can terminate. That is my view of the law."[39]

Marcilla retired to Albuquerque, New Mexico, embittered by the turn of events; Therrien and his co-directors at Comercio continued to operate as usual. But their situation became more difficult in 1982 when the bank crisis in Colombia focused press attention on banks with a record of self-lending. A new government enacted sweeping financial reforms, such as placing a limit of 7 percent of a bank's capital on loans to any one borrower, including bank directors and their companies. The government also warned the banks that they would be nationalized if they did not stop "playing with the people's money." One was.

This was bad news for Comercio, whose directors admitted that a large portion of the bank's loan portfolio consisted of credits to companies owned by them. But their most serious mistake was greed: In mid-1982 they tried to take over one of the country's largest sugar mills, Riopaila, which had substantial loans with Comercio.[40] Their predatory action was not unusual: One of the major economic problems in Colombia and elsewhere in Latin America has been the seizure of industrial and agricultural concerns by financial organizations that take advantage of extraordinarily high interest rates to gain control of companies unable to repay their debts. The practice of self-lending has accelerated the process because the only companies with access to cheap credit are owned by bank directors. To compensate for 4 percent interest loans of the sort given Chase representative Therrien, banks must charge unusually stiff rates to outside borrowers, which in Colombia were running as high as 50 percent in 1982. As in other Latin-American countries, hundreds of Colombian companies went bankrupt because they could not afford the cost of working capital. Industry and agriculture stagnated, finance being the only sector to show a high return on capital.

However, when Comercio's directors set their sights on Riopaila, they did not reckon with the hostility of the sugar mill's owners. They also mistimed their move, attempting the takeover just when the collapse of Correa's financial conglomerate set off a string of bank failures. Public confidence in the country's financial institutions dropped precipitously—63 percent of those questioned in a local poll said they had little or no faith in Colombia's banks. After Correa's exposure, the slightest rumor could set off a bank run, and when Comercio's savings and loan subsidiary, Ahorramás, was denounced at a stockholders' meeting for giving loans totaling 200 percent of its capital to the company's director, Comercio was forced to publicly defend Ahorramás. This so alarmed its depositors that they withdrew $33 million in less than a week.[41]

Angered by Comercio's designs on Riopaila, its board of directors employed Fernando Londoño Hoyos, a lawyer and president of the Latin American Federation of Banks, to defend their interests; he opened a Pandora's box for Chase Manhattan. Quite apart from the behavior of Comercio's Colombian directors, Londoño confirmed Marcilla's charges that Therrien had taken advantage of his position as Chase's representative to obtain Comercio loans and gain control of stock in the bank.[42] A company owned by Therrien's wife and daughter was also involved in the takeover of 20 percent of the $50 million Riopaila sugar complex. Incredibly, the total capital of the Comercio directors' companies in the deal was worth only 1/33 of the stock they intended to acquire. "Chase Manhattan will have to explain the wheeling-dealing of its representatives in this country," said Londoño, "as well as how Mr. Therrien . . . acquires shares in some of the most important companies in Colombia, which happen to be indebted to the bank he administers. The board of directors of Riopaila does not want its stock in the hands of a foreigner, much less the representative of one of the most powerful banks in the world."[43]

Although Londoño wrote Chase Chairman Willard Butcher about the matter, no action was taken, just as nothing changed after Marcilla's complaints. Nevertheless Therrien's involvement in the Riopaila affair hurt Chase's image in Colombia. Most other foreign banks forbid their overseas representatives to own local companies, the conflict of interest being obvious, and there certainly appeared to be a conflict between Therrien's position as Chase's man in Bogotá and his part in the controversial attempt to grab one of the largest companies in Colombia. Nor was Chase's "when in Rome" argument convincing, since it suggested that American bankers can ignore U.S. banking laws and ethics when abroad. And in this case Comercio's foray was also questionable under Colombian law. As in the United States, Colombian banks may not own industries and agricultural enterprises, but Comercio's directors argued that the bank had nothing to do with the acquisition of the sugar mill by companies owned by the bank's directors. It was mere coincidence, they insisted, that the buyers of Riopaila stock also controlled Comercio, which also happened to have large loans outstanding to Riopaila.[44]

While Comercio's directors were at that time technically correct when they said that Colombian law did not prohibit a bank from lending money to companies controlled by the bank's directors, the law changed substantially in the fall of 1982, when the government decreed stiff fines and prison sentences for self-lending. Strict limits were placed thereafter on insider loans, and bankers were told that they, like everyone else, would have to pay the going interest rate and provide genuine collateral. Meeting such conditions put a number of banks in a bind—including Comercio, which already was overextended through its savings and loan subsidary. If Ahorramás ran into trouble, Comercio would be called upon to pay up; and if Comercio could not do so, the buck would pass to Chase. But Chase's management in New York had apparently never considered such possibilities when it dismissed Marcilla's charges, along with Marcilla.

As in the Drysdale and Penn Square affairs, when Chase paid dearly for its loose management, Comercio's easygoing ways proved expensive. After a branch manager had made off with $4 million from a Comercio letters-of-credit operation, Comercio followed Chase's example in the Drysdale scandal by at first refusing to pay creditors, forcing them to take the case to court.[45] Like some Miami banks, Comercio was similarly lax in its choice of clients. Miryam Luengas Echavarría, one of Medellín's major cocaine traffickers and a well-known launderer of drug money, kept her account at Comercio's Medellín subsidiary.[46] Comercio was also charged by the Colombian authorities with making illegal payoffs to a former comptroller general in return for government deposits.[47]

ROGUES' GALLERY—Chapter 8

GUILLERMO HERNANDEZ CARTAYA, Cuban exile banker who founded the World Finance Corporation (WFC), which was involved in laundering, terrorist politics, and drugs, and was connected to organized crime, the CIA, and Fidel Castro's government.

EDWIN WILSON, former CIA agent and notorious arms trafficker (see Chapter 4).

SANTO TRAFFICANTE, JR., organized-crime leader, headquartered in Tampa, who worked with the CIA in attempted assassination of Fidel Castro.

JAIME GUILLOT, Colombian drug trafficker involved in arms traffic with Colombian Castroite guerrilla movement called the M-19.

SALVADOR "GALLEGO" ALDERGUIA, Hernández Cartaya's right-hand man in WFC and an alleged double agent.

RICHARD FINCHER, former Florida state senator, with alleged narcotics connections, who was employed by the CIA; business associate of Bebe Rebozo and partner of drug trafficker in Miami pest control company that led to the WFC investigation.

ALBERTO ARGOMANIZ, alleged drug trafficker and partner of Fincher in pest control company.

ENRIQUE "KAKI" ARGOMANIZ, half brother of Alberto Argomániz; employed by Fincher and WFC; allegedly involved in gun and drug smuggling.

MARIO ESCANDAR, Cuban exile involved with drugs and "in tight" with Fincher (see Chapter 6).

ORLANDO BOSCH, a notorious Cuban exile terrorist.

DUNEY PEREZ ALAMO, WFC building manager, former CIA agent, and member of Bosch's terrorist organization; helped Hernández Cartaya plan terrorist attack on Cuban consul in Mexico.

GASPAR JIMENEZ, co-member of Bosch's terrorist group; involved in attempted kidnapping of Cuban consul and murder of his bodyguard.

NESTOR "TONY" IZQUIERDO, Cuban exile, formerly associated with the Defense Intelligence Agency, who helped Jiménez escape from a Mexican prison.

RICARDO "MONKEY" MORALES, Cuban exile terrorist; former Castro, CIA, FBI, and Venezuelan secret police agent and self-admitted assassin; involved in bombing of a Cuban airplane (see Chapter 6).

MITCH WERBELL, notorious arms dealer.

REGINALD DENTON, president of insurance group who worked with Hernández Cartaya.

ROBERT VESCO, international swindler who lived in Costa Rica.

CARLOS HERNANDEZ, former CIA agent, drug trafficker, and member of death squad organized by Bureau of Narcotics and Dangerous Drugs; bodyguard of former Costa Rican President José "Pepe" Figueres.

FRANCISCO J. FERNANDEZ, WFC executive; found guilty of tax evasion with Hernández Cartaya.

VINCENTE CARRODEGUAS, WFC executive; also found guilty of tax evasion.

MARCELO HERNANDEZ CARTAYA, father of Guillermo; indicted with his son for bank embezzlement in Texas.

CAMILO A. PADREDA, also indicted for bank embezzlement in Texas.

JAIME MOSQUERA, WFC representative in Panama and Colombia; jailed on charges of bank fraud in Colombia in 1982 after suggesting bailout for Colombian banker Felix Correa (see Chapters 5 and 7), also in jail.

Chapter 8

The World Finance Corporation, a spectacular scam with a pin-stripe name. How a glib Cuban refugee built an international pyramid on money laundering and tax evasion, abetted by the CIA, Fidel Castro, right-wing terrorists, and Arab potentates.

"Among Cubans appearances are more important than reality," a Cuban exile banker told me in Miami. The man had been a witness to the bizarre and as yet unfinished story of the World Finance Corporation (WFC), which included banks, drugs, the arms traffic, CIA agents, and Fidel Castro's regime. Some of its aspects—particularly the drugs-for-arms deals—were even more incredible than the Nugan Hand scandal in Australia.* Yet WFC was essentially little different: Just as the Australian bank cashed in on Southeast Asia's CIA-supported opium industry, so the Miami bank fattened on the Florida drug traffic, dominated by CIA-trained Cubans.

The principal character in the WFC affair is the banker Guillermo Hernández Cartaya, a Cuban exile and veteran of the Bay of Pigs invasion. While a man of that background might be expected to associate with a "Monkey" Morales or Paul Helliwell,† one would hardly imagine him doing business with Castro. But Hernández Cartaya, say those close to WFC, would deal with anyone so long as there was a profit. In that respect he was as impartial as the notorious arms dealer Edwin Wilson, who supplied all who could pay—and who frequently relied on the same criminal network that was behind WFC. The Cuban Government's motives for dealing with WFC are less clear, but a prime

* See Chapter 4.
† See Chapters 5 and 6.

consideration may have been the politics of drugs: Castro has publicly conceded that his government trained members of the Colombian Castroite guerrilla movement known as the M-19, and the guerrillas have admitted that they used drug traffickers to secure weapons on the arms black market.[1] WFC appears to have played a part in this exchange.

Hernández Cartaya's financial empire offers a field day for students of conspiracies. Its agents dealt with everyone from Robert Vesco to Santo Trafficante, Jr., and the U.S. Government so botched its investigation of the case that congressmen and others were convinced there had been a CIA cover-up. Even after WFC was disbanded, its roots kept cropping up—in Colombia, Venezuela, Texas, Florida, and wherever else it had operated. And when they reappeared, the roots gave off a whiff of corruption: extortion in Texas, bank fraud in Colombia, and again and again the politics of drugs.

***

In 1971, when Colombia's marijuana and cocaine traffic was just getting started, Hernández Cartaya opened WFC in Coral Gables. A smooth, fast-talking Cuban with a taste for expensive living and beautiful women, Hernández Cartaya had worked briefly as a banker in Havana before the revolution. In Miami he joined the Bay of Pigs invasion and was captured in Cuba. He languished there in prison until 1962, when President Kennedy ransomed him, along with other volunteers. Back safely in the United States, he joined the giant Citizens and Southern Bank of Atlanta. When he was thirty-nine, he left the bank to found WFC.[2]

R. Jerome Sanford, a Miami assistant U.S. attorney who became deeply involved in the WFC investigation, said that when he was looking into the origins of WFC he found that it was first called the Republic National Corporation and had six stockholders and directors. In addition to Hernández Cartaya, Walter Sterling Surrey signed the incorporation papers as a stockholder and director. One of Washington's power-broking lawyers and, like Paul Helliwill, a charter member of the old boy network in U.S. intelligence, Surrey had been with the OSS during World War II. All the corporation's founders gave his law firm as their address.

Surrey maintained his connection with WFC until 1976, by which time it had become notorious.[3]

Everyone who has dealt with Hernández Cartaya describes him as a brilliant financial manipulator, and he certainly showed his ability in the six years after WFC's founding. By 1977, when his empire started to collapse, the corporation had, in addition to nine Miami companies and a bank, subsidiaries in eight Latin-American countries, the Netherlands Antilles, the Cayman Islands, London, the United Arab Emirates, and Texas. Its loan business alone came to more than $500 million a year—quite a feat for a company that had started six years earlier with five employees and a capital of $500,000.

As revealed by government investigations on three continents, WFC was a giant money-cycling machine, but it was infinitely more complex than the run-of-the-mill laundering schemes of the sort operated by Isaac Kattan.‡ Hernández Cartaya milked banks and investors in several countries, including the United States; he played for high stakes in the international currency market; and he masterminded several brilliant if fraudulent schemes. A flamboyant con man he made his entrance into Ajman, one of the United Arab Emirates, in a private jet. A Cuban exile chauffeur awaited him in "the biggest limousine in the country," said one witness, but the clincher was a red carpet that the chauffeur would roll out whenever the banker emerged from the car. The Arabs, duly impressed, agreed to invest $37 million in one of his loan schemes. When they discovered they had been duped, they seized Hernández Cartaya's passport while he was on a later visit to Ajman and threatened to jail him. Hernando Barjuch, the Colombian ambassador to Iran and an acquaintance of Hernández Cartaya, was reported to have come to his rescue by providing a diplomatic passport to enable him to leave Ajman by posing as a Colombian citizen. (Barjuch denied the charge). Arrangements for Hernández Cartaya's flight were made by the Colombian airline Aerocóndor, with which WFC had business dealings and which was suspected of drug smuggling.[4]

Such goings-on were of only peripheral interest to U.S. author-

‡ See Chapter 7, pp. 127–29.

ities, who were more concerned with WFC's drug connections with the Santo Trafficante, Jr., crime syndicate in Tampa.* They were exercised even more by a $2 million loan made to WFC in 1975 by the Narodny Bank, a Soviet institution that lends in Western fashion to help the U.S.S.R. relieve its chronic hard-currency shortage and, according to some spy experts, is a conduit to pay the Soviet's undercover agents.

At the same time, evidence came to light that WFC was working with the Castro government, possibly in a laundering operation, and that Hernández Cartaya's top lieutenant, Salvador Alderguía, was a foreign agent—whether for Cuba or some other foreign government was unclear. To complicate matters even more, WFC also had dealings with Cuban exile terrorists and ex-CIA agents. According to one former employee, it was deep in the arms-for-drugs exchange with Venezuela and Colombia, its chief client in the latter nation being the Castroite guerrilla group M-19. The man's story was open to question, since he himself had been an arms mercenary with CIA contacts and claimed to have worked with Edwin Wilson in the WFC drugs-for-guns trade. On the other hand, Jaime Bateman, undisputed leader of Colombia's M-19, publicly admitted to using a well-known Colombian drug trafficker, Jaime Guillot, to obtain arms on the black market, and Guillot was known to have had contacts with the Cuban ambassador to Colombia in late 1979.† For his part, Wilson worked with at least one close associate of Hernández Cartaya, Cuban exile and former CIA "asset" Rafael Villaverde, who was recruited by Wilson for a Libyan hit squad. Implicated by "Monkey" Morales in a Miami narcotics network,‡ Villaverde disappeared in 1982 during an alleged boating accident in the Bahamas.⁵

Sanford, who became involved in the investigation while prosecuting drug and Cuban exile terrorist cases, said that it "became obvious that international narcotics; homegrown, exported ter-

---

* See Chapter 6, pp. 106–7.
† Guillot fled to Europe in 1982, after his association with the M-19 was revealed, and is presumed to be in hiding there.
‡ See Chapter 6, pp. 105–6.

CHART OF WFC HOLDINGS
(February 4, 1977)

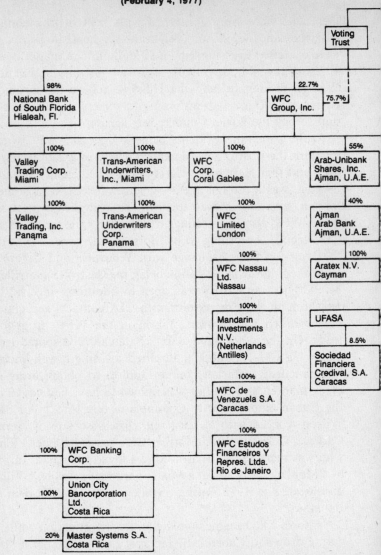

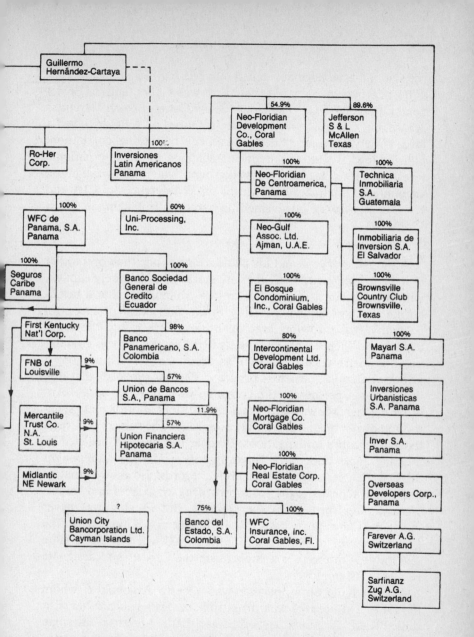

rorism; and espionage dovetailed into one big ball of yarn. There is no question in my mind that there was Cuban and/or Soviet penetration of WFC." The House Select Committee on Narcotics Abuse and Control agreed that the activities of WFC involved a large variety of crimes, "including aspects of political corruption, gunrunning, as well as narcotics trafficking on an international level . . . It is against this background that our investigation encountered a number of veiled or direct references to CIA and KGB complicity or involvement in narcotics trafficking in South Florida."[6]

***

Although everyone and his uncle seems at one time or another to have investigated WFC, the case started out routinely enough, with a complaint to the police from a Miami firm that a neighboring business known as King Spray Service, a pest control company, was throwing large quantities of trash into the firm's dumpster. When the police investigated, they found bags containing marijuana residue as well as credit card receipts from a known narcotics dealer. Corporate checks revealed that the dealer was a partner in the company owning King Spray. Another partner was Richard Fincher, a former Florida state senator and owner of a large Miami car agency. The subject of several federal narcotics investigations, Fincher had been subpoenaed by a grand jury; undercover investigators said they had bought drugs in Fincher's agency. Telephone records also showed that he had made repeated calls to known drug traffickers and underworld figures throughout the country. But Fincher was never indicted. It later turned out that he had been "of interest" to the CIA from 1962 to 1972, roughly the period when he was a state senator. "Of interest" is a euphemism the CIA uses to designate people in its employ.[7]

A third King Spray partner was Alberto Argomániz, whom the DEA had ticketed as a drug trafficker. His half brother, Enrique "Kaki" Argomániz, worked as a Latin-American salesman and consultant for Fincher's auto agency and made frequent trips to Latin America. When investigators tried to locate "Kaki" Argomániz, they were told to "try the WFC Corporation," where they disovered he was on Hernández Cartaya's payroll.

Federal investigators were aware of "Kaki" Argomániz as a suspected gunrunner and his association with prominent drug traffickers. In 1974 he pleaded guilty to income tax violations and received three years' probation.[8]

Fincher had other interesting connections. He was a business partner and claimed to be "a very close friend" of Bebe Rebozo, President Nixon's confidant. His associate, Alberto Argomániz, also had ties to the Rebozo family, having worked with Rebozo's nephews, Michael and Fred, in an aborted scheme to import marijuana from Mexico. (Michael Rebozo was later sentenced to a year in jail for possession of narcotics.) Fincher was also reported to be "in tight" with Mario Escandar, who was arrested during the 1970 drug bust that first revealed the "Cuban Connection."* As noted by crime expert Hank Messick, it was a tight circle. "Escandar was a friend of Hernández Cartaya, who was a friend of Dick Fincher, who was a friend of Bebe Rebozo, who was a friend of Richard Nixon, who once told John Dean he could get a million dollars in cash."[9]

Six months after the police examined King Spray's trash, WFC's name came up again when Myriam Rogers, the daughter of Miami's most notorious terrorist, Orlando Bosch, was arrested at Miami International Airport for allegedly attempting to import seven pounds of cocaine. In her address book under "W" was WFC and its Coral Gables address. Local police also learned that WFC had been printing and selling "bonds" as a way to obtain money for Bosch's terrorist group, either because of political convictions or for prudent motives of self-survival. As pointed out by the Dade County Organized Crime Bureau, few Cuban exiles decline to cooperate with Bosch lest they be accused of Communist subversion and end up dead.

But WFC gave more than a little help to the terrorists' cause. Dade County intelligence reports revealed that Duney Pérez Alamo, the supposed building manager for WFC and a former CIA agent, had admitted to being a member of Bosch's organization. He was a neighbor and close friend of Gaspar Jiménez, who was also part of Bosch's group and one of three Cuban exiles arrested in Mexico in 1976 for trying to kidnap the Cuban consul

* See Chapter 6, pp. 105–6.

in Mérida and for killing his bodyguard. According to the Organized Crime Bureau, "Hernández Cartaya financed and planned the Mexican action, with help from Pérez Alamo." In March 1977 Jiménez escaped from a Mexican prison, apparently using for the purpose $50,000 supplied by WFC. Jiménez's sister was given the money on the "stipulation that Jiménez would not talk to authorities about WFC activities," government investigators learned.[10]

One of those who aided in the escape was Nestor "Tony" Izquierdo, a Cuban exile formerly associated with the Defense Intelligence Agency (DIA). He was arrested while attempting to reenter the United States from Mexico, but was released on low bail when a retired Navy commander who had once worked with the DIA vouched for his "good character." CIA documents examined by *Newsday* reporter John Cummings, who has specialized in Cuban exile affairs, disclosed that the same former DIA official had met with Izquierdo in Miami only three days before he left for Mexico to spring Jiménez. Government files further showed that Izquierdo's bond and legal fees were paid by WFC.[11]

One of Jiménez's co-terrorists in the Mérida affair was subsequently connected to the 1976 bombing of a Cubana Airlines flight after it took off from the Caracas airport, killing all aboard. According to "Monkey" Morales,† self-admitted murderer and drug trafficker who claimed to have provided the plastic high explosives that destroyed the plane, the man who built the bomb was Gustavo Castillo, who participated with Jiménez in the attempted kidnapping.[12]

Acting as a counterweight to the exile-CIA connections, Salvador Alderguía, the alleged foreign agent and Hernández Cartaya's right-hand man, conducted WFC's relations with Havana. The telex room in WFC's Coral Gables headquarters was closely guarded; telex managers were hired by Alderguía and dealt directly with Hernández Cartaya. One telex operator told Dade County investigators that numerous coded cables were sent to Cuba via Panama as, for example, a seemingly innocent announcement of the birth of a red-haired baby. The operator said that once she even got a call from the Cuban central bank.[13]

† See Chapter 6, pp. 101–2.

The authorities discovered that Alderguía had met with the Cuban consul in Jamaica on several occasions, and in 1978, when assistant U.S. attorney Sanford was preparing to indict Hernández Cartaya and Alderguía, he got a tip from a local FBI agent, Willis Walton, that Alderguía was about to flee to Cuba on an Air Jamaica flight. Alderguía was detained at the airport and his briefcase was searched by Walton, who told Sanford that it contained documents referring to U.S. "national security" and what became known as the "Samuel letter"—a message addressed to someone named Samuel with coded instructions. Sanford was not allowed to see the letter or other documents, since the evidence wasn't relevant to any prosecution, but later leaks from the FBI indicated that it had been written in Havana.[14]

After Congressman Lester Wolff, then head of the House Select Committee on Narcotics Abuse and Control, told CBS's "60 Minutes" about the Cuban connection, there was an enormous brouhaha among government agencies and in the press, yet Alderguía was never arrested for spying. The most he was charged with was a passport violation for his part in helping Hernández Cartaya escape the angry Arabs in Ajman. After hearing how the Arabs had intended to cut off Hernández Cartaya's hand, a sympathetic jury acquitted the pair.[15]

While Alderguía was awaiting trial, his cousin, who had posted the $25,000 bond for Alderguía, was found dead, under suspicious circumstances, in the spring of 1978. The cousin, Dr. Emilio Alderguía, was a gynecologist who had offices in the professional building next to Miami's Mercy Hospital, which backs on Biscayne Bay. One evening at about ten o'clock he left the professional building, but instead of taking the usual way out (i.e., by driving from the building's parking lot to Bayshore Drive), he apparently circled round to the back of the hospital, where his car supposedly jumped a concrete seawall, and he drowned in five feet of water. According to Sanford, unidentified divers with scuba tanks arrived almost immediately; when questioned, they claimed to be friends of the doctor and continued searching for his personal effects. Although the city police called the death an accident, the medical examiner refused to classify it as such. "The police closed the file and marked it confidential, so no one could get at it," Sanford said.[16]

Alderguía, who told Sanford he was convinced that his cousin had been murdered, took to carrying an Uzi submachine gun in his car. His chief fear centered on "Monkey" Morales, everybody's helpful informer. On the surface it appeared that Morales had reason to be gunning for an alleged Castro agent, and as Sanford said, "The FBI claimed it was hot to get [Alderguía] as a foreign agent."[17] On the other hand, when investigators from another federal agency (not the FBI) checked with the CIA about Hernández Cartaya and Alderguía, they got back a categorical message that Hernández Cartaya had nothing to do with the agency, whereas they did not deny Alderguía had worked for them. More specific proof that Alderguía was a double agent came from a letter, found on the body of Alderguía's cousin, addressed not to the doctor but to Alderguía. The letter was written by an FBI agent in New York and was addressed to Alderguía by his nickname, "Gallego." *Newsday* reporter Cummings, who uncovered the letter, quoted at length its suggestions for FBI contacts in Miami. The writer particularly urged Alderguía to get in touch with FBI agent Willis Walton—the same Walton who told Sanford that Alderguía was a Cuban spy and wanted him arrested because he feared that Alderguía was fleeing to Cuba.[18]

Most of those who did the real digging on the WFC case, including Sanford, the Dade County Organized Crime Bureau and the IRS, are convinced that they were looking at a maze of double-dealing in the style of Le Carré, with Alderguía and Hernández Cartaya playing both sides of the fence. Since several of the people working at WFC listed the CIA as a former employer, and the CIA's contacts with Bosch's terrorists are well documented,[19] there is a certain plausibility to the belief of local law enforcement officers that by means of the drug trade the CIA was using WFC to finance counterrevolutionary activities by Cuban exile terrorists—a pattern already established in Southeast Asia during the Vietnam War.‡ On the other hand, WFC's connections with Castro's Cuba—as revealed by the telex messages, the strange loans from Moscow's Narodny Bank, and Alderguía's

‡ See Chapter 4.

meetings with the Cuban consul in Jamaica—were difficult to refute.

***

Intrigue was, of course, Hernández Cartaya's forte. Though he is well regarded by associates in Texas, where he now lives, he left a string of enemies in Latin America, including Panama's president, Ricardo de la Espriella, a former business associate who found himself holding the bag in Panama when the WFC empire collapsed. Other acquaintances had equally unpleasant experiences. One was Reginald Denton, president of the Foreign Credit Insurance Association, which represents some fifty large companies that insure loans made by the Export-Import Bank of the U.S. Government. Hernández Cartaya had met Denton when they were both enrolled at Georgia State University. According to attorney Sanford's investigations, Denton was a protégé of Surrey, the Washington lawyer who helped found WFC. After he became president of the insurance association, Denton began dealing with WFC, which, said Sanford, loaned Denton $500,000. Later investigations by Sanford's office and the Export-Import Bank revealed that Denton used the association's money to buy WFC bank certificates through the Cayman Islands. Denton was also involved in loans to WFC bank partners. A search of his office turned up WFC seals, stationery, and correspondence from Hernández Cartaya. Denton was dismissed from his job in 1976, but two intriguing details remained unanswered. One was a letter from the CIA to the FBI, telling the latter to lay off Denton after its agents had questioned him in the WFC case. The second was the insurance of a loan for a paper plant in Costa Rica. Denton had intended to approve the insurance until someone at the insurance association complained of a possible connection between the paper plant and the international swindler Robert Vesco.[20]

That was in the mid-1970s, when Vesco had evaded U.S. justice by fleeing to Costa Rica, where then President José "Pepe" Figueres became his patron after Vesco invested $2.1 million in one of the president's enterprises.[21] That was also the period when WFC executive Fernando Capablanca opened a WFC subsidiary in Costa Rica. Vesco knew Hernández Cartaya, and at one point it was suggested to the Cuban exile that Vesco become an investor in WFC. But Capablanca said that Hernández Cartaya vetoed the idea because he figured that Vesco, being the bigger shark, would simply swallow WFC.[22]

Other residents in Costa Rica in the same period included Orlando Bosch, the Cuban exile terrorist whose organization received funding from WFC, and Santo Trafficante, Jr., the anti-Castro Mob leader,* who left his Florida home in early 1974 to spend eighteen months in Costa Rica. Congressional hearings and investigations by the DEA showed that WFC was linked to Trafficante's organization and that one of Trafficante's associates was even on the WFC payroll. Trafficante arrived just when Vesco was beginning negotiations with arms merchant Mitch WerBell to set up a submachine gun factory. A mysterious White Russian, WerBell had a long association with the CIA dating back to World War II, when he had worked with Paul Helliwell's OSS China section.† One of his associates was the arms mercenary who claimed that WFC was involved with Colombian guerrillas in an arms-for-drugs trade (see p. 149). Completing the cozy circle was Cuban exile Carlos Hernández, a former CIA agent and drug trafficker who was recruited by the DEA's predecessor, the Bureau of Narcotics and Dangerous Drugs, to form part of a death squad to knock off important drug traffickers. Himself convicted of drug trafficking in the United States, Hernández skipped to Costa Rica, where he soon became second-in-command of that country's narcotics division and the bodyguard of President Figueres, who was also at one time in the pay of the CIA. To add to the conspiratorial atmosphere, Vesco, like Trafficante, was alleged to have been in the narcotics traffic.[23] As *Harper's* Washington editor, Jim Hougan, observed in his book *Spooks,* "Clearly, the timing of these events, and the milieu they comprised, are claustrophobic with coincidence."[24] Since all the

* See Chapter 6, pp. 106–7.
† Investigations by *The National Times* of Australia showed that the Nugan Hand Bank (see Chapter 4) funneled money to WerBell: "According to a former deputy director of the CIA who did not want his name used, 'Werbell conducted operations for U.S. intelligence on a regular basis, and we paid him on occasion through the Nugan Hand Bank'" *(The National Times* [Sept. 12, 1982]).

characters had links to exile politics, smuggling, and the CIA, Hougan theorizes that their "coincidental" gathering in Costa Rica had to do with terrorist plots and the drug trade. Whether or not he is right, there is no doubt that after Costa Rica, terrorist attacks, formerly confined to Miami, spread throughout the hemisphere.

***

After the Arabs lowered the boom on Hernández Cartaya, his WFC empire rapidly fell apart. The Ajman subsidiary had been the linchpin in a round-robin operation whereby Hernández Cartaya had been taking money from one bank to pay another. When the Arabs refused to play anymore, the merry-go-round stopped. By 1978 WFC was under investigation by the FBI, DEA, Customs, the IRS, the Dade County Organized Crime Bureau, and the Miami district attorney's office, as well as an interagency task force. Two congressional investigations were started, in addition to federal grand jury hearings. A year later most of WFC's international subsidiaries were in liquidation or closed by host governments. Investors lost at least $55 million, and many firms associated with Hernández Cartaya hurriedly removed his name from their board of directors.

One of the first casualties was Hernández Cartaya's National Bank of South Florida. When examiners from the Comptroller of the Currency moved in, they found massive evidence of laundering, self-lending, and misuse of bank funds. Accounts belonging to WFC and Hernández Cartaya were often overdrawn by as much as $2 million, cash deposits were never entered in the bank's books, and dozens of cash transactions had not been reported to government authorities, as legally required. Bank employees told the examiners of how trash bags full of cash were routinely but haphazardly left on bank officials' desks. One such official had previously been convicted of bank fraud.[25] "Hernández Cartaya didn't care where the money came from: He would launder it," said an IRS agent. "At one point there was a big hullabaloo because it was discovered that some money had been moved through WFC's Panamanian branch to buy arms for the Sandinista rebels in Nicaragua, but Hernández Cartaya had nothing to do with the Sandinistas. He was just making money."

The Cuban banker was a wonder at laundering. "In one day," said the agent, "he withdrew $3 million from the Ajman bank and sent it to 130 accounts in seventeen different countries!"[26]

Hernández Cartaya was not at all pleased by the arrival of examiners from the Comptroller of the Currency. Bank directors who cooperated with them received death threats, the examiners themselves being warned that Hernández Cartaya had a lot of "muscle." Board meetings were decidedly uncomfortable, with Alderguía, the alleged Castro agent, playing bodyguard at the door, "a large bulge under his coat."[27] The Comptroller of the Currency stood firm, however, and Hernández Cartaya was forced to sell his interest in the bank.

The examiners were right to be frightened: Government investigators said that Hernández Cartaya was in the big-time criminal league. One of his associates in WFC, according to the DEA, was an alleged narcotics wholesaler and member of the Trafficante organization. Another link to the underworld was the Dominion Mortgage Corporation (DMC), which had the same Coral Gables address as WFC. DMC financed the construction of a condominium, spa, and lounge in Las Vegas, constructed a housing division there, and used a fictitious name to purchase a local detective agency run by former Las Vegas police officers. DMC also bought a $2 million professional plaza with funds from WFC, and opened negotiations to buy several casinos, including Caesar's Palace. Information obtained from DEA arrests indicated that DMC was working with the Trafficante organization to supply the narcotics flow into Las Vegas. An IRS surveillance team confirmed that on one occasion a courier took $1 million in two suitcases from a Las Vegas casino to Miami, where his first stop on leaving the airport was the WFC address in Coral Gables. The courier left the building empty-handed.[28]

Despite all the leads—and with some four dozen agents on the case—the U.S. Government finally had to take the course used during Prohibition with well-known mobsters. In 1981 Hernández Cartaya was indicted not for bank fraud, espionage, or laundering but for income tax evasion. Six of his associates were also indicted, but a federal grand jury ruled that only Hernández Cartaya and two lieutenants, Francisco J. Fernández and Vicente Carrodeguas, were guilty. Hernández Cartaya was sentenced to five years in prison and was slapped with a $50,000 fine, a conviction he immediately appealed.[29]

A year later Hernández Cartaya was hit with another indictment, this time from a federal grand jury in Texas, where he also held extensive interests, including a country club–residential complex. He was charged with embezzlement of the Jefferson Savings & Loan Association, a WFC subsidiary in Texas. Also indicted were Hernández Cartaya's father, Marcelo, aged seventy-one, and Miami building contractor Camilo A. Padreda.‡ A longtime associate of Hernández Cartaya, Padreda formerly headed Florida's Latin American Businessmen's Association. According to the Miami *Herald,* he was also a "dedicated money man" (or fund-raiser) for Manolo Reboso, who ran for mayor of Miami in 1981 and lost, possibly because of allegations—never proven—by "Monkey" Morales that drug dealers were planning to finance Reboso's campaign [30]

***

The roots of WFC kept reappearing in places where it supposedly had ceased to exist. One was Colombia, which, in combination with Panama, had been the most important link in Hernández Cartaya's Latin-American network. The Colombian connection began while he was still at Atlanta's Citizens & Southern Bank. There he met Jaime Mosquera, a Colombian banker who represented Citizens & Southern in Bogotá. After WFC was founded, Mosquera joined the team as head of its Panamanian subsidiary, Unibank, which in turn controlled WFC's holdings in South America. Thanks to Mosquera's business and political connections, Hernández Cartaya was quickly accepted in Colombian society, and Unibank opened an office in Bogotá. Hernández Cartaya then bought into a small provincial bank, Banco del Estado, which soon expanded by absorbing two other local banks. Mosquera became head of Estado while also negotiating large loans to Colombian companies through Unibank.[31]

---

‡ The indictment stopped an $18 million hotel project in Brownsville, Texas, that Padreda and Marcelo Hernández Cartaya had intended to develop with a $3 million federal grant from the Department of Housing and Urban Development. (Brownsville *Herald* [Oct. 24, 27, and Nov. 10, 14, 1982].)

In 1975 Unibank nearly pulled off a major coup by serving as the lead bank for a $100 million syndicated loan to Idema, a government agricultural institute; at the time it was the largest loan Colombia had ever sought. The then banking superintendent, Christian Mosquera, a cousin of Jaime, approved the loan over the protests of other banks, which doubted WFC's ability to carry so large a loan—and at interest charges well below the going rate. Colombia's president, Alfonso López Michelsen, overruled the superintendent, replacing WFC with Irving Trust Company as the lead bank in the loan. But Christian Mosquera's role in the affair was not forgotten, and seven years later, when he was jailed for his part in negotiating the purchase of the Bank of Perrine in Miami for the Colombian speculator Felix Correa,* it was recalled that he had also had dealings with WFC.[32]

The $100 million loan caused a stir in the United States during congressional investigations of WFC, when it was suggested that the Cuban Government, hoping thus to persuade the López government to restore relations with Cuba, had been WFC's financial backer in the deal. It was also suggested that as another condition for the loan highly placed officials in the Colombian Government had agreed to cooperate in the northbound drug traffic.[33] But while the López administration did reestablish relations with Cuba, and while its policy toward the drug traffic was one of laissez-faire, neither had anything to do with the loan. Politically independent in foreign affairs, López had announced his intention to normalize Colombian-Cuban relations long before he became president. As for the drug traffic, he argued that Colombia had neither the financial resources nor the security apparatus to stop it—which was true—and that in any case it was a gringo problem. With an excellent rating in the international loan markets, Colombia did not need to make deals with WFC or Cuba to obtain external financing.

After WFC collapsed, the López administration was doubly glad that it had not gone with WFC on the loan. The closure of Unibank in Panama cost depositors (mostly Colombians) some $18 million, and when a Panamanian banking commission appeared in Bogotá to demand an accounting, the government

* See Chapter 5, p. 97.

closed the Colombian subsidiary of Unibank.[34] But Jaime Mosquera, Hernández Cartaya's man in Colombia, was still active in running the Banco del Estado, and after a change in government and bank superintendents in 1978, he was allowed to resume the presidency of Estado. No official records exist to document what happened, but sometime between 1977 and the end of 1978, when WFC had crashed, Estado's board of directors changed and there was no more mention of WFC or Hernández Cartaya, although a Comptroller of the Currency/IRS chart had shown that WFC owned 75 percent of the bank. Estado continued to grow, and in 1982 it was poised to take over a Medellín bank, which would have made Estado the fourth largest financial institution in Colombia. It had also applied to the Federal Reserve to buy a bank in Georgia.[35]

But Mosquera then made the fundamental error of talking too much. Instead of following the example of more discreet bankers, he rushed to the defense of Medellín banker Felix Correa when the latter's financial empire went under in mid-1982. Mosquera told the press that Colombian banks should form a pool to bail out Correa, a proposal that astonished the other bankers. No one could understand why Mosquera wanted to help Correa, whom the banking authorities had accused of massive fraud and self-lending and against whom there was evidence of association with the Medellín cocaine traffic.† So the investigative unit of the Colombian newspaper *El Tiempo* began to look into Mosquera's affairs, only to discover that he had been guilty of the same self-lending practices as Correa, using fictitious cattlemen to obtain loans for himself and his family. In September 1982 Mosquera joined Correa in jail, the Banco del Estado collapsed, and presumably that was the end of the WFC Colombian connection.[36] It was not, however, the end of the WFC story.

***

At the time when Jaime Mosquera was on his way to jail, two other former associates of WFC from Venezuela were trying to gain control of Flagship Banks, the fifth largest bank holding company in Florida. The takeover bid was led by Juan Vicente

† See Chapter 5, pp. 95, 99, and Chapter 7, pp. 129, 131.

Pérez Sandoval, with the backing of his powerful brother-in-law Oswaldo Cisneros. Of Cuban origin, the Oswaldo Cisneros family wields substantial political and financial influence in Venezuela through its holdings in the Pepsi-Cola Venezuela franchise, a television station, and a chain of supermarkets formerly owned by the Rockefellers. Among the family's indirect holdings is Sociedad Financiera Credival, the parent of Inversiones Credival, which is headed by Pérez Sandoval, and the intended co-purchaser with him of as much as 24.9 percent of Flagship stock (anything over that amount would have to be approved by Florida state regulators). Pérez already held 9.9 percent of the stock and was negotiating to acquire another 11.7 percent from Florida's politically powerful Smathers family. (Its most celebrated member, former Senator George Smathers, was for a time known as the "Senator from Cuba" because of his enthusiasm for the Batista regime.)[37]

When Flagship learned of the takeover attempt, it filed suit, asking the Federal Reserve to turn down the Venezuelan application on the ground that the documents filed for stock purchase were "materially false and misleading concerning the background and identity of Pérez and Credival."[38] In addition to not acknowledging Credival's close relationship with the Cisneros family, Pérez did not disclose that he and Oswaldo Cisneros had been associates of Hernández Cartaya in the mid-1970s.[39]

After some hard lobbying by Flagship, the Federal Reserve told Pérez that his application to buy bank stock was incomplete and returned it, demanding a thorough financial accounting by Pérez and his partners—one of the few occasions in the Fed's history when it did not automatically approve a foreigner's application.[40] Pérez nevertheless seemed determined to continue with the bid, and the Smathers interests still seemed disposed to sell.

Founded by George Smathers' father, the bank went through a stormy period in 1975–76, when it was on the danger list of the Comptroller of the Currency, but after Philip F. Searle became chairman, Flagship became one of the most profitable banks in Florida. A professional with a good reputation in the banking community, Searle failed to get on with George Smathers' older brother, Frank, who looks after the family's interests at the bank. Unable to make Searle accept his views on how the bank should be run, Smathers put the family's block of shares on the market in early 1981, although bank analysts were sure he would have a hard time finding a buyer for the $28.5 million package. They were quickly proved wrong when the Venezuelans showed up, money in hand.[41]

That the Smathers family knew of the buyers' WFC connections was unlikely. Even if they did, it probably would have made no difference, since the Cisneros family is highly regarded in Venezuela and Hernández Cartaya, despite his record, is still respected by many members of Miami's Cuban exile community.

*   *   *

"The bad guys really aren't very good at it," observed Florida State Attorney Janet Reno of the likes of Hernández Cartaya, but she conceded, "we're worse."[42] That certainly seemed to be true of the WFC case, which, after more than two years of investigation by dozens of government agents, turned out to be like an elephant giving birth to a mouse. Many of those who worked on the case are convinced that it went nowhere because of CIA pressure to drop it, and there is no doubt that the CIA had an interest in WFC, as evidenced by its warnings to the FBI to lay off insurance executive Denton and by the number of WFC employees who had formerly been employed by the agency.‡ Yet the evidence also suggests that the investigation failed to develop leads on drug and arms smuggling or organized-crime connections because the investigators lacked the tools to follow up on them. "Most of the guys on the investigation were good people, but they were street-smart cops who didn't know how to read a balance sheet or go into a bank and know what documents to look for," said a former undercover agent who worked on the WFC investigation. One of the few accountants assigned to the case, he said it took him a year to convince the law enforcement agencies that they needed a computer to put money and drugs together. "You cannot teach the ordinary cop how to follow a

‡ In response to the author's request for files on WFC under the Freedom of Information Act, the CIA disclaimed any knowledge of the case.

paper trail overnight," he said, "and they shouldn't be asked to do it."[43]

His comments go to the heart of the matter. While WFC provided the most bizarre and far-reaching case of a drug laundromat, it was essentially the same as other financial institutions that profit from the narcotics traffic.* "Throughout the WFC case," said the undercover agent, "my battle cry was that if we can cut the money source, you will see a sharp decline in the traffic." But the traffic has not declined, which means that for all the arrests and publicity about presidential task forces, the money source has not been touched. "What people don't realize," he warned, "is that this is a national security issue, because if these people [i.e., criminals] control the economy, they can cause chaos."[44]

Similar opinions were expressed by another financial specialist assigned to the WFC case. "The reason the FBI investigation went nowhere was because these people have no expertise in money investigations. When they see a conglomerate like WFC, with something like 100 companies, they rush off in all directions, without ever zeroing in on anything. It was the worst FBI investigation I've ever seen," he concluded in disgust.[45]

If the FBI really did "screw up," as most of the other agencies seem to think, that would be as logical an explanation for a cover-up as a CIA connection. As the lead agency in the investigation, the FBI received a treasure trove of boxes containing all the files assembled on WFC by congressional investigations, the U.S. attorney's office in Miami, and the Dade County Organized Crime Bureau. But the FBI asserts it cannot say anything about the files, neither who has them nor what they're doing with them. In fact, it cannot say anything at all about WFC![46]

All the people on the Miami side of the investigation also agree that another reason why the case failed to develop was that they got no support from their bosses in Washington. Despite constant prodding by the House Select Committee on Narcotics Abuse and Control, the bosses "never did prove to be too eager," said the committee's then chairman, Lester Wolff. As shown by committee hearings, most of those responsible in Washington didn't know what was going on and didn't want to know. Members of

---

* See Chapter 7.

the committee constantly complained of their frustration. "I don't think it is our role to be . . . sitting here like we are some kind of undercover agents doing your work," Congressman Tennyson Guyer told government officials. He said that government witnesses were "in a vacuum, that they knew nothing about what we were talking about," and that "if Jack Anderson wrote one article on this, there would be a lot of red faces."[47]

Looking back on the case, former Chairman Wolff thinks it indicative of the "posturing" of U.S. administrations on the drug issue. "The problem of drug abuse is a multifaceted one, and unless you attack it from the social side, the financial side, from the criminal element and the health side, you're not going to get anyplace." But, said Wolff, those appointed to stop the traffic have either ended up in jail (as in the Nixon administration†) or have "absolutely no credentials to head up the effort." Whether Republican or Democratic, the government always treats the drug traffic as a political issue, he said, "and that's the basic problem. We have declared so many wars on drugs that if we lost that many wars the United States wouldn't be around anymore."[48]

If Wolff is correct, then the "politicization" of crime becomes the key issue. Throughout the WFC case there were cover-ups by government agencies to protect people suspected of crime. The Miami police covered up the suspected murder of Dr. Alderguía because of local political pressures, according to investigators involved in the case. The CIA covered up for its former employees, including self-confessed assassin "Monkey" Morales. The FBI played the same game, as with Alderguía, the suspected double agent, and then proceeded to botch the case. Those who tried to take the investigation further, like assistant attorney Sanford, the Dade County Organized Crime Bureau, and the House Select Committee on Narcotics Abuse and Control, met a wall of hostile secrecy. "I'll be honest about it, I'm bitter," said one investi-

† Nelson Gross, a New Jersey politician and Nixon's Coordinator for International Narcotics Affairs, was convicted of conspiracy to bribe and tax evasion. (Hank Messick, *Of Grass and Snow* [Englewood Cliffs, N.J.: Prentice-Hall, 1979], p. 29.)

gator. "I spent two years of my life on this case, only to see it go nowhere because of 'national security.' "

Two questions arise from the cover-ups. One is whether "national security" can be used as a blanket excuse to prevent criminals from being brought to justice. If such is the case, then the laws of the United States have no meaning and crime will continue to flourish. The second is whether the "politicization" of crime is not an excuse to ignore it, either because those involved are politically powerful or because the courage to stop it is wanting. But to ignore something is not to remain innocent; in the eyes of the law it is to be an accomplice.

ROGUES' GALLERY—Chapters 9 and 10

PIERLUIGI PAGLIAI, Italian neofascist terrorist, head of Bolivian death squad/drug ring and member of Ordine Nuovo, the paramilitary arm of the fascist Mason lodge Propaganda-2 (P-2); died in shoot-out in Bolivia with DEA and Italian police agents.

STEFANO DELLE CHIAIE, alias the "Black Pimpernel," the father of Italian right-wing terrorism and member of Ordine Nuovo; worked with Pagliai in Bologna railroad-station bombing and in Bolivia; organized attempted assassination in Rome of Chilean Christian Democrat leader in cooperation with Chilean secret police; colleague of Michael Townley, who masterminded the assassination of Orlando Letelier, the former Chilean ambassador to the United States; believed to be in Argentina.

LUIS ARCE GOMEZ, Bolivian colonel who played leading role in the military's "cocaine coup" in 1980; major drug trafficker who used Pagliai and Delle Chiaie to organize paramilitary death squads known as "The Colonel's Syndicate"; in exile in Argentina.

KLAUS BARBIE, alias Klaus Altmann, a former Gestapo chief who lived in Bolivia; extradited to France in 1983 to stand trial for his role as the "Butcher of Lyons"; recruited German and Austrian neo-Nazis who worked with Delle Chiaie and Pagliai in training Bolivian death squads.

JOACHIM FIEBELKORN, a German Nazi terrorist recruited by Barbie to work with Delle Chiaie and Pagliai in Bolivia; later captured in Frankfurt for his part in the Bologna railroad-station bombing.

JOSE LOPEZ REGA, chief hatchet man in the corrupt government of Isabel Perón in Argentina and founder of the paramilitary death squad, the Argentine Anticommunist Alliance (AAA); also involved in Bolivian cocaine traffic; leading member of the P-2; believed to be in hiding in Spain.

VALERIO "BLACK PRINCE" BORGHESE, prominent Italian fascist who worked with Delle Chiaie in attempted 1970 coup in Italy; had contacts with Chilean junta in 1974; member of the P-2.

MICHELE SINDONA, Sicilian banker who established international banking network; principal financial adviser to the Vatican Bank until 1974, when the collapse of the Sindona-controlled Franklin National Bank in the United States brought down his European banks and landed him in a U.S. prison; charged with Mafia-connected murder in Italy; the financial brains behind the P-2; alleged conduit for CIA funds to right-wing groups in Italy.

ROBERTO CALVI, Milanese banker and close associate of Sindona, who became the Vatican Bank's principal business partner after Sindona was jailed; provided extensive financial support for P-2 political activities in Latin America through his Ambrosiano Bank in Milan, in association with the Vatican Bank; died under mysterious circumstances in London in mid-1982.

LICIO GELLI, grand master of the fascist P-2 lodge; a Nazi collaborator during World War II; wanted in Italy on charges of military and political espionage, illegal possession of state secrets, tax fraud, and possible involvement in the Bologna railroad-station bombing; arrested in Switzerland while attempting to withdraw some $60 million from numbered accounts belonging to Calvi's Ambrosiano Bank; escaped Swiss prison in 1983 and believed to be in hiding in Uruguay.

ADMIRAL EMILIO MASSERA, member of the Argentine military junta that overthrew Isabel Perón's government in 1976; head of an infamous torture center in Buenos Aires; key Argentine member of P-2.

ROSARIO and GIUSEPPE GAMBINO, members of the New York Gambino crime family; alleged accomplices of Sindona in arranging his fake kidnapping to Italy during Sindona's trial in New York; charged with smuggling heroin into New York via Milan, Sindona's bank headquarters.

GULF & WESTERN, U.S. conglomerate charged by Securites and Exchange Commission with engaging in stock manipulation in association with Sindona; partners with Sindona and the Vatican Bank in large Italian real estate company; owned shares in Sindona's Franklin National Bank.

PETER SHADDICK, former vice president of Continental Illinois Bank, who headed foreign-exchange department of Sindona's Franklin Bank, bribed by Sindona.

WILLIAM J. ARICO, an Italian-American and reputed Mafia gunman arrested in connection with the murder of the Italian court-appointed liquidator of the Sindona empire, which Sindona was said to have instigated.

LUIGI MENNINI, managing director of, and the highest lay official in, the Vatican Bank; indicted in an investigation of the Sindona case by the Italian authorities; under investigation for possible bank fraud in connection with Calvi's Ambrosiano Bank.

PELLEGRINO DE STROBEL, chief accountant of the Vatican Bank; also indicted in the Sindona case and under investigation for possible bank fraud.

ARCHBISHOP PAUL MARCINKUS, American-born director of the Vatican Bank; under investigation for possible bank fraud.

MONSIGNOR DONATO DE BONIS, Vatican Bank's secretary; under investigation for possible conspiracy to defraud the Italian tax authorities.

GENERAL VITO MICELI, CIA financial conduit, P-2 member, and representative of neofascist Italian Social Movement (MSI) of "Black Prince" Borghese.

FLAVIO CARBONI, a Sardinian business associate of Calvi, with alleged Mafia connections and member of the P-2; accompanied Calvi on his ill-fated trip to London; arrested in Switzerland after Calvi's death while attempting to withdraw money from secret Ambrosiano/P-2 accounts.

SILVANO VITTOR, a bodyguard provided by Carboni to accompany Calvi to London; well-known Italian smuggler.

COUNT UMBERTO ORTOLANI, sinister Italian businessman and Gelli's alter ego in the P-2; has extensive bank and real estate holdings in Uruguay; now living in São Paolo, Brazil.

JUAN DOMINGO PERON, Argentine dictator and master of the "strategy of tension" used by the extreme right in Italy and Argentina; friend and promoter of Gelli.

ANTONIO VIEZZER, head of disbanded Italian intelligence agency and P-2 member; arrested on suspicion of murder of Italian journalist who accused Gelli of working for the CIA.

Chapter 9

Razzle-dazzle banking reaches the Vatican, as Archbishop Marcinkus involves the Holy City in the schemes of Italian fascists, the Sicilian Mafia, and Latin-American death squads. An example of the high cost of credulity.

An oddly assorted group was gathered at La Paz's international airport one cold Andean night in October 1982 to watch the takeoff of a chartered Alitalia DC-10 with a dying man on board. Among those present were U.S. Ambassador Edwin G. Corr, CIA and DEA agents, and twenty-two members of the Italian secret police.[1] The injured passenger on the Rome-bound flight was Pierluigi Pagliai, an Italian neofascist terrorist, more recently head of a Bolivian death squad/drug ring, who had participated in a bizarre affair involving the Institute for Religious Works, better known as the Vatican Bank. As in the WFC scandal, with which it had some links, the trail led through a maze of organizations with terrorist, drug, and organized-crime connections, but while money had been the overriding objective of the conspirators in WFC, neofascist politics were the driving force in the Vatican affair.

A handsome young man whose code name was "Angel," Pagliai frequented the netherworld of right-wing European and Latin-American terrorists. His boss in Bolivia, Stefano Delle Chiaie, is known as the father of Italian right-wing terrorism. Among the "exploits" of Delle Chiaie and Pagliai was the bombing of the Bologna railroad station in 1980, causing eighty-five deaths and nearly two hundred injuries. After that incident the pair fled to Argentina, where Delle Chiaie had contacts through the paramilitary, neofascist Ordine Nuovo, an Italian terrorist group that had been involved in an unsuccessful military coup against the Italian Government in 1970.[2] They arrived in Bolivia shortly after the military's "cocaine coup,"* which was supported by Argentina's military regime.[3] Thousands of Bolivians were being rounded up, tortured, and murdered in the coup's aftermath. Pagliai was employed as a torturer by Colonel Luis Arce Gómez, the well-known cocaine trafficker and then minister of the interior.[4]

DEA agents became aware of Pagliai and Delle Chiaie in mid-1981, when a group of German and Austrian neo-Nazis were caught by the Brazilian federal police while crossing the border from Bolivia. Police found hand grenades, machine guns, Nazi propaganda and paraphernalia, a German-language military manual, and six pounds of high-grade cocaine. It turned out that the "Boys from Bolivia" had formed a paramilitary squad and were headquartered with the Italians at a ranch on the outskirts of Santa Cruz de la Sierra, in the eastern part of Bolivia. Santa Cruz is the capital of Bolivia's $1.6 billion annual cocaine traffic and the most pro-Nazi city in South America.[5]

The ranch was run by Joachim Fiebelkorn, a German Nazi terrorist who, with Delle Chiaie and Pagliai, was responsible for the Bologna train-station bombing. Fiebelkorn escaped to Paraguay after his colleagues were arrested at the Brazilian border and later turned up in Frankfurt, where he was caught by the German police.[6]

Bolivia's military regime conceded that the Germans and Italians had close contacts with Klaus Barbie, who earned the title of "Butcher of Lyons" as Gestapo chief of the French city during World War II. In his two-year reign, according to French authorities, he was responsible for 4,342 murders and 7,591 deportations to death camps.[7] Notwithstanding this fact, after the war U.S. intelligence installed him in a safe house in Augsburg and gave him a sanitized identity and $1,700 a month in return for information on the Soviets. Erhard Dabringhaus, a former U.S. counterintelligence agent who was one of Barbie's interrogators, admitted that the Americans kept his hiding place secret

---

* So named because many of the military officials who led the coup were involved in the cocaine traffic.

from the French, who were urging the U.S. authorities in Munich to surrender him. According to French Nazi hunter Serge Klarsfeld, the French made twenty different requests for Barbie's surrender, none of which was answered. In 1983, thirty-eight years after the war, the Justice Department belatedly recognized that U.S. intelligence officers had arranged for Barbie's escape to Bolivia and that they had lied when denying that he was under their protection. According to the Justice Department's 218-page report on Barbie, he left Europe with Red Cross papers supplied by a Croatian priest. (Some fifty thousand Nazi war criminals were aided by the International Red Cross, which sent them to South America on Bishop Alois Hudal's "underground railroad," some with fake Vatican passports and clerical robes.) Barbie was not the first war criminal to receive American aid; the Justice Department also documented several cases in which prominent Nazis were smuggled into the United States for training as anti-Soviet agents.[8]

Using the assumed name of Klaus Altmann, Barbie lived quietly with his family in Santa Cruz, where he opened a sawmill. Among his acquaintances was former SS Colonel Frederick Schwend, a leader in the Nazi escape organization Odessa. Barbie also worked with Hugo Banzer, who was implicated in Bolivia's cocaine traffic; and when the colonel seized the government in 1971 in a right-wing, U.S.-backed coup, Barbie became his security adviser, with instructions to reorganize the secret police. During the period leading up to the coup, Barbie made several trips to Miami, allegedly to buy arms for Bolivian paramilitary groups. Miami was—and still is—the principal U.S. port of entry for Bolivian cocaine, and there is evidence that Barbie and Schwend were part of a guns-for-drugs trade financed by Florida drug importers.[9]†

Although Barbie's cover was blown in 1971 after a German executive in Peru recognized a picture of him circulated by Klarsfeld, his military connections in Bolivia protected him from the French and West German governments, which fruitlessly sought his extradition. After the cocaine coup in 1980, Barbie reached new pinnacles of power. He was feted as an official guest

† See Chapters 6, pp. 104–17, and 8, pp. 146, 147, 149, 152, 157, 159.

in the presidential palace and apparently was given official support for his recruitment of the German and Italian neo-Nazis, who used the Santa Cruz ranch to train paramilitary squads for the Bolivian military's drug syndicates. Known as "The Colonel's Syndicate" (for Colonel Arce Gómez) or "The Black Eagles," they sowed terror in Santa Cruz.[10] In one case involving Pagliai, the band slaughtered seven Colombian drug traffickers in a Santa Cruz mansion, stealing the $8 million kitty with which the Colombians had intended to buy cocaine.[11]

U.S. and European authorities were powerless to do anything about the Santa Cruz killers and dope dealers as long as the coke-smuggling generals remained in control of the government. But in the fall of 1982, when the military could no longer keep its hold on Bolivia in the face of bankruptcy and severe general unrest, an honest civilian was recalled to take over the mess. Hernán Siles Zuazo, a left-of-center politician whose election as president in 1980 had sparked the cocaine coup, wanted to rid Bolivia of the Nazis and drug traffickers; he therefore agreed to a CIA–DEA–Italian secret police plot to whisk Pagliai and Delle Chiaie off to Italy. The plan was to seize the pair during the weekend celebrations for Siles Zuazo's inauguration in order to avoid publicity and a possible counterattack by the Italians' powerful paramilitary squad. In an ensuing gun battle with U.S. and Italian agents, Pagliai was wounded in the neck and spine. (He died shortly after his arrival in Rome, dashing the Italian authorities' hopes that he might shed some light on Ordine Nuovo.) Delle Chiaie, apparently forewarned, fled Bolivia.

Believing that his military connections would protect him, Barbie carried on as usual, but when he appeared at a government office in early 1983 to pay a fine, he was seized by the Bolivian authorities. A few days later he was on a plane bound for Lyons, where the French Government charged the sixty-nine-year-old Nazi with "crimes against humanity." But Barbie remained unrepentant. "What is there to regret?" he told an interviewer. "I am a convinced Nazi . . . and if I had to be born a thousand times, I would be a thousand times what I have been."[12]

***

Of the principals in the Santa Cruz network, Barbie was the most notorious, but Delle Chiaie was probably the more dangerous. Known in Latin-American circles as the "Black Pimpernel," the Italian terrorist had arrived in Bolivia on an Argentine passport and, according to Bolivian press reports, now took refuge in Argentina, along with Bolivia's Colonel Arce Gómez, who was given official sanctuary.[13] Delle Chiaie's Argentine contacts went back to the 1970s, when the Argentine Anticommunist Alliance (AAA), a paramilitary death squad, was founded by José López Rega, chief hatchet man in the corrupt government of Isabel Perón. Like Pagliai and Delle Chiaie, López Rega and his son-in-law Raul Lastiri, who served briefly as Argentine president, were implicated in the Bolivian cocaine traffic, using the northern Argentine province of Salta for a three-nation cocaine operation involving Argentina, Bolivia, and Paraguay.[14]

Orlando Bosch, the notorious Cuban exile terrorist,‡ also worked with the AAA, and he and Delle Chiaie were associated with a death squad organized by the Chilean secret police after Salvador Allende's overthrow in 1973.* Among that group's victims was Orlando Letelier, Allende's ambassador to Washington, who was blown to bits by a terrorist bomb on Washington's Embassy Row in 1976. Eugene M. Propper, the assistant U.S. attorney assigned to the case, discovered that the Chilean police's "most enthusiastic Italian contact" was a person called "Alfa," code name for Delle Chiaie, who was also known as "The Black Bomber." According to Propper, Delle Chiaie set up the attempted assassination of former Chilean vice president Bernardo Leighton and his wife in Rome in 1975.[15]

Delle Chiaie also had links to Michael Townley, the American-Chilean agent accused of masterminding Letelier's assassination. Townley and Delle Chiaie collaborated with a neofascist Chilean group, Patria y Libertad, which was subsidized by the CIA and played an important role in the 1973 coup in Chile. Delle Chiaie and his friend, the Italian fascist Valerio "Black Prince" Borghese, visited the Chilean junta in 1974; according to Propper,

‡ See Chapter 8, pp. 153, 154.
* Bosch was also involved with "Monkey" Morales in blowing up an Air Cubana plane (see Chapter 6, pp. 101–2).

Delle Chiaie also secretly met with Chilean dictator Augusto Pinochet in Madrid in 1975 during the funeral of Generalísimo Francisco Franco.[16]

What had all this plotting to do with the Vatican Bank? The bank's two principal financial advisers and partners, Michele Sindona and Roberto Calvi, were members of P-2, a neofascist Masonic lodge in Milan headed by the Italian fascist financier Licio Gelli, who had dropped from public sight. Gelli was wanted in Italy for, among other things, his connection with the Pagliai and Delle Chiaie bombing of the Bologna railroad station.[17] Other members of P-2 who used Delle Chiaie's terrorist organization for equally sinister purposes included: López Rega and his son-in-law Raul Lastiri; the fascist "Black Prince" Borghese; General Vito Miceli, former head of a disbanded, scandal-ridden intelligence agency in Italy and a representative in parliament of the neofascist Italian Social Movement (MSI), founded by Borghese; and Admiral Emilio Massera, member of the Argentine military junta that overthrew Isabel Perón's government in 1976 and head of a torture center in Buenos Aires.[18] As shown by Italian authorities, P-2 was "a state within the state," its aim being to restore fascism in Italy and buttress its hold on Latin America. Calvi's Ambrosiano Bank in Milan was employed to finance P-2's political and financial interests in Latin America, and Delle Chiaie's Ordine Nuovo was P-2's paramilitary arm.[19] That Archbishop Paul Marcinkus, the American-born head of the Vatican Bank, knew of such connections is considered unlikely, although the Vatican Bank was perhaps the largest shareholder in Ambrosiano and Calvi worked closely with Marcinkus on financial matters. More to the point, the Vatican's own investigation of the Calvi connection disclosed that the Vatican Bank owned ten Panamanian shell companies that were used to advance the political ambitions of Calvi and Gelli in Latin America and, through them, the P-2.[20]

**

The P-2 lodge in Milan might never have been exposed had it not been for a self-kidnapping arranged by the Italian-American banker Sindona. In 1979 he had been accused, and was later convicted of bank fraud and perjury in the United States, for having robbed the Franklin National Bank—America's twentieth largest—of $45 million in 1974, causing Franklin to fail. A month before the date of his trial in New York, Sindona disappeared, supposedly having been kidnapped by left-wing Italian extremists. That, at least, was his tale when he reappeared two and a half months later on Forty-second Street with a bullet wound in his thigh and armed with documents, somehow gathered during his "abduction" in Europe, which he claimed would exonerate him. When U.S. and Italian agents checked his story, they established that he had arranged his own disappearing act with no great subtlety (e.g., booking his own European flights). It was also discovered that his accomplices included Rosario and Giuseppe Gambino, of the New York Gambino crime family, who had been charged with smuggling heroin into New York via Milan, Sindona's Italian headquarters.[21]

While checking Sindona's abduction story, in March 1981 the Italian police obtained a warrant to search the Arezzo villa of P-2 Masonic master Licio Gelli. There they discovered a cache of sensational documents, among them a list of 953 P-2 members, including: the heads of Italy's intelligence agencies; numerous generals and admirals; and key men in government ministries, the courts, industry, banking, and the press. The only major political organization not represented was the Italian Communist Party. The revelations set off a major scandal in Italy, causing the fall of the government of Arnaldo Forlani. P-2 files also implicated Gelli and Milan banker Calvi in Sindona's fake kidnapping, documenting Gelli's role in helping Sindona find a hiding place in the Palermo home of two well-known members of the Sicilian Mafia. Papers found at the villa also raised the possibility that Gelli had been involved in the Bologna railroad-station bombing.[22] When the P-2 story broke, Gelli fled to South America, but Calvi, already enmeshed in legal difficulties in Italy, had to brazen it out in Milan. By that time Sindona was in a New York federal penitentiary serving a twenty-five-year sentence for his part in Franklin's collapse.

Of the four principals in the Vatican mystery—Sindona, Calvi, Gelli, and Archbishop Marcinkus—Sindona was probably the most important, for without his expert financial jiggery-pokery Calvi's Ambrosiano Bank would have remained a small provincial institution incapable of underwriting Gelli's political projects for Italy and Latin America. And but for Sindona—once known as "God's banker" because of his close ties to the Vatican Bank— Marcinkus would have been spared much grief.

A thin, balding man in his early sixties, Sindona still retained the aura of a multimillionaire banker when reporters besieged him in his New York prison after the P-2 scandal broke. Like many bankers, the Sicilian-born financier entered banking through a law practice, which he had established in Milan after World War II. His specialty was Italian tax law, and he earned a reputation for arranging profitable acquisitions and mergers. In the 1960s he began to develop his own financial empire through a holding company, Fasco, which he created in the bank haven of Lichtenstein. Fasco thrived, and before Sindona's empire collapsed the holding company owned 125 corporations in 11 countries, including 6 banks in Europe and the Franklin National Bank in New York, in which he acquired a controlling interest in 1972. Contrary to later dismissals of Sindona as a second-rate mobster, he was well regarded in international financial circles and did business with such establishment pillars as Continental Illinois National Bank; Hambros Bank Ltd., a leading British merchant bank; and the important Banque de Paris et des Pays Bas. In 1963, for example, Sindona joined with the French bank to buy a controlling interest in Libby, McNeill & Libby, Inc., the American food-processing company. Through such partners, Sindona developed excellent contacts around the world. "Banking is a matter of connections," he once said, adding that he had "personal connections in all important financial centers."[23]

One such was Mudge, Rose, Guthrie and Alexander, the law firm of President Nixon and his attorney general, John Mitchell, which represented Sindona in the United States. Another was David M. Kennedy, chairman and chief executive officer of Continental Illinois Bank, Nixon's Secretary of the Treasury from 1969 to 1971, and U.S. ambassador to NATO. After leaving government work, Kennedy joined the board of Fasco in 1973 and served as adviser to Sindona, providing him with connections to public and private banking officials in the United States and abroad. After Sindona bought the Franklin shares, Kennedy agreed to take responsibility for voting the stock for one year.

Kennedy later testified that he received a $200,000 loan from Sindona in early 1974, which he said he fully repaid. In 1982 Kennedy was sued for $54 million by the Italian Government, in New York, on charges that he conspired illegally with Sindona to defraud a bank owned by the latter.[24]

Yet another associate was Gulf & Western (G & W), the U.S. conglomerate with large sugar interests in the Dominican Republic and elsewhere in Latin America. But this connection proved more controversial, offering the first glimpse of Sindona's piratical style. In a wide-ranging suit, the Securities and Exchange Commission (SEC) accused G & W of engaging with Sindona in stock manipulation to rig the values of companies in which they were partners. These included Paramount Marathon movie studios and the Società Generale Immobiliare (SGI), a giant Italian real estate company that counted the Watergate complex in Washington among its many holdings. The SEC also charged that G & W took a $6 million loss on shares in Franklin Bank when it collapsed, but failed to report the loss to stockholders; instead it inflated its profits by at least $4.5 million.[25]

Two aspects of Sindona's G & W connection related significantly to his other activities. One was the conglomerate's alleged links with organized crime, as revealed in hearings by the Illinois Racing Board in connection with G & W's hotel and sports holdings. The other was that the third partner with G & W and Sindona in the Italian real estate company was the Vatican Bank.[26]

Sindona's contacts with the Vatican began in 1969, when he became financial adviser to Pope Paul VI, who had known him in Milan. The son of a bankrupt farmer, Sindona had early learned to manipulate church patronage when, as a young man in Sicily, he had used the influence of the bishop of Messina to acquire a truck to transport suspect goods. After graduating from the University of Messina, he wrangled an introduction to the powerful Monsignor Giovanni Montini in Milan, who would later become Pope Paul VI. Montini introduced the smooth-talking Sicilian to his friend Giulio Andreotti, a pillar of the Christian Democratic Party and frequent cabinet minister in Italy's revolving-door governments. With such contacts Sindona soon prospered, buying one bank after another, until he had assembled a multinational empire worth hundreds of millions of dollars. As he had done in his youth in Sicily, he assiduously courted those with power; and when Andreotti's Christian Democrats faced electoral peril from the Communists, he was an unstinting contributor as well as a funnel for supporting funds from the CIA.[27]†

The Pope was also impressed by the towering Marcinkus (six foot three inches tall and weighing well over two hundred pounds), who served as bodyguard and advanceman for Paul's trips abroad and helped save his life during a visit to Manila, when a fanatic Bolivian artist tried to stab him. Thus the same year that Sindona became "God's banker" Marcinkus was put in effective charge of the Vatican Bank (he was appointed president in 1971). Sindona, who had no respect for him as a banker, used Marcinkus for his own murky purposes. He was, said Sindona, "a nobody who had pretensions to become a financier. He thought that because he had a position as a banker, he was a banker—two weeks at Harvard University lectures and he thought he had become a banker."[28]

Italy in those years was undergoing its usual political convulsions, aggravated by terrorism on the extreme left and right. Also worrying Pope Paul was a growing threat of an elected Communist government. The Vatican Bank had been established in 1942 by Paul's predecessor, Pope Pius XII, to secure certain Vatican monies from the effects of World War II. Most of its holdings came from a 1929 agreement with Benito Mussolini, who paid the Holy See $83 million as compensation for papal territory seized by the Italian republic in the previous century. But Pius had no idea how to run a bank, and most of its advisers were relatives, princes, and counts without financial experience. The majority of the bank's money was invested in poorly run Italian companies, including a ceramics firm. Some of the Vatican's investments were downright embarrassing—an Italian firearms factory, for example, or a Canadian pharmaceutical company that manufactured contraceptives. When Sindona appeared on the scene in 1969, he was given a free hand to divest and diversify, primarily into banks outside Italy and into U.S. stocks and securities.

† See pp. 187, 190.

The problem was that Marcinkus was no banker and Sindona's style was less than heavenly. Born into a working-class family of Lithuanian background in Cicero, Illinois, Marcinkus studied at local Catholic schools and an Illinois seminary before becoming a priest. After graduating from Rome's prestigious Pontifical Gregorian University, he joined the Vatican's diplomatic corps. The experience was good training for a bishop but provided no background in finance, which has always been a weak point in church administration. Thus Marcinkus, despite his organizational talents, was no match for Sindona, who used the Vatican's name and, by some accounts, its financial holdings to enrich himself.[29] On the one hand, the idea that the Vatican might be involved in shady deals would not have occurred to those who dealt with Sindona, its representative. On the other, Sindona knew that the Vatican Bank, owned by the Vatican State, was not subject to any controls by the Italian central bank, or beholden to stockholders, and therefore could do many things forbidden to other banks, such as the export of capital.[30] If Sindona is to be believed, Marcinkus was perfectly aware that he was being manipulated. "We used his name a lot in business deals," Sindona later claimed in prison. "I told him clearly that I put him in because it helps me get money."[31]

During the first years of the association all seemed well, but in 1972 Sindona made a fundamental error in acquiring 21.6 percent of the Franklin Bank at $8 a share above the going market price. A large U.S. bank noted for its growth, Franklin may have seemed like a useful vehicle for Sindona's international financial manipulations. In fact, the bank was so overextended and had so many bad loans that in 1965, and again in 1970, it had been classified as a problem bank by the Office of the Comptroller of the Currency. Even before Sindona took over, Franklin's foreign-exchange trading division was in "chaos," with virtually no internal controls. But instead of correcting this situation, Sindona urged his executives to engage in an orgy of speculation on the Eurocurrency market at a time when the market was little understood even by the biggest multinational banks. Then, as now, the Eurocurrency market was a giant floating crap game in which exchange dealers (mostly banks) bet on the rise or fall of national currencies.

Sindona's Italian banks had made money on the game. Figur-
ing that Franklin would do the same, he employed two aggressive
foreign-exchange traders and gave them all the bank's chips to
bet. One of the two had a decidedly poor reputation as a reckless
dealer, but the other, Peter Shaddick, had been a vice president
of Continental Illinois Bank. When Continental bought an interest in one of Sindona's Italian banks, Shaddick joined its board,
and after Sindona gained control of Franklin, he recruited Shaddick to help run the foreign-exchange department. According to
testimony at Sindona's trial, he bribed Shaddick "for the purpose
of corruptly influencing his conduct at the bank." If so, the bribe
misfired, because Shaddick had a bad losing streak in the foreign-
currency game, causing Franklin to suffer massive losses. For a
time Sindona was able to hide the situation by transferring
money from his European banks to Franklin, but when the large
international banks, led by Morgan Guaranty Trust, ceased dealing with Franklin, the bank collapsed, setting off an immediate
run on Sindona's European banks, which fell like dominoes.[32]

While foreign-exchange speculation was a major cause of
Franklin's failure, Sindona's looting of the bank to bolster other
companies in his empire also contributed to its demise. The Vatican seemed unaware of what was going on to the very end. Indeed, banking sources said that the Vatican Bank raised $30 mil-
lion to prop up Franklin. SGI, the Italian real estate company,
was also heavily involved in Sindona's last-ditch transactions,
and when his empire collapsed, the Italian central bank seized
SGI as collateral. The Vatican Bank, which was also a minority
shareholder in two of Sindona's Italian banks, lost upwards of
$240 million.[33] Nevertheless, two cardinals, including a former
head of the Vatican Bank, were prepared to testify as character
witnesses at Sindona's New York trial. John Paul II forbade them
to do so.[34]

In all fairness, the cardinals were no more naive than U.S.
bank regulators, who, though aware of Franklin's distress and
though repeatedly warned of impending disaster by Morgan and
other banks, did nothing to save the bank because Franklin's
management assured them that everything was in order. During
congressional hearings James Smith, Comptroller of the Currency, whose office was responsible for Franklin, vehemently de-

nied any intercession on the bank's behalf by his old boss David Kennedy, though he did admit to meeting Sindona under Kennedy's auspices. In any case, the record shows that the Comptroller's office failed to conduct the legally mandated number of inspections, just as in the Penn Square case,‡ and that it approved Franklin's overseas expansion at a time when it knew the bank was in serious trouble.[35] Italy's central bank proved equally remiss. Italian banking authorities, who knew of irregularities and possible criminal activities in Sindona's Italian banks, not only failed to inform their counterparts in Washington but even told the Federal Reserve that Sindona was an exceptionally endowed banker whom the world needed! That was in February 1974, a few months before Franklin was declared insolvent.[36]

The collapse of Sindona's banks cost investors and depositors on both sides of the Atlantic, including important sectors of the Long Island economy dependent on Franklin. Yet, incredibly, Sindona still played the Italian guru, lecturing to packed halls at Harvard, UCLA, the University of Chicago, and other schools on free enterprise and the perils of communism. Convicted *in absentia* in Italy in 1975 on charges arising from his financial manipulations, he continued to hold court from his luxurious eleventh-floor apartment in New York's Hotel Pierre, where he would amuse visitors with paper sculptures called origami boats.* When Italy formally requested his extradition in 1976, Sindona boasted that his friends in Washington would never allow him to go back to Italy, where, he alleged, he was a victim of political persecution. Three years later, when he was indicted in the United States, the Italian Government's request was still being processed by the State Department.[37]

Sindona turned out to be more than a financial manipulator: He was charged with murder, as well as embezzlement of some

‡ See Chapter 2, pp. 26, 28.
* Since childhood, Sindona has had a peculiar compulsion to fold origami boats of the kind called "heaven or hell" in Italy. His desks would later be filled with piles of these paper sculptures, which were meant to be folded and unfolded with the fingers. Moving his hands one way, he would make the inside of the boat open on blue paper, for heaven; moving them another way, the interior would be red, for hell. (Charles Mann with Dale McAdoo, "Sindona: An Investigative Report," *Attenzione* [December 1979].)

$225 million from Italian banks. Since the murder charge was Mafia-related, it raises questions about the source of Sindona's fortune, which has always remained a mystery. After World War II Milan emerged as Italy's financial hub, so it was only natural that Sindona should be drawn there, but his origins lie in Sicily, which took over from Marseilles as the world's heroin center when the French Connection was broken in the early 1970s. As one Italian newspaper noted in regard to Sindona's currency manipulations, "It's foolish to think that clandestine capital traffic is entrusted to hoodlums with false-bottomed briefcases. [Such traffic] assumes more abstract, less risky forms, hiding behind apparently innocuous bookkeeping. But it is not innocuous." Carlo Bordoni, an associate of Sindona and his right-hand man at Franklin, agreed; he told the newsmagazine *Panorama* that "Michele Sindona was (and still is) one of the Mafia's bankers, the route through which organized crime money passes across the Atlantic."[38]

Undoubtedly the new mafias emerging from Italy's drug boom are more sophisticated than were the old dons with their secret rites. One skill that they have been quick to learn is money laundering: Dozens of banks have opened in Sicily to handle its estimated $6 billion annual heroin trade with the United States. And, unlike the old Mafia, which was content to coexist with the state, the new generation is challenging Italy's government at every turn. More than a thousand people have been killed in Sicilian drug wars since 1979, many of the victims government officials under orders to stop the Mafia. General Alberto Dalla Chiesa, Italy's top antiterrorist fighter, directed a string of successful raids against the Red Brigades, only to be murdered in Sicily four months after he was sent there to clean up the region. Other Mafia victims included Palermo's public prosecutor, its chief investigating judge, and Sicily's regional president. Seventy-six people have been indicted for these killings, among them Sindona.[39]

Sindona was also charged with instigating the murder of Giorgio Ambrosoli, the Italian court–appointed liquidator of the Sindona empire. One of those said to have carried out the killing was William J. Arico, an Italian-American and a reputed Mafia gunman, who was arrested in Philadelphia in 1982. Italy immediately requested his extradition.[40] Ambrosoli had spent four years investigating "il crack Sindona," as Italians dubbed the empire's collapse. In 1979, only hours after talking to U.S. authorities about the Vatican Bank's relations with Sindona, he was shot to death by three men in the street outside his home in Milan. Ambrosoli told American investigators that in 1973 Sindona had sold two companies to Milan banker Calvi for what was considered the greatly inflated price of $100 million. Ambrosoli said that Sindona paid a $5.6 million commission as part of the deal to "an American bishop and a Milanese banker." Official Italian sources later confirmed that Ambrosoli was referring to Marcinkus and Calvi. Sindona subsequently admitted giving the money to Calvi but said it was to purchase shares in Calvi's Ambrosiano Bank and other stocks. "None went to Marcinkus unless Calvi gave it to him," he said.[41]

Adding to the embarrassment and financial losses consequent on "il crack Sindona," the name of the Vatican Bank kept coming up in indictments related to the case. Among the twenty-five prominent Italian bankers indicted by the Italian Government were Luigi Mennini, the highest lay official in the Vatican Bank, who acts as managing director under Marcinkus; Pellegrino de Strobel, the bank's chief accountant; and Massimo Spada, a former top financial adviser to the Vatican.[42]

The 1982 indictments were more salt in the already smarting wound of Marcinkus' involvement with Calvi and his fascist friend Gelli, whose dealings made Sindona's seem humdrum. But Sindona remained the key figure throughout the unfolding Vatican drama because he was Calvi's financial and political godfather and had introduced him to Marcinkus and Gelli. Sindona stated that he did not meet Gelli until 1973, and then only during a chance encounter at the Grand Hotel in Rome, but other information suggests he had dealings with the P-2 before then, as a go-between for the CIA.

In the years after World War II the CIA pumped some $65 million into Italy to support centrist and right-wing political parties, as revealed by the House of Representatives' Pike Report on CIA activities. Despite this massive support, the beneficiaries "suffered repeated electoral setbacks," and the CIA apparently concluded that another "quick fix" was necessary in the form of

$10 million for the 1972 parliamentary elections. But Nixon's White House, the CIA, and Graham Martin, the then U.S. ambassador to Italy, could not agree on who should get the booty. Martin worried that Sindona had a direct line to the White House because of his association with David Kennedy and Nixon's former law firm.† Sindona had also been active in the 1972 Nixon reelection drive, when he put together fund-raising campaigns, offered $1 million to the reelection committee on the condition of anonymity (it was refused), and orchestrated rightwing Italian efforts to woo Italian-American voters into Nixon's camp. Ambassador Martin concluded that Sindona was too extremist, his preference for CIA funding being Vito Miceli, a rightist general who headed the scandal-ridden SID, the Italian counterpart of the CIA. Martin wanted total control over the CIA's purse strings in Italy lest "certain people"—meaning Sindona—push the White House into a "disastrous program." There were bitter fights between the ambassador and the CIA station chief over who was crazier, Sindona or Miceli, Martin at one point threatening to put the chief spook on the first plane back to Washington. "It was a mess," said an embassy official. "There was lots of money floating around and everybody and his uncle was giving it to Sindona and Miceli. Sindona was a money channel years before Martin asked for control of the funds."⁴³

The irony is that Martin and the CIA bickered for nothing, since the Sindona and Miceli pipelines both led back to the same neofascists. Both men belonged to the P-2; Miceli, who received at least $800,000 from Ambassador Martin, was also a member of the neofascist Italian Social Movement of "Black Prince" Borghese.‡ According to the Italian press, some of the CIA money went to finance an aborted fascist coup against the Italian Government, which was organized by Borghese in December 1970. Also implicated in the coup were Miceli and the Italian terrorist Delle Chiaie, of Ordine Nuovo, the paramilitary arm of the P-2, as well as John McCaffrey, chief of the European resistance movement for Britain during World War II. The Scotsman met Sindona after the war when he represented Hambros Bank in

† See pp. 180, 181.
‡ See pp. 177, 178.

Italy. Hambros was a partner with Sindona in an Italian bank, and McCaffrey became close friends with the Sicilian, who shared the same right-wing ideology. In an affidavit signed in Ireland in 1981 shortly before his death, McCaffrey stated that he helped Sindona plan the 1970 coup and that he was "sure to a moral certainty" that the CIA was aware of the plot. Convinced that the coup would "exclude any attempt at neo-fascist dictatorship," McCaffrey seemed unaware of Sindona's P-2 links, although everyone on the Italian side of the conspiracy was connected to the neofascist lodge. Miceli and Sindona were involved in another unsuccessful coup conspiracy in 1973, known as the Rosa dei Venti. Italian judicial authorities uncovered additional evidence implicating Miceli's SID and Delle Chiaie in the 1969 explosion at Milan's Piazza Fontana, in which seventeen died. The bombing was part of the "strategy of tension," hatched by right-wing SID officials and Borghese's neofascists, to cause a shift to the right on the part of Italian voters alarmed by phony "leftist" bombings.[44]

In addition to CIA funds, the P-2 crowd obtained money from kidnappings of well-to-do businessmen in Europe and from the drug traffic in South America. Sindona's Milan bank laundered money for the notorious Mafia kidnappers of *Anonima Sequestri,* who worked with Delle Chiaie's Ordine Nuovo. A London-connected bank, Universal Banking Corporation, performed a similar service for *Anonima* and financed European fascists on the run. A Scotland Yard investigation of Universal Banking Corporation revealed that the mastermind behind the bank was none other than Meyer Lansky, financial genius of America's organized crime.* To complete this unholy alliance, several Italian priests were also members of *Anonima,* including four Franciscan monks who were convicted for their involvement in kidnappings and Mafia money laundering, allegedly through Vatican-controlled banks.[45]

***

The Sindona-Miceli connection again raises questions about the CIA's Mafia and fascist links.† Like Klaus Barbie, who was

* See Chapters 3, pp. 40, 47; and 5, p. 81.
† See Chapter 5, pp. 79–82.

saved from French vengeance by U.S. intelligence officers, coup plotter Borghese was rescued from execution at the hands of the World War II Italian resistance by intelligence agent James J. Angleton, one of the CIA's future "whiz kids" and an expert on Vatican affairs. After the war against fascism in Europe, the CIA proceeded to finance the fascists' cause in Italy through men like Borghese, Sindona, and Miceli.[46]

When Martin was replaced by Ambassador John Volpe, Sindona's relations with the embassy returned to normal: The same year he ran the Franklin National Bank into bankruptcy, Sindona was given the "Man of the Year" award by Volpe at a luncheon at the American Club in Rome.[47]

Chapter 10

The Vatican resists its creditors and throws a chill into world banking.

After Milan banker Roberto Calvi's body was discovered hanging from a bridge in London in mid-1982, Archbishop Marcinkus and the Vatican Bank were engulfed in a second wave of scandal. The question everyone was asking, including cardinals as well as bankers, was how Marcinkus could have become involved with yet another crook after his experience with Sindona. But not only did Marcinkus take part in the intrigue that led to Calvi's death, he also continued to deal with Calvi after his connection with the P-2 had become known and the banker had been sentenced to four years in prison for illegal currency dealings.[1] The kindest thing to be said of Marcinkus is that he was extraordinarily naive —not a quality one hopes to find in the sole keeper of the Vatican's purse strings.

Like Sindona, Calvi was caught in a trap of his own devising when he borrowed excessively on the Eurocurrency market to buy shares in his own Ambrosiano Bank (in itself an illegal procedure) and to finance Gelli's murky P-2 operations in Latin America. When Calvi could no longer cover old debts with new loans, he found himself cornered by the Italian banking authorities, who demanded to know why some $1.4 billion had disappeared into the accounts of certain mysterious Panamanian companies. On June 11, a few days after receiving an ultimatum from Italy's central bank, Calvi disappeared from Milan, fleeing first to Yugoslavia, then to Austria, and finally to England. Normally accompanied by eleven bodyguards, Calvi had only two companions on this journey—Flavio Carboni, a Sardinian businessman and fellow member of the P-2, with alleged Mafia connections, and Silvano Vittor, a bodyguard provided by Carboni.[2]

By all accounts the flamboyant Sardinian played a major role in the last months of Calvi's life. He constantly warned the banker of impending danger: Calvi was not to trust his own bodyguards; he should not sleep at his own house; and he should be very careful wherever he went, for "they" were out to kill him. Calvi took it all seriously. He told the Italian newspaper *La Stampa:* "I really am frightened. It is a question of surviving in a climate that is becoming like a religious war. The atmosphere favors every sort of barbarism."[3]

Vittor arranged for Calvi's escape from Italy in a smugglers' launch, the *Ouragano,* which took the banker across the Gulf of Trieste to the small fishing village of Muggia in Yugoslavia. From there he was driven through the night to meet Carboni at a safe house in Austria. Three days later—after Calvi had methodically burned dozens of documents, by Vittor's account—Vittor flew to London with Calvi, whose crudely doctored passport aroused no suspicion. Calvi's escape reportedly was aided by Hans Kunz, a self-described "Swiss businessman" who chartered the plane that flew Calvi to London. According to the Italian press, Kunz and his brother Albert were actually part of a giant Mafia guns-for-drugs operation busted in late 1982. Carboni, who followed the banker to London, claimed that Calvi had insisted on a secure place to stay, but Carboni's choice—a seedy flat off King's Road —depressed and angered him (Carboni, by contrast, was staying at the Hilton Hotel with two girlfriends). Vittor and Carboni claimed that Calvi grew increasingly frightened and morose. On the evening of the third day of the stay Vittor said he went out about 11 P.M. for a sandwich with Carboni and his girlfriends, and that when he returned he found the apartment empty. No one had seen Calvi leave. At seven-thirty the next morning the banker's body was found hanging from the scaffolding at Blackfriars Bridge.[4]

During Calvi's flight his personal secretary of thirty years jumped—or possibly was pushed—to her death from a fourth-floor window in the bank's Milan headquarters. She left a note saying that Calvi should be "twice cursed for the damage he caused the bank and all its employees." A judge investigating the case was then murdered. And Calvi's body was found dangling beneath Blackfriars Bridge. In the pockets of Calvi's expensive gray suit were $20,000 in foreign currencies and twelve pounds of bricks and stones. A London coroner, whose ruling was later questioned by British authorities, decided that Calvi had committed suicide; the banker, facing prison in Italy, his financial empire in ruins, had enough reason to take his own life. He had tried to kill himself once before, during his 1981 trial for illegal currency dealings, though it is questionable whether that attempt was genuine or merely intended to attract political sympathy (which it did). Most of those involved in the affair were convinced he had been murdered. Roberto Rosone, Ambrosiano's senior deputy chairman, said he was certain that Calvi had been killed. Two months before the banker fled Italy a gunman had wounded Rosone in an episode generally regarded as a "warning" to Calvi. A slight, unathletic man, Calvi, sixty-two, "just wasn't the sort to do a contortionist's act by hanging himself from a London bridge with his pockets full of bricks," said Rosone. The Italian press agreed. They published diagrams of the alleged suicide showing that Calvi would have had to climb down a twenty-foot ladder to reach the bridge scaffolding from which he was found hanging. And he was known to suffer from vertigo.[5] *

Sindona and Calvi's family also believed the banker had been murdered. Carlos Calvi, the dead man's son and a representative of an Ambrosiano subsidiary in Washington, said that his father kept in contact with the family after he left Milan, and that he had been on the verge of completing a business deal that would have extricated him from his financial difficulties in Italy. (London's *Financial Times* speculated that Calvi had gone—or was perhaps lured—to London to complete that deal.)[6] Another reason the family suspected foul play was that Calvi's bulging black briefcase—which Vittor admitted the banker had had with him in Austria—was not to be found in London. According to the European press, the missing briefcase may have been smuggled out of London by a small plane chartered from Geneva by "Swiss businessman" Hans Kunz. The plane arrived at Gatwick Airport

---

* The London coroner based his finding of suicide on the lack of any signs of violence save for two deep rope marks on Calvi's neck.

the same day Calvi died. It arrived without luggage, remained on the ground for ninety-nine minutes, and left with a medium-sized suitcase. Italian police speculated that it contained the key to secret P-2 accounts in Switzerland. (Carboni and then Gelli were caught trying to withdraw the money.) "In the last year of his life, my father lived in fear," Carlos Calvi said. (In 1982 Calvi had budgeted more than $1 million in Ambrosiano funds for his personal security.) Sindona, who agreed that Calvi was frightened, believed that his enemies were Communists in South America. Vatican sources, on the other hand, thought that Calvi had more to fear from the P-2's Gelli.[7]

***

Calvi's rise and fall was inextricably intertwined with the fortunes of Sindona. As the latter tells it, Calvi approached him around 1969 to say that he shared Sindona's right-wing politics and to ask for help in building Banco Ambrosiano. By that time Sindona had designs on Franklin National Bank. "I told Calvi, 'You take care of Italy. We'll help you from America. You must be the *bastione,* the bulwark, against communism.'" Sindona claimed he also told Calvi, " 'You are the man who must keep the relationship with Marcinkus.' "[8]

Described by the Italian press as having "eyes of steel," Calvi was a professional banker from a banking family—his father was a Milanese bank director. Like many young Italians in the 1930s, he became a fascist militant while attending the university. After the war he took a low-level job in the foreign department of Ambrosiano Bank. Quiet, methodical, and hardworking, he became a protégé of one of the bank's leading managers, Carlo Alessandro Canesi, and rose with his patron through the hierarchy. He succeeded Canesi as president in 1974. The proverbial bank gnome, Calvi worked twelve-hour days and had no outside interests, save for the clandestine P-2. He refused to delegate authority and developed a reputation for being extraordinarily secretive. Unlike the polished Sindona, Calvi was never at ease in international finance circles and spoke in convoluted, almost unintelligible phrases. "It wasn't easy to talk to him," said one banker. "He wouldn't make any attempt to find a common ground." Sindona had a different impression of the man that was probably nearer the truth. Though he may have appeared "cold-blooded," Calvi was impressed, said Sindona, by counts and barons, the sort of society that Gelli attracted to the P-2. "He was no good at choosing other people," Sindona added.[9]

That observation applied as well to Calvi's relationship with Sindona. Wise bankers distanced themselves from the Ambrosiano Bank after learning that as early as 1973 Calvi had been using Ambrosiano funds to backstop Sindona's dubious operations. When Ambrosoli, the murdered state liquidator of the Sindona empire, charged that Calvi had received a $5.6 million payoff for collaborating in one of Sindona's fraudulent schemes,† it became apparent, said one banker, that "Sindona and his crowd had long had their hooks in Calvi. Calvi took the money, and after that he could be manipulated—blackmailed."[10] ‡

As Sindona's "man" at Ambrosiano, Calvi quickly learned to ape his patron. He was determined to transform his bank from a relatively small regional bank with strong religious overtones (Ambrosiano was known as the "priests' bank," and at one time would-be shareholders had to present baptismal certificates to prove their Catholicism) into a major international financial institution. Provided with Sindona's introductions to international bankers, Calvi created Italy's largest financial group, with huge banking, financial, and insurance interests throughout the world. Just as a Lichtenstein holding company had been the linchpin in the Sindona empire, Ambrosiano's global interests were controlled through a bank holding company in Luxembourg, a haven beyond the reach of Italian banking authorities. Parts of the Ambrosiano empire, such as its Nassau bank, were built on the ruins of Sindona's network, but the key connection was Marcinkus, whom Sindona introduced to Calvi in 1971.

Marcinkus denied that he had ever had more than cursory dealings with either man, although the Vatican Bank acquired 1.6 percent of Ambrosiano's parent bank in Milan—and possibly

† See Chapter 9, p. 187.
‡ According to *The Sunday Times* of London, in 1978 Calvi paid Sindona $500,000 through Swiss banks to stop a Sindona-orchestrated poster campaign in Milan that accused Calvi of fraudulent bank deals in minute detail *(The Sunday Times* [Feb. 13, 1983]).

more if, as the *Financial Times* speculated, it held any of the anonymous equity in the Luxembourg holding company (32 percent of the company's bearer shares were owned by unknown investors). And the archbishop became involved with Ambrosiano in other ways. In 1971, a few months after Sindona and Calvi set up Banco Ambrosiano Overseas in the Bahamas, a "Mr. Paul Marcinkus" was listed as one of its directors. In return for Marcinkus' patronage, the Vatican Bank received 8 percent of the Nassau bank's stock and 4 percent of the Luxembourg holding company. Sindona and other Italian financial sources noted that the Vatican Bank was able to perform valuable services for Ambrosiano and other Italian banks—as, for example, moving funds out of the country, an operation forbidden to Italian banks. Sindona asserted that in return for such favors Calvi's banks paid the Vatican an interest rate on its deposits that was one percentage point higher than other customers received. Vatican officials denied that the bank helped to export Italian funds.[11]

The Italian central bank began pressing Calvi to clean up Ambrosiano's financial mess in Latin America when a 1978 audit revealed huge gaps in the bank's overseas accounts. But the secretive and evasive banker, using political influence and bribes, managed to put off the reckoning until May 1982. Later investigations by the Italian banking authorities showed that some $1.4 billion had been drained through Ambrosiano's Luxembourg holding company to its branches in Nassau, Managua, and Lima. These banks, in turn, loaned the money to Vatican-controlled shell companies in Panama. Approximately $400 million was used by Calvi to buy shares in the Milanese parent bank in a bid to take personal control of Ambrosiano. Another $400 million consisted of interest on that debt, which Calvi had borrowed on the Eurocurrency market before 1978. Because no interest was paid, it was simply tacked onto the $400 million owed, which meant that by 1981 the original debt had roughly doubled. Apparently Calvi intended to offset the debt with shares from Ambrosiano. Instead, interest rates rose and the dollar increased in value, thus adding to the Panamanian companies' indebtedness, while the Italian lire fell, diminishing the value of the Ambrosiano stock pledged as collateral. A further $400 million went for a host of P-2 activities in Latin America, from arms purchases to under-the-table payments to right-wing newspapers. Additional Euromarket borrowings by Calvi in 1981–82 increased the total debt to about $1.4 billion. In the last days before his death Calvi tried to negotiate the sale of Ambrosiano stock at values well above the market price—apparently the reason for his trip to London—but if there was any deal in the works, Calvi died before it could be completed.[12]

The Vatican Bank was involved four ways in Calvi's venture. First, Marcinkus was a member of the board of directors of the Nassau subsidiary. Second, the Vatican Bank had borrowed $250 million from Ambrosiano's Lima subsidiary, Banco Ambrosiano Andino. Third, in September 1981, the Vatican Bank gave Calvi letters of patronage ("comfort letters," in bank parlance) for the Panamanian companies' debt. Calvi needed the letters to appease the directors of Ambrosiano's bank in Lima, who were insisting that he produce written proof of his assertion that the Vatican owned the Panamanian companies. The Vatican Bank obliged with letters stating that it directly or indirectly controlled the companies that had received the loans, and that the bank was fully aware of their borrowing activities. Giorgio Nassano, chairman of the Lima bank, said the letters were accompanied by signed loan-account statements acknowledging interest details and repayment dates on the loans themselves.[13]

Such letters of patronage have been widely used in the international banking community as a guarantee securing the borrower's obligation to repay. No bank had ever failed to honor repayments covered by such letters until the Vatican announced, in 1982, that it had no obligation to pay the Panamanian companies' debt because at the time he received the letters of patronage Calvi had given Marcinkus a secret letter releasing the Vatican Bank from any financial responsibility for the loans. Naturally none of the directors of the Lima bank saw the secret letters, which came to light only after Calvi's death, when Italian banking authorities were pounding on Marcinkus' door. To Italian officials the affair smacked of fraud. "The Vatican must have known that the two [sets of] letters could not be genuine at the same time," argued a senior financial official. There is also a question of timing. According to the *Financial Times,* some of the Ambrosiano loans were made to the Panamanian companies only *after* receipt of the comfort letters from the Vatican. But Vatican officials claimed that the Ambrosiano loans involved "prior financial dealings with which the [Vatican Bank] is not connected." On the other hand, "Calvi had been saying for years that he was working for the Vatican," said an Ambrosiano source. "We still don't know that he was lying." One result of the argument over who was responsible is that bankers have ceased to use letters of patronage.[14]

The fourth Vatican tie was the most damaging, because it proved conclusively that the bank had owned the Panamanian companies that were used by Calvi to buy Ambrosiano stock and to finance the P-2. After the Calvi scandal broke, Pope John Paul appointed a blue-ribbon investigative commission composed of Joseph Brennan, an American Catholic and former chairman of the Emigrant Savings Bank in New York; Phillippe de Wech, a former president of Switzerland's Union Bank; and Carlo Cerutti, a high-ranking Italian civil servant with strong ties to the Vatican. Among their findings was the fact that the Vatican Bank owned ten of the Panamanian shell companies. According to the commission's report, the Vatican Bank had been "exploited" by Calvi, who had made the bank the owner of the companies without its knowledge. But the report also acknowledged that Marcinkus had learned of Calvi's manipulations in July 1981, and yet two months later he had given the banker the Vatican's letters of patronage.[15]

In fact, Marcinkus may have known of—and been a party to—such manipulations long before that. *The Sunday Times* of London turned up a document, dated November 1974 and signed by Vatican Bank officials, instructing a Swiss bank to arrange the formation of a Panamanian company called United Trading Corporation. Some $226 million of the missing $1.4 billion owed by Calvi passed through Ambrosiano's Latin-American subsidiaries to United Trading, and since United Trading was one of the companies named in the letters of patronage issued by the Vatican Bank, *The Sunday Times* believed it "could have been used to help the Vatican's financial problems." The newspaper also reported that the Vatican Bank used another Panamanian shell company, Laramie, in a secret transaction with Ambrosiano. The same paper said it had evidence that the Vatican Bank put an inflated price of $20 million on shares it owned in a Rome construction company that it sold to Ambrosiano through Laramie. But the Vatican Bank "never delivered the shares and kept both the $20 million and the shares." Denials by the Vatican Bank that it received money from Banco Ambrosiano or Calvi "must be suspect," the newspaper concluded.[16]

Calvi's wife Clara agreed. She said that during his trial for illegal currency dealings her husband had summoned her and their daughter Anna to visit him in prison. Clara recalled that "he gave us some papers on which he had written: This trial is [about] IOR [the Institute for Religious Works, or the Vatican Bank]. He told us that we should go to Marcinkus and Mennini [Luigi Mennini, the bank's managing director] and ask them for the secrecy to be removed so it would be known he had not done it." As the two women left the prison, there was an astonishing incident. They were climbing into a waiting car when Mennini's son Alex—who was an official at the Banco Ambrosiano—jumped in as well. "When he saw the papers in my daughter's hand, he tried to grab them," said Clara. "But I sat on them and wouldn't let go." Clara claimed that Alex Mennini said, "You must not mention this name [Vatican Bank] even in confession."[17]

But if some people were worried by what Calvi might reveal, Marcinkus himself showed little apparent concern. Calvi's son Carlo repeatedly telephoned Marcinkus at the Vatican in an attempt to enlist his support. Eventually the archbishop responded. "Tell your father, don't bring up our problems with the bank because they are *his* problems."[18]

Despite evidence to the contrary, the Vatican's report concluded that the Vatican Bank had no obligation for the $1.4 billion debt incurred by the companies. The problem with the investigative commission's report, said *The Wall Street Journal,* was that it raised more questions than it answered. One that any banker would have asked is why Marcinkus agreed to go on playing Calvi's game by issuing the letters of patronage, particularly after Calvi had been convicted of illegally exporting $26.4 million. Another is why Marcinkus did not inquire into the business of the Panamanian companies once he had learned that the Vatican Bank owned them (or, as suggested by *The Sunday*

THE AMBROSIANO MONEY-GO-ROUND

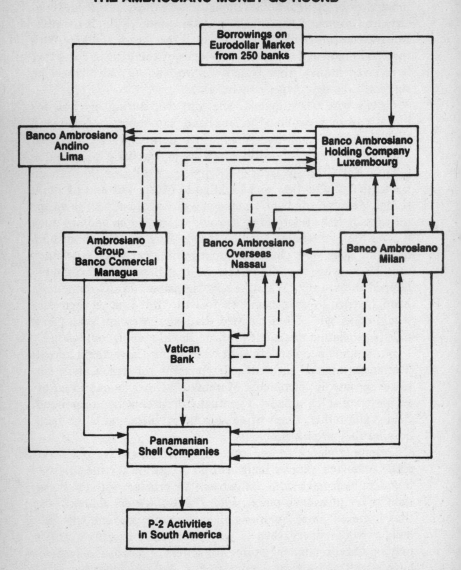

Times, perhaps he did know). Yet another is why the archbishop told the Italian press in October 1982—more than a year after learning that the Vatican Bank owned the Panamanian companies—that he had no knowledge of, and "nothing to do" with, their operations. As noted by Peter Hebblethwaite, a prominent writer on Vatican affairs, Marcinkus seemed to be afflicted with "extraordinary blindness."[19]

***

In addition to possible financial liability, there were strong political and institutional reasons for denying Vatican links to the Panamanian companies, since the latter financed the P-2's activities in Latin America. According to Sindona, the Ambrosiano Bank's connection with the Masonic lodge dated to the early 1970s, when he introduced Calvi to "Grand Master" Gelli and Calvi became a Mason. "Calvi was Catholic, but Gelli said he had a relationship with some cardinals [who made it] very clear the church was not against it," said Sindona. "Gelli told Calvi he was free to be Catholic—[Freemasonry] does not interfere with religion."[20]

But Gelli's interpretation did not accord with canon law, and to remind Italians of the church's position on Freemasonry after the P-2 scandal broke, the Sacred Congregation for the Doctrine of the Faith published a statement forbidding Catholics "under pain of excommunication from joining Masonic or similar associations." (The Italian Government followed up by seizing membership lists that identified some thirty thousand Masons in Italy.) One of the clues to why Gelli chose the Masons to further his political ambitions was found among his papers when the police raided his Arezzo villa. It was an exchange of letters between himself and Philip A. Guarino—national chairman of the Italian-American division of the U.S. Republican National Committee and a P-2 member—on how to help "our brother, Michele" (i.e., Sindona), then on trial in New York. Although the correspondence came to nothing, it outlined the role played in Italy by American Masons after World War II.[21]

In eighteenth-century Europe Freemasonry was the semisecret party of republican revolution. In Latin America the Masons played a similar anticlerical role, although they tended to remain a conservative force, often allied with the military, as in Chile. In nineteenth-century Italy the liberal revolution was led by secret societies called *Carboneria,* which were similar to Freemasons (Garibaldi, Italy's national hero, was a Mason). To curry favor with the Vatican Mussolini banned the Italian Masonic orders, but the ban was not seriously enforced. Thus the Americans were able to build on an existing network after World War II.

The Americans wanted to fill key positions with people who were neither fascists nor leftists, and a solution was to rely on the Italian-American international organizations. For Sicily this meant mainly the Mafia, but the Masonic lodges were probably more helpful in the rest of Italy. At that time, Italian-American Masons tended to be Democrats, like New York Mayor Fiorello La Guardia. Some were immigrants, such as unionist Guiseppe "Joe" Lupis, who channeled American union money into Italy to splinter the labor movement and create anti-Communist unions during the cold war. According to one former prominent Italian Mason, the split in the Italian Socialist Party (PSI) that created the Italian Social Democratic Party (PSDI) was "entirely provoked by Freemasons in the United States and Italy." Thus the anti-Communist imperative pulled Italian Freemasonry to the right, and in the 1950s the lodges provided ex-fascists with democratic cover and contacts with American brothers ready to raise funds to stop communism. The lodges in general, and the P-2 in particular, began to recruit heavily among military men eager for promotion. Membership in a lodge was reliable evidence of the anticommunism required for a successful career in a NATO military force.[22]

Gelli came to Freemasonry well along in his career. Unlike Calvi, he had been more than a rank-and-file fascist in his youth. He was a militant member of the party and joined an Italian Blackshirt division to fight for Franco in Spain when he was seventeen. The son of poor laborers in Piamonte, he was a high school dropout who "made up for intelligence with shrewdness," according to a Christian Democrat politician who belonged to the P-2. His first business venture was a mattress factory and textile-import operation, which thrived because Gelli early learned to cultivate people in the right places. After the war he went to Argentina, where he made his fortune. How he amassed so much wealth and influence has never been established, although it is known that his principal associate was the sinister Italian Count Umberto Ortolani, who has extensive operations in Uruguay and was Gelli's alter ego in the P-2. Some Latin Americans who have followed the pair's career claim that after the war they helped wealthy fascist fugitives transfer their fortunes to South America, keeping up to 40 percent of the money. Their clients were unable to protest for fear of being denounced, a form of blackmail that became a key feature in the P-2's success. Later they used Calvi's connections to expand into banking, and Ortolani was made head of Banco Financiero Sudamericano (Banfisud), the second most important private bank in Uruguay, with branches in Argentina, Brazil, and Paraguay. Banfisud was a subsidiary of Calvi's Ambrosiano Bank in Milan. Gelli's political ambitions were encouraged by Juan Domingo Perón; his second wife, Isabel; and their henchman, José López Rega, whom Gelli met when the trio was in Spanish exile. Gelli became a frequent visitor to Perón's Madrid mansion and is believed to have helped him recover the body of his first wife, the legendary Evita, through contacts with the Argentine military.[23]

Gelli's relations with Perón are interesting for what they suggest about P-2 strategy in Italy. Italian sociologists, historians, and journalists are largely in agreement that in the 1970s extreme-right terrorism formed part of a "strategy of tension" designed to provoke the extreme left into responding in kind. The strategy was successful in that it became increasingly difficult to determine which terrorist organization was responsible for what atrocity, and the confusion contributed to a breakdown in government institutions. The aim was to trigger a military coup that would restore "order" (i.e., fascism) to Italy.[24] Though it may have appeared peculiarly Italian at the time, the strategy was well known among Latin-American revolutionaries as early as the 1960s, particularly among the guerrilla columns of local Communist parties, which used it to goad the military into seizing the state. The theory was that once a right-wing military regime had taken over, it would so alienate the population by its ruthless methods that the people would rise up in spontaneous rebellion. It never worked in South America because the people were too disorganized and apathetic to revolt; even in Nicaragua, where such a revolution occurred, it took the guerrillas forty-three years to achieve their objective.

However, from his exile in Madrid Perón proved himself a master at stirring up unrest. Unlike other Latin dictators, Perón had shrewdly organized Argentina's labor movement as his principal power base during his first period in government (1943–55). Though he was deposed in 1955, successive military and civilian governments were unable to lay his ghost, and in 1973 he was allowed to return to Argentina, where he won the presidency in popular elections.

That Perón had never intended to champion the left became apparent during a brief visit to Buenos Aires in 1972, when an estimated two million Argentines gathered at Ezeiza Airport to welcome him. The reception was marred when leftist Peronists were ambushed by right-wing supporters of the dictator. Later evidence suggested that Perón knew of the impending attack but did nothing to prevent it. After he became president, he ordered a crackdown on dissident labor leaders and generally supported the suppression of the center-left by fascist paramilitary groups that had come into existence during his first period in government. The disillusioned young turned to the guerrilla movements that Perón himself had earlier encouraged from exile in Madrid. Thus the stage was set for a national bloodbath when the old man died and Isabel succeeded him in the presidency. Had Perón lived, his government probably would not have been much different from the repressive military regime that replaced his wife in 1976 and wiped out the political center as well as the left. Statements by leading generals, in addition to the swastikas and other Nazi paraphernalia on display in the military's torture centers, left no doubt of the regime's neofascist philosophy. Several of the government's most powerful members, such as Admiral Emilio Massera, the navy chief, were members of the P-2. Unlike Italy, with its older, more complex traditions, Argentina proved a successful experiment in the strategy of tension by restoring "order" to the nation. But the cost was horrendous: some twenty thousand died or disappeared and the Argentine economy was destroyed.[25]

When Perón flew to Argentina in 1973, Gelli was on the plane with him. Under the Peróns the Italian's fortune prospered. He was appointed economic adviser to the Argentine embassy in Rome and was given an Argentine diplomatic passport, thereby providing him with diplomatic immunity on his travels. When Isabel succeeded her husband, López Rega became the all-powerful minister for social welfare. He also founded the infamous Argentine death squad, the AAA, and helped Gelli establish a P-2 chapter in Buenos Aires, which attracted important representatives of the military and financial establishments.[26]

Gelli's spiel contained an inextricable mixture of nostalgia for fascism, political opportunism, and self-interest, with the last usually dominating. For example, it was through his efforts that Calvi's Ambrosiano group came to control the Argentine publishing empire, CREA Editorial Abril, with eighteen magazines and other publications, including the popular weekly *Siete Dias*. Abril had been set up by Víctor and César Civitá, two Italian brothers who arrived in Latin America in 1940. The Brazilian side of the operation, under Víctor, still flourishes, but César had to abandon the Argentine branch in the 1970s, when López Rega was virtually running the country. César's son-in-law, a left-wing Peronist, was kidnapped in 1974 and is presumed dead. At the same time, Civitá himself was accused of collaborating with the Argentine guerrillas. As a result of threats to his life, Civitá began to sell his various companies. It is believed that the harassment, along with the kidnapping of his son-in-law, was engineered by López Rega on behalf of the P-2. The buyer of Civitá's Argentine empire was the Rizzoli group, Italy's largest publishing organization and the owner of Milan's influential daily *Corriere della Sera*. Rizzoli, in turn, was controlled by Calvi's Ambrosiano Bank, which helped finance the Argentine acquisition through the Vatican's famous Panamanian shell companies. Executives of Abril and Rizzoli were members of the P-2. According to *Il Mundo*, an Italian business magazine and part of the Rizzoli group, 80 percent of the Rizzoli shares were controlled by the Vatican Bank between 1977 and 1981, when Calvi's empire began unraveling. The magazine reported that Marcinkus had personally approved the purchase through intermediary companies in Milan, Panama, and Geneva. Although the archbishop denied the story, Angelo Rizzoli, the family representative of the Rizzoli group, told an Italian parliamentary commission that he had seen the Vatican's seal of ownership endorsed on the shares. (Il Mundo published the charges in 1983 after the Ambrosiano Bank had collapsed and the Rizzoli group had been placed under government supervision.)[27]

Gelli was careful to cover his military flank, and when Isabel Perón was overthrown in 1976, his connections served him well. His principal patron in the new junta was Admiral Massera, head of the Navy,* but other military officials also belonged to the P-2, including a retired admiral, who was on the board of Banco Ambrosiano's Argentine branch, and an army commander, who became president of the state-run oil company. It was an indication of Gelli's continuing good relations with the military that he remained in his post at the Argentine embassy in Rome until 1981, when the P-2 scandal forced him to flee to Uruguay.[28]

Gelli was doubly useful to Admiral Massera: He arranged arms sales and harassed the Argentine exile community in Europe. At that time the Italian military attaché in Buenos Aires was a member of the P-2, and through such connections Massera arranged the purchase of Italian frigates. It was also said that Gelli's contacts with Muammar el-Qaddafi enabled him to arrange arms shipments to Argentina through Libya. Apparently the quid pro quo was to have been Argentine nuclear technology to help Libya develop nuclear weapons. (Argentina has the most advanced nuclear technology in Latin America and is capable of making a nuclear bomb; the Argentine Navy controls the Atomic Energy Commission in charge of nuclear policy.) Whether Gelli had a part in obtaining Libyan arms supplies for Argentina during the 1982 conflict with Britain over the Falkland Islands is unknown, but the Argentine military regime did confirm the receipt of such arms.[29]

A more spectacular charge was that Calvi and Gelli tried to secure French Exocet missiles for Argentina during the Falklands conflict. Money for the purchase was reportedly funneled through Ambrosiano's Lima subsidiary and represented Calvi's

---

* Some Argentine journalists believe Massera warned López Rega to escape to Spain before the coup; Isabel was imprisoned but later released under the military government of General Roberto Viola, who was also believed to have had links with Gelli.

last major borrowing on the Eurocurrency market (some $200 million). The deal apparently fell through because of a shipping mix-up in Europe, so that by the time the Peruvian vessel that had been sent to pick up the missiles had located them in Genoa, the war was over. Whatever the truth of the allegations, Peru was Argentina's closest ally during the conflict and the Peruvian Government offered to send arms and men to aid the Argentines. Moreover, the Peruvian central bank maintained close links with Calvi's Lima bank and was its largest depositor. Thus the Peruvian Government would have had no objection to the Exocet deal.[30]

If such a purchase was indeed attempted, the trail would have been hidden through the Vatican's Panamanian shell companies, since virtually all financing by the Lima branch was booked through them. The possibility that these companies were used to obtain Exocet missiles for Argentina is especially serious, because at the time of the Falklands war Archbishop Marcinkus knew the Vatican Bank owned the companies. While it may be inconceivable that he was privy to such an arrangement, it is an embarrassing footnote to Pope John Paul's visit to Argentina during the height of the conflict, when he urged the regime to end the war.

When later confronted with evidence of his membership in the P-2, Admiral Massera claimed that Gelli's work on behalf of the junta had been of "undeniable merit in the fight against subversion," and that he had "collaborated actively to spread the truth of our war against terrorism in Europe." But the eulogy took on a sinister note when it was learned that a naval intelligence operation Massera had been directing with Gelli in Paris was linked to several murders, including those of two Argentine diplomats.[31]

Massera was also linked to the 1977 disappearance of the Argentine ambassador to Venezuela, Héctor Hidalgo Sola. According to court testimony, Gelli and Massera wanted an ambassador who would do their bidding in the petroleum-rich nation, but Hidalgo Sola refused either to cooperate or to give up his post. He was replaced by a diplomat who was a member of the P-2.[32]†

† Massera was arrested in mid-1983 on charges of involvement in the disappearance and presumed murder of an Argentine businessman (Latin America Weekly Report [London], June 24, 1983).

Though Argentina was the P-2's headquarters in Latin America, it also had important lodges in Uruguay, Paraguay, and Brazil. In Montevideo Gelli's associate, Count Ortolani, built up a membership of at least five hundred, including prominent military hard-liners. Using the diplomatic cover of ambassador of the Order of Malta, he also acquired large real estate holdings in association with Gelli. After the P-2 scandal broke in Europe, Gelli fled to Montevideo, where he hired a private plane to fly him to a ranch he owned in southern Brazil. Ortolani sought refuge in São Paolo, Brazil. The Uruguayan military obligingly waited until he left the country to act on an Interpol request for a search of his house. But Uruguayan authorities refused to release the papers found there, presumably because they contained incriminating evidence against military officials. In Brazil, by contrast, the P-2 lodge was still in an incipient stage, with only nineteen members, mostly businessmen and none politically important. Ortolani's Banfisud bank had a branch in Brazil, and Gelli owned property in São Paulo and Rio de Janeiro, where his sister and daughter lived. But the atmosphere in Brazil, which was undergoing a process of democratization, was not conducive to P-2 penetration.[33]

Paraguay has traditionally been the last refuge in Latin America for right-wing villains on the run, a haven for German Nazis as well as for former Nicaraguan dictator Anastasio Somoza. General Alfredo Stroessner, the region's longest-ruling dictator, has also given sanctuary to drug traffickers and neofascist terrorists, such as Elio Massagrande and Gaetano Orlando, prominent members of Delle Chiaie's Ordine Nuovo and wanted for murder in Italy. Stroessner later invited a leader of the neofascist Italian Social Movement (MSI), also linked to the P-2, to indoctrinate the youth wing of his ruling Colorado Party.‡ And when the Chilean secret police wanted diplomatic passports for two of the conspirators involved in the Letelier assassination in Washington,* Stroessner obliged. Thus Paraguay would have been a logical place for Ortolani to rebuild the P-2 from his base in São Paolo, the principal bridge between Asunción and Europe.[34]

‡ See Chapter 9, pp. 177, 178, 188–89.
* See Chapter 9, p. 177.

Calvi might have aided Ortolani, but by 1982 he had become a liability. His financial empire was in ruins, and the publicity arising from Ambrosiano's problems had refocused the spotlight on Gelli and the P-2. Sindona said he warned Calvi not to link up with Ortolani, "who had pretensions like Marcinkus to be a financier." Sindona claimed that Ortolani encouraged Calvi to "finance newspapers for ideological reasons in Buenos Aires and Montevideo. But money to dictators and generals was sometimes under the table." Sindona also insisted that Marcinkus knew and generally approved of Calvi's Latin-American ventures, although he was unaware of the details. "I had told Calvi to tell Marcinkus that if they [the Vatican] can help, it is in their own interest. South America is Catholic. They don't want to lose this big a part of their account." The Vatican, however, denied any involvement.[35]

***

Three months after Calvi's body was found hanging from Blackfriars Bridge, Gelli was arrested in a Geneva bank while attempting to withdraw some $60 million using an Argentine passport. The funds were part of $100 million in Banco Ambrosiano money that had been stashed in numbered Swiss accounts —and Gelli knew the numbers. What he did not know was that such accounts were no longer immune to police investigation. Before Gelli flew in for the money, the Geneva bank had frozen the accounts and permitted a police stakeout. The Italian authorities requested his extradition for political and military espionage, illegal possession of state secrets, tax fraud, and possible involvement in the Bologna railroad station bombing.† But in August 1983, just nine days before a Swiss court was due to rule on the Italian request, Gelli disappeared from his Geneva prison. Bloodstains and a hypodermic needle were found in his cell, and there were signs of a struggle in a prison patio, giving rise to the suspicion that he had been kidnapped. Gelli's ruse was soon disproved when a prison guard confessed to taking an $8,500 bribe from Gelli to open his cell door and drive him across the French border in a small van. Press reports suggested that Gelli had fled to

† See Chapter 9, p. 173.

Uruguay, where he was being protected by the right-wing South Korean Moonies sect, which has extensive financial and property holdings there. Italy's disgusted interior minister said he had warned Swiss authorities of Gelli's probable escape and had even given them a list of likely accomplices (it presumably did not include Swiss guards).[36]

Other members of the P-2 lodge also ran into trouble. Antonio Viezzer, the head of a disbanded Italian intelligence agency and a P-2 member, was arrested on suspicion of complicity in the 1979 murder of journalist Mino Pecorelli, whose sensationalist newsletter had been funded by Gelli and fed by piquant leaks from Gelli's files. Pecorelli had accused Gelli of "working both sides of the street" by collaborating with the CIA. Also jailed was General Raffaele Giudice, a P-2 member and former commander of the Finance Guard, which is responsible for customs, tax collection, and fraud investigations. Giudice was given a seven-year sentence for his part in a huge petroleum tax scandal in which more than $2 billion in tax revenues were diverted into private pockets and spirited abroad.[37]

The tax scandal caused the Vatican Bank yet more embarrassment when two priests were arrested for their part in the affair and three others—including Monsignor Donato de Bonis, the bank's secretary—were notified by Italian authorities that they were under investigation for possible conspiracy to defraud the tax authorities. The priests, Fathers Simeone Duca and Francesco Quaglia, were accused of accepting bribes for helping to arrange financial transfers for tax officials who were part of the scheme. Also under investigation was Monsignor Mario Pimpo, assistant to Cardinal Ugo Poletti, the Pope's vicar of Rome. It turned out that Poletti had written a letter to Giulio Andreotti, a bigwig in the ruling Christian Democratic Party who had earlier befriended Sindona on Pope Paul's recommendation,‡ to suggest General Giudice as head of the Finance Guard. Though Poletti himself was not accused of any wrongdoing, he drew criticism during Giudice's trial for denying, under oath, that he had written the letter. When a local magazine then published it, Poletti claimed that it had slipped his mind.[38]

‡ See Chapter 9, p. 181.

Other P-2 members, such as the under secretary of defense and the head of the Supreme Council of Magistrates, were forced to resign their posts; and the commanders of Italy's three major intelligence services—all members of Gelli's lodge—were suspended, as were the commander of Italy's equivalent of the Joint Chiefs of Staff and General Giudice's successor at the Finance Guard. They were among thirty generals and eight admirals who belonged to the P-2. Perhaps most significant, an application to join the P-2 had been made by General Dalla Chiesa, who was in charge of operations against the Red Brigades and was later murdered in Sicily when he tried to combat the Mafia.[39]*

How Gelli was able to attract such people—the group included three cabinet ministers and forty-three members of parliament—is an Italian mystery, but one explanation might have been blackmail. Among Gelli's early recruits was a high-ranking member of SIFAR, an intelligence agency closed down for its involvement in the 1970 attempted coup led by the fascist "Black Prince" Borghese and other colleagues of Gelli.† The Italian parliament had ordered SIFAR's files burned because they were full of gossip about leading figures, but they turned up at Gelli's villa when the police raided it, along with tapes, a list of informers, and photos, including pictures of Pope John Paul in swimming trunks at his country retreat of Castel Gandolfo.[40]

There are some who ascribe the Vatican Bank's involvement with Calvi and the P-2 to the atmosphere of intrigue that permeates Italian institutions, but bankers argue that the bank became embroiled in the scandal mainly because of its extreme centralization, with all decisions in the hands of Marcinkus and two elderly aides, managing director Mennini and chief accountant de Strobel. The trio apparently was under pressure, possibly of Marcinkus' own devising, to produce large profits for the papacy's favorite causes—in John Paul's case, the Solidarity movement in Poland. Such pressures, said a former Bank of Italy governor, "can lead to mistakes." Added a senior Italian official, "Being essential allowed the bank too much freedom." Although a commission of five cardinals theoretically oversaw the bank's

* See Chapter 9, p. 186.
† See Chapter 9, p. 188.

operations, they met rarely, were given little useful information by Marcinkus, and probably would not have understood detailed financial statements if they had seen them. Until John Paul's appointment of an independent investigative commission after Calvi's death, there was no outside audit, and the only person Marcinkus had to report to was the Pope himself.[41]

According to the *Financial Times*, European bankers had long been unhappy about how the bank was being run; at one point they had suggested to a senior Vatican official that Marcinkus was not entirely suitable for his post. The Bank of Italy also warned high Vatican officials that a scandal might well arise from the archbishop's dealings with Calvi, but no action was taken. After the Ambrosiano affair broke, Chase Manhattan reportedly was approached for a $500 million credit line to shore up the Vatican Bank, but while the bank was "prepared to respond to any desire on their part for us to be of assistance," according to a Chase official, such help would be forthcoming only if the bank were reorganized.[42]

Marcinkus insisted that he had "never done anything that can be considered a fraud" and claimed that he had no intention of resigning from the bank. He has withstood all criticism because of his special relationship to the Pope. Some Vatican insiders have alleged that this closeness rests on the bank's considerable contributions to Poland's Solidarity movement. In any case, the American advanced rapidly under John Paul, assuming the office of governor of the Vatican City and personal travel secretary to the Pope, this in addition to his bank duties. His prospects for a cardinal's red hat must have seemed good until the Ambrosiano scandal engulfed the Vatican. According to Sindona, Marcinkus never sought money for himself, an opinion supported by the archbishop's relatively simple lifestyle (his only diversion is golf). What Marcinkus wanted, said the imprisoned banker, was power: "He was greedy because he wanted to give the money [he made] to the Pope because he wanted to become a cardinal." The archbishop, Sindona added, wanted to appear to know everything about banking and therefore never consulted with other bankers or a lawyer. Otherwise he would not have signed the letters of patronage for the Panamanian shell companies, which Sindona described as "unbelievable."[43]

Intrigue and jealousy are rife in the Roman Curia, and Marcinkus was the only high-ranking American in the Italian clique. He was accepted, reluctantly, because most of the Vatican's investments were (and are) in the United States and it was considered essential to have someone who knew the American banking community and spoke fluent English. Marcinkus' knowledge of English has never been in doubt, but one wonders if he ever mixed with the likes of David Rockefeller. For the titans of U.S. finance, the Vatican Bank, with only $300 million in capital, was no more important than a provincial bank in the Midwest. Both Sindona and Calvi knew that the bank itself was of no great significance; the institution that stood behind it opened all the doors. But Marcinkus' American defenders bridle at the suggestion that the archbishop might not be a first-rate banker. "Anyone who says that Marcinkus is ignorant about the techniques of international banking doesn't know what he is talking about," fumed Cardinal John Joseph Krol of Philadelphia. Such a line of defense only made Marcinkus' case look worse, in the opinion of Italian banking authorities, who said that if the archbishop knew what he was doing when he authorized the letters of patronage, he was probably guilty of fraud.[44]

After judicial authorities served notice on Marcinkus, Mennini, and de Strobel that they were under investigation for possible bank fraud, the three took refuge in Vatican City, beyond the reach of Italian law. Marcinkus has stubbornly refused to discuss the matter or meet with Italian banking authorities, who worried that they would be left holding the bag for the default of Ambrosiano's Luxembourg subsidiary on more than $1 billion in Eurocurrency loans to the Panamanian shell companies. Unable to leave Vatican City, Marcinkus did not accompany John Paul on his trip to Spain in the fall of 1982—the first time he had not served as the Pope's bodyguard.

John Paul's investigative panel cleared the Vatican Bank of any legal responsibility for the debts of the Vatican's Panamanian companies on the ground that the bank had been gulled by Calvi, but the scandal would not die. One reason was the moral question of confusing God and mammon. Not only had the Vatican Bank been involved with two extremely shady bankers, but also its directors had been so eager to make money that they failed to inquire into the P-2 connections of Ambrosiano's Latin-American subsidiaries. As pointed out by Vatican specialist Peter Hebblethwaite, "To be engaged in international finance at all is to be engaged in 'speculation' in one form or another, [such as] playing the market, buying cheap and selling dear, and watching the vagaries of gold and international currencies. Speculation is not a crime, even though it does seem to go against the 'priority of labor over capital' asserted in *Laborem Execrens* [an encyclical on labor by John Paul]; and if Pope John Paul wants to 'keep priests out of politics,' it would seem sensible to keep consecrated archbishops out of international finance." As for the Sindona and Calvi connections, said Hebblethwaite, they involved something much more sinister than "speculation."[45]

With collections from Catholics in the United States and Europe on the decline because of the Ambrosiano scandal, the Pope took the unusual step of airing the problem at a meeting of the Sacred College of Cardinals. Though primarily intended as a "morale booster" for the shaken cardinals, the meeting did establish two important guidelines for the Vatican Bank. The Pope made it clear that henceforward voluntary contributions, not dubious transactions on the international money market, would be the main source of Vatican support. And the investigative commission in charge of examining the bank's links with Calvi was made a permanent auditing body, with the addition of a fourth member, German banker Hermann J. Abs. Still, there was an unsatisfactory feeling among the cardinals—who listened to an ambiguous explanation of the bank's problems in Latin—that they had not heard the last of the affair.[46]

In the richer nations, particularly the United States and West Germany, a chorus of complaint was demanding an end to the secrecy surrounding Vatican finances. Clerics and laity said they wanted "fundamental changes in the way the Vatican handles its finances," including regular publication of balance sheets, as is the practice in most North American dioceses. As pointed out by the *National Catholic Reporter*, "We have the right to ask the U.S. bishops and the Vatican if it is proper for them to call upon us to support the Vatican when it wastes money through careless policies 10 times faster than the bishops can collect the cash." As to the Vatican's constant pleas of poverty, said the newspaper, that was nonsense, because profits from the Vatican Bank were never factored into the annual deficit. "That's the sort of jiggery-pokery the Securities and Exchange Commission in this country prevents."[47]

North American Catholics also noted with suspicion that the Vatican has been reporting deficits since 1975, the year after Sindona's empire crashed at great cost to Vatican finances. Contributors have no idea how much the Vatican takes in each year during the "Peter's Pence" collection, for instance, since the figures are kept secret. Evidence also exists to suggest that the Vatican has been putting pressure on North American and European cardinals to funnel contributions made for the Third World through a Vatican agency, COR UNUM, instead of sending it to the people intended.[48]

Another aspect of the scandal that does not seem to go away is the alleged connection between Calvi's ill-fated trip to London and the secretive, right-wing Catholic movement Opus Dei. Calvi's ideological outlook was not unlike that of Opus Dei, which flourished in Spain under General Franco, and since its membership includes some of Europe's leading financiers, it is not inconceivable that Calvi appealed to the organization to rescue him and the Vatican Bank. Such, at least, was the story told by Calvi's family, which claimed that he had gone to London to negotiate the sale of Ambrosiano stock with Opus Dei representatives. However, two days after his arrival in London, trading in the rapidly plummeting Ambrosiano shares was suspended and the bank's directors resigned. So Calvi had nothing to sell. Calvi's son Carlo contended that his father had discussed the operation with the Pope, and that John Paul had approved it. But, said the family, the arrangement was controversial within the Vatican because it would have mixed politics with finance, presumably because in return for assuming the debt Opus Dei would have sought leverage within the Vatican—for example, in the formulation of Vatican policy toward Communist and Third World countries.[49]

Both Marcinkus and Opus Dei categorically denied that any deal had been in the works. Opus Dei spokesmen insisted that its concerns were "exclusively spiritual and apostolic" and that it had "never engaged in business or finance." The statement was

true as far as it went, but it failed to point out that many Opus
Dei members engage in business and finance—and quite successfully. Indeed, the movement's secular emphasis has been one of
the main reasons for its growth. Both in Spain and Latin America Opus Dei has sought out and cultivated lay people with
promising political careers, such as future cabinet ministers (Colombia) or dictators (Argentina). Vatican sources said that Cardinal Sebastiano Baggio, the powerful prefect of the Vatican's Sacred Congregation for Bishops and a known Opus Dei
sympathizer, had long wanted the organization to take over the
running of the Vatican Bank, a claim also made by Calvi's son.
Two months after Calvi's death Baggio announced the recognition of Opus Dei as a "personal prelature," giving the movement
the prestige and power of a major religious order.[50]

Equally suggestive was the claim by Francesco Pazienza, who
worked as a consultant for Calvi, that he had found a group of
buyers who were willing to pay $1.2 billion for 12 percent of
Ambrosiano's stock. Pazienza claimed that he represented U.S.,
Iranian, and Saudi interests and that his partner in the deal was
Roberto Armao, president of the Vatican Foundation of Sts. Ben-
edict, Cyril, and Methodius, who was asked to help the Vatican's
investigative commission in sorting out the Vatican Bank's affairs
after the Ambrosiano scandal. According to Pazienza, Armao
had worked for many years with the Shah of Iran as his head of
protocol and was "a close collaborator of [David] Rockefeller."‡
Pazienza himself had good contacts in the Middle East, particularly Saudi Arabia, through missions there on behalf of Italy's
military intelligence service (SISMI). Pazienza acknowledged to
an Italian parliamentary commission investigating P-2 links that
SISMI had paid him for his services through a secret Swiss account during the period when the intelligence service was run by
a general who belonged to the P-2. Pazienza also claimed to be a
friend of Michael Ledeen, a consultant for the under secretary of
political affairs at the State Department and formerly employed
by the Center for Strategic and International Studies, a right-
wing think tank. Ledeen helped popularize the imaginative thesis
of "international terrorism" as one big Soviet plot to destabilize

‡ See Chapter 1, p. 6.

the West, Italy being an example, but his interpretation of Italian affairs was questioned by the European press, which suggested Ledeen had links with Gelli and the P-2, and that Ledeen, on behalf of the State Department, had tried to buy 480 P-2 files photocopied by the Uruguayan interior ministry after the raid on Ortolani's mansion in Montevideo (see p. 208). Pazienza also reportedly told the Italian parliamentary commission that he was friendly with former Secretary of State Alexander Haig "when he was head of NATO, because we were both involved together in some business incidental to an American industry that produces arms." The reports of Ledeen's P-2 links and Haig's relations with Pazienza were based on leaks from the secret hearings by the Italian parliamentary commission and were therefore unconfirmed. Still, if Gelli were to be believed, Pazienza had some powerful friends in Italy and Washington. "Beware that Pazienza is important; he maintains relations with the Mafia, Haig," Gelli wrote in a letter of introduction for Pazienza. "They also say that he belongs to the CIA, or wants to . . ." Such relations would not be unusual. Both the Nixon and Reagan administrations dealt with the same milieu, as shown by Sindona's high-level connections in the former's administration* and by some of the guests at the latter's political functions. They included Gelli, who was invited by Republican bigwig Phil Guarino† to Reagan's inaugural ball, which Gelli attended, and Miguel Angel Napout, reputedly Paraguay's biggest smuggler, with links to Nixon's confidant, Bebe Rebozo,‡ and South American heroin traffickers. Napout received an invitation to attend the Republican convention, where he interviewed presidential candidate Reagan.[51]

Another persistent issue concerned who was to be made responsible for picking up the pieces of Calvi's empire. While the Italian central bank pooled seven banks to rescue the Milanese parent, renamed Nuovo Banco Ambrosiano, the bank's 38,336 shareholders derived no solace from this move, because their shares in the old bank, once valued at around $200 million, were worthless. The Italian treasury minister, Beniamino Andreatta,

* See Chapter 9, pp. 180–81, 187, 188.
† See p. 201 in this chapter.
‡ See Chapter 8, pp. 153, 165.

said that "the Italian government expects a clear assumption of its responsibilities on the part of the Vatican Bank," if not on legal grounds then on moral ones, but Marcinkus insisted that the Vatican Bank had no liability. "I can only say I'm sorry for the [Ambrosiano] shareholders who saw their investments go up in smoke," he said. "I must say frankly that I'm sorry for us, too; our investment, too, went up in smoke."[52]

However, the Italian banking authorities would not let Marcinkus off the hook for payment of at least part of the missing $1.4 billion owed by the Panamanian shell companies. They were determined to salvage from the Ambrosiano debacle a definitive clarification of ties between the Vatican Bank and Italy, and the status of the bank in regard to Italian laws. While assuming responsibility for the Milanese parent's debts, the Italian central bank refused to answer for debts to some 250 foreign banks incurred by the Luxembourg holding company and its Nassau and Lima subsidiaries, telling foreign creditors to take the matter up with the Vatican Bank, which owned the Panamanian companies.[53]

The Italian authorities' decision sent shock waves throughout the international banking community, which had unwisely assumed that the Italian Government would stand behind the subsidiaries of the Milanese bank as the "lender of last resort." The phrase came into use in 1974 when central bankers of the Western nations met in Basle, Switzerland, to discuss responsibility for bank failures after the collapse of Sindona's Franklin National Bank in the United States and the Herstatt Bank in West Germany, which also went under because of heavy foreign-exchange speculation.* The intent was to set some ground rules for supervision of banks operating in more than one country, but the Basle Concordat "is not and was never intended" to be a government bailout for troubled banks, said Peter Cooke, the head of banking supervision at the Bank of England and chairman of the Basle Committee of Supervisors. In other words, contrary to the widely held belief among bankers that their governments will always finally come to the rescue, there is no lender of last resort.[54]

* See Chapter 9, pp. 183–84.

There were other problems in defining responsibility. While the Basle Concordat holds banks responsible for their foreign branches, foreign holding companies and subsidiaries fall between the cracks, the host country and the government of the parent bank sharing vague responsibilities. Ambrosiano's Luxembourg offshoot was not a branch but a holding company, and under Luxembourg's bank-secrecy laws the authorities had no right to supervise it. Italian laws regarding foreign subsidiaries placed similar restraints on local banking authorities (the laws were changed after the Ambrosiano debacle). But even had the Milanese parent accepted responsibility for the Luxembourg company, it did not have the assets to repay its creditors. Moreover, there was a big question about who really owned the Luxembourg company, since 32 percent of its shares were in bearer form, making it impossible to identify the owners (Europe's financial press speculated that the Vatican Bank held the unidentified one third). Italian authorities claimed that "from a juridical point of view, we are under no obligation to rescue foreign operations of Banco Ambrosiano." To drive home Cooke's point about the lender of last resort, the Italians added, "We are not bound to bail out insolvent banks."[55]

Although international bankers threatened dire repercussions for Italy's credit rating if the central bank did not pay up, the banking authorities stood fast, referring all complaints to the Vatican Bank. By the end of 1982 the pressure was beginning to pay off, with Pope John Paul agreeing to cooperate with Italian authorities in a joint investigation into the scandal. The decision reflected the pontiff's concern over the continuing bad publicity, as well as a desire to head off lawsuits against the Vatican Bank. The Italian authorities said they believed that foreign creditors would drop such suits if the Vatican paid them a negotiated sum. Just how much became a favorite Roman guessing game. "Anything between 1 percent and 99 percent," said one official. In getting to the bottom of the affair, banking authorities said they also hoped to encourage the Vatican to reform its finances and make them less secretive.[56]

Whether the slow-moving Vatican bureaucracy could really be persuaded to change its secretive ways was open to question, but there seemed little doubt that Catholics in North America and

Europe would be asked to provide the money to cover the Vatican's settlement with Ambrosiano's foreign creditors. If anyone knows the Vatican, it is the Romans; and their opinion of the affair was neatly summarized by the letters on Vatican City automobiles: SCV (Santa Città Vaticana). Romans now insist the letters stand for *Se Cristo Vedesse* (If Christ could see!).

***

The Ambrosiano affair marked a turning point in international finance not because a prominent banker proved to be a crook but because it showed how fragile the fabric of international finance has become. Until the Italians refused to serve as lender of last resort, many bankers had assumed that if worse came to worst their governments would step in. But the Calvi disaster showed how nebulous are central bank understandings, particularly those involving bank havens like Luxembourg and the Bahamas. It was the threat to such understandings, rather than the loan losses themselves (which are relatively minor when shared among 250 banks), that threw such a scare into the international money market. Bank analysts pointed out that there were no clear rules governing bank havens and that even if they existed they might be impossible to enforce because of the stringent bank secrecy laws that are the havens' principal attraction. Ambrosiano's collapse also pointed up the weakness of a system of international banking that does not have a complementary system of controls. European bankers complained that they had lent to Ambrosiano's Luxembourg company in the belief that it formed part of an integral group backed by the parent in Milan. But, unlike large U.S. banks, Italian banks do not prepare consolidated accounts, nor do their managements or banking authorities think in consolidated terms. So what is assumed in one country to be standard procedure may not be followed in another.[57]

After the Ambrosiano default, serious fears were expressed about the stability of the $1.8 trillion Eurocurrency market, which consists primarily of interbank transactions and is therefore susceptible to a chain reaction of bank failures. It was a perilous place for any banker to be without a safety net, and Peter Cooke, head of the Basle committee, reminded all the players that if they should fall the central banks have no strategy for putting Humpty Dumpty together again. Surprisingly, quite a few bankers agreed that it would be unwise to stretch a safety net, since that might encourage the freewheeling practices that had led many banks into trouble with Ambrosiano. For all their grousing about Italy's failure to pay up, the bankers should have known they were taking a big gamble when they loaned money to Ambrosiano's Luxembourg company. Italian Treasury Minister Andreatta estimated that banks got one-sixteenth to one-quarter percentage point of additional interest by lending to Ambrosiano's foreign subsidiaries rather than to the parent. Greedy for the extra money, the bankers did not take the precaution of getting a guarantee for the loans from the bank in Milan, and when the responsibility squabble broke out, that failure looked foolish. "You can't get more return and have the same risk," said Andreatta. "I think it's useful for the international community to know that banks are risky enterprises and that it's possible and necessary to evaluate risk." A London banker who did not lend to Ambrosiano agreed. "For two years the Italian press had been speculating that Calvi was in trouble with his foreign operations. You could have called anyone in Italy to ask if you should lend to the foreign [subsidiaries], and they would have said, 'Don't do it.' " But the many banks that failed to call included Bank of America, Manufacturers Hanover Trust, First National Bank of Boston, Britain's National Westminster Bank, plus German, Arab, and Swiss banks, all of which lent money to the Ambrosiano subsidiaries.[58]

Archbishop Marcinkus' willingness to take risks without checking the credentials of those he dealt with was the crux of the Vatican Bank's problems. That sort of irresponsibility is also the source of much of the nervousness—some would say near-hysteria—that has infected the international banking system since mid-1982, when the banks were hit by a chain of disasters: the Drysdale and Penn Square defaults; the bankruptcy of major corporations in West Germany, Canada, and the United States; the collapse of the commercial real estate market; and, of course, Ambrosiano. But none of these crises compare with what may be in store if the Third World defaults on its staggering foreign debt.

The threat is particularly severe in Latin America, where Mexico, Argentina, and Brazil have led a pack of eighteen nations seeking relief from crippling interest payments—never mind the principal. As bankers began bolting their doors in preparation for the coming storm, international credit dried up, making the financial situation of many countries and corporations unsustainable. To be sure, not everybody was talking doomsday, but the chorus was growing, and for the first time since the Depression bankers admitted there were cracks in "the very foundations of the banking system."[59]

Part III

Chapter 11

The big commercial banks find that lending money to Third World countries is a habit hard to break. Ronald Reagan rides to their rescue with taxpayers' money.

The neighborhood is dark and the man looks for his house key under the only streetlamp. A night watchman approaches and asks, "What did you lose?"

"The key to my house." The watchman joins the search. "Are you sure you lost it here?" "Oh no, I lost it over there," pointing to the darkest part of the street.

"Then why the devil are you looking for it here?"

"Because I can't see anything over there."

The senseless search was a favorite joke in Munich's cabarets during the 1930s. Recently it has become popular again, this time in Brazil, where nightclub entertainers have developed a whole repertory around the foreign debt. But the humor is bleak because the Brazilians know they will never find the money to repay the debt. At the beginning of 1983 it was close to $100 billion (the highest in the developing world) and had become a major political issue. Foreign debt is front-page news, the subject of frequent discussions among Brazilian laborers, who—most bankers might be surprised to learn—can cite precise figures and how much each American bank holds.[1]

Brazil is hardly alone: At least thirty-five countries are in the same bind scrounging for money on a hand-to-mouth basis, teetering on the brink of default. But if they are afraid to search in the dark, their creditors in the First World are just as frightened, particularly those in the United States, who have recklessly entrapped themselves with the Latin Americans. Essentially the problem is that faced by Michele Sindona and Roberto Calvi: To repay the banks the debtor countries must borrow still more, until finally the speeding merry-go-round spins them off into bankruptcy.

Two critical issues emerge from the deepening international financial crisis. One is the ethics of international financiers, who increasingly resemble professional gamblers. The other is the effect of such gambling on the people of the United States as well as the Third World. If nobody wants to look into the dark side of the street, that may be because it appears uncomfortably like 1929, when the bank crash in the United States triggered a world depression. As one Swiss banker observed, the international banking system is technically bust, only bankers won't admit it because the truth could cause "a panic of unforseeable consequences."[2]

The seriousness of the situation was borne home to bankers and governments alike in August 1982, when Mexico announced that it could not pay $26 billion due on its $85 billion debt, which is second only to Brazil's among Third World nations. The announcement sent shock waves through U.S. banks, which had sunk $25.8 billion into Mexico, or more than the combined equity capital of the eight largest U.S. banks. Some, like Citibank and Chase Manhattan, were also heavily exposed in Brazil, which suspended payments in January 1983, requesting banks to reschedule $4 billion of its debt. Citibank's loans to Brazil are believed to total more than its equity capital of $4.8 billion; and when overdue and shaky loans to other Latin-American countries are included, the bank appears to be hanging by its fingertips over financial ruin. "In effect," said Senator John Heinz (R-Pa.), "the officers of these banks literally 'bet the bank' on the continued health and prosperity of one country."[3]

Bankers are less concerned about repayment of principal than the maintenance of interest, since the latter means that a loan is still "performing" and need not be written off as a loss. They will keep such loans on their books to the bitter end, with the result that in a few years total interest can equal or surpass principal, as Calvi learned to his dismay when the Panamanian companies' debt ballooned from $400 million to $800 million because of unpaid interest charges.* Even as late as mid-1982 bankers were saying that if worse came to worst they could always roll over, or stretch out, payments on principal for countries like Brazil (which, in fact, they had been doing all along). But the bankers did not foresee their nation-clients running out of cash to pay the all-essential interest, since few had thought to monitor the rapid buildup of short-term debt (180 days or less) that the developing countries were amassing. (Why short-term loans are not included in debt statistics is one of the mysteries of the banking world.) When these stopgap loans were added to the "bunching" of medium- and long-term debts due in 1982–83, the bill for many countries became impossible to pay. Those that tried to borrow on the Eurocurrency markets to stave off default found that funds had dried up after the Ambrosiano shock.† Due to the world recession and an almost vertical drop in the price of commodities (the main source of foreign exchange in the developing countries), many nations resorted to selling their gold and running down foreign reserves. By the winter of 1982 the Third World was engulfed in a liquidity crisis, and many countries lacked the foreign exchange to pay for such essential imports as grain, never mind the interest on foreign loans.

Latin America was in the eye of the hurricane because its debt accounts for nearly half the $626 billion owed by the developing countries, and more than 20 percent of it is held by a handful of U.S. banks. The crisis quickly took on epidemic proportions. In addition to the biggest debtors (Argentina, Brazil, and Mexico), fifteen other Latin American nations either applied to the International Monetary Fund (IMF) for emergency relief or asked their foreign creditors to reschedule their debts, postponing payment of interest as well as principal. (The only Latin country to call rescheduling by its real name was Cuba, which asked its Western creditors for a ten-year moratorium.) Some, such as Costa Rica, Bolivia, and Mexico, simply stopped paying the interest. Nor was the Latin-American crisis temporary. No amount of financial patchwork could remedy a situation in which the region's export earnings and recent foreign loans were almost

* See Chapter 10, p. 196.
† See Chapter 10, pp. 220–22.

entirely earmarked for old debts instead of productive investments. In Brazil the situation rapidly became untenable. Of the
country's export earnings, 60 percent went for debt service in
1982; in 1984 that figure will be an incredible 93 percent!

Latin America has always been a financial gamble. In the nineteenth century Argentine defaults nearly brought down Barings
—then the foremost British merchant bank—and England's
economy with it. During the Depression all but three Latin-
American countries defaulted on their debts, the exceptions being
Argentina, Haiti, and the Dominican Republic. (At the time,
U.S. Marines were stationed in the latter two countries, which
goes a long way toward explaining their decision not to default.)
While economic conditions of the 1930s and the 1980s are different in many respects, three parallels clearly apply to Latin America: A crucial reason for the 1930 defaults was the freeze on new
loans and investments, a problem also facing the region in the
1980s; in both periods commodity prices collapsed; and, finally,
the ratio between debt service and export earnings is about the
same today as it was in 1929. Some nations, among them Brazil,
took more than two decades to resume repayment; even after
adjusting for inflation, the debt then was miniscule compared to
the $300 billion now owed by Latin America.[4]

Nor were the big U.S. banks so exposed in the 1930s. Indeed,
the key ingredient in the threatened financial explosion of the
1980s is that foreign loans now comprise more than half of all
lending by the big U.S. banks. For some (e.g., Citibank) the percentage is even higher. While a Citibank affiliate lost $90 million
when Peru defaulted in the 1930s (the bank had paid the son of
the president of Peru $450,000 to arrange the loan), the loss was
minor compared to the risks bank chairman Walter Wriston is
taking in Brazil: If the Brazlian people repudiate their bondage to
foreign debt, Citibank, popularly known as the "Brazilian Bank,"
will go under.

As long as hard-line army generals were in charge of the Brazilian Government, American bankers could be reasonably certain that Brazil would remain in harness, but the country is now
undergoing a process of democratization, during which the hard-
liners have been shunted to the sidelines. Brazil's rulers have
always been political pragmatists, so if it comes to a choice be-

tween revolution or Citibank, the Brazilians will not hesitate to ditch Mr. Wriston.

Looking back, historians may say that Citibank and other U.S. banks were the victims of their own greed, but that may be true only in part. In the 1970s, when the world was awash in petrodollars from the newly rich oil-producing nations, many bankers were convinced that they had a unique opportunity to make enormous profits, while providing a service by recycling oil money through loans to the developing countries. The stampede to lend money began in 1973, when oil prices skyrocketed and private banks, stuffed with Arab cash, sought new customers in the Third World. Until then most developing countries had borrowed primarily from governments or multilateral institutions, such as the World Bank; but in less than a decade that situation had reversed, with commercial banks funding up to two thirds of the loans. When the boom started, most large U.S. and European banks already had branches in the Third World to serve the needs of the multinational corporations, but it was only when small- and medium-sized banks joined the majors that Third World lending was raked with the fever of a gold rush.

As bankers readily admit, lending tends to be a sheeplike exercise. If one or more well-known banks are lending to a certain country, all the other banks want part of the action. But the "loan-pushing" bankers did not pause to consider the likelihood of interest default, let alone the loss of principal. So billions upon billions of dollars were thrown at the Latin Americans—and sometimes even shoved down their throats.[5] Of course, many of the governments were corrupt and only too glad to take the handouts, which were diverted to private Swiss accounts or spent on flashy palaces and costly armaments. (The people seldom had any say in the matter, since they were largely ruled by military regimes.) Some money did go into useful investments, like hydroelectric schemes, but even in Brazil, still generally regarded by bankers as a nation that tried to administer its debt wisely, much of the money was squandered on luxuries by a small social and military elite. (At one point the ultimate status symbol for the ruling military caste was a government-paid butler.)

The point missed by outside creditors—to Iran as well as Brazil—is that modernization does not necessarily signify progress.

While Brazil's economy ranks eighth among Western nations, its society is as unequal as that of any feudal land. According to World Bank statistics on income distribution, Brazil's richest 10 percent of the population possesses more than 50 percent of the country's wealth (compared to 26 percent for the wealthiest 10 percent in the United States). Meanwhile, the bottom 20 percent of Brazil's population receives a mere 2 percent of the nation's income. Nearly one third of the country's 118 million people live in extreme poverty, 10 million are mentally retarded, and 14 million are abandoned children. Since 1965, when the military regime enforced a wage freeze, infant mortality rates have increased to 80 per 1,000 live births and illiteracy rates have risen 10 percent. Yet studies by the World Bank and other international institutions show that there is no justification for such abysmal social standards in a country with an annual per capita income of $1,140. (Costa Rica, with an $884 per capita income, provides adequate public services.)[6]

Brazil has also become one of the most dependent nations in the world—dependent on the banks because of its foreign debt, overwhelmingly dependent on foreign trade to service that debt, and dependent on foreign multinationals, which dominate industry and agriculture. When the world recession struck in the early 1980s, that dependence became a tremendous burden: Export earnings fell, while the cost of debt service rose. Inevitably Brazil was forced to apply to the IMF for help. But the austere conditions that the IMF imposes on the granting of loans are dreaded in the Third World because they mean yet greater hardship for the majority of the people. Even before Brazil applied to the IMF, the majority suffered extreme want—a poverty much worse than that in 1964, when the military seized power to "modernize" Brazil and when the foreign debt was a mere $2 billion.

In the rush to modernize, Brazil's bankers and generals ignored the country's single most important resource—its people. But history has shown that this was a perilous oversight, and in 1982 the combined pressures of Brazilian business, the Catholic Church, and the labor unions—all of which oppose economic growth without social progress—forced the military government to hold direct elections for the first time since 1964, marking a gradual return to democracy. The new governors, when they emerge, may well repudiate the old debts.

Brazil's story is similar to that of many Latin-American nations, although the details vary and the social pressures for change may be different. The invariable common factor is that poverty grows along with debt. Put another way, the money borrowed by Latin America did not go to develop its human resources, and only rarely (even in Brazil) was it used efficiently for agricultural and industrial development. This creates a vicious circle: If a people have no chance to advance in the workplace, the economy will eventually stagnate; and if the economy is not performing adequately, the government cannot repay its debts.

Most large banks try to include political risk in their country assessments, but their knowledge of the social, economic, and political forces at work is often extraordinarily scant. Witness the advertisements for Mexico in U.S. bank publications even as late as August 1982, when the government had effectively defaulted on its foreign debt. Bank of America, which has some $2.5 billion in questionable loans to Mexico, was telling its clients that "now is a great time to lay the foundation for 1983 and beyond." Chase Manhattan was no less effusive, promising high growth rates despite the growing evidence of an oil glut that was to batter Mexico's oil-dependent economy. Citibank advertised that under the leadership of then President José López Portillo, "Mexico is entitled to view its future with optimism," yet it was López Portillo's government that defaulted on the debt and nationalized the country's banks. Eight months before the roof fell in, U.S. banks were queuing up to lend to Third World Mexico at rates only a quarter of a percent above their loans to Western Europe. Despite storm warnings, the bankers poured $3.6 billion into Mexico in the second quarter of 1982—more than in the same period in 1981. The $6 billion shortfall in Mexico's 1981 oil earnings was a clear sign that the economy was in serious trouble, but the bankers seemed not to care. Smaller U.S. banks were particularly rash, going far beyond their strength to play in the league with the majors.[7]

Bankers Trust of South Carolina, for example, was one of hundreds of smaller banks to rue the day it joined a syndicated loan to Mexico. On the widely held assumption that such loans were a

guaranteed gold mine, the bank's international division decided
to chip in $5 million toward a six-month, $300 million package
put together in early 1982 by Banco Nacional de Mexico
(Banamex), then Mexico's second largest private bank. As Bankers Trust officials later admitted, they fell for the bait because
they were dealing with a country about which they knew little.
Most of the statistics available, such as data from the IMF, were
from 1979, when Mexico was not in such serious financial trouble. Banamex responded to queries about Mexico's economic
health with a glowing report, that was also based on outdated
statistics. Most telling of all, when officers of the South Carolina
bank questioned their New York colleagues, the latter proved to
be "most avid recommenders," saying that Mexico was the "best
thing since sliced bread"—this when the country was only
months away from default. Richard Fearrington, senior vice
president in charge of the Bankers Trust loan, said that while he
had sense enough to stay out of Zaire, since he didn't even know
where it was, Mexico seemed a safe bet because he had once
visited the country. "Unfortunately," he later admitted, "my
knowledge was a little rusty." In August 1982, a week before
Bankers Trust was to be repaid, the Mexican Government pulled
the rug from under 1,400 foreign banks, including the small
South Carolina institution, by announcing that it could not repay
its debts.[8]

Bankers claim they were caught out because they did not know
just how big a lump of Mexico's debt was short-term, but they
should have made it their business to know. Any foreign businessman operating in Latin America is aware that government
statistics are usually twisted for political reasons. Official figures
for Mexico's debt, oil income, cash-flow estimates, and other economic yardsticks were notoriously unreliable during the López
Portillo administration, but apparently the bankers never
thought to question them.

In most risk surveys twenty or so factors are listed on a chart,
with numerical ratings ascribed to each—as if it were possible,
for example, to quantify such complex sociopolitical issues as the
likelihood of insurrection. Even then the information is lopsided,
because most of the bankers' sources are like-minded businessmen and government officials. And the bank may entirely ignore

the survey if it suits its interests to do so. A former officer in Citibank's planning division said that the decision to make a loan to a given country usually hangs not on the division's statistical projections of good or bad risk but on whether the foreign branch manager is in the good graces of the head office in New York. And the primary consideration for that, said a Citibank manager in Latin America, is how well he or she has met Citibank's ambitious goal to increase annual earnings by 15 percent.

One could argue that because the statistics are faulty, it is better to depend on the "man on the spot," but it is highly improbable that the latter has ever spent time in a slum or rural village, talked to a labor or student leader, or had contact with a dissident priest. Such people represent the "bottom line" for any sociopolitical assessment of Brazil. They were the "bottom line" in Iran, only there the priests were mullahs.

The U.S. Treasury Department's reporting is no better. "We do not include socio-political analysis in our economic reporting," said a department spokesman, who appeared shocked by the suggestion. Some banks also take a cavalier attitude toward political assessment. Multinational Strategies, a New York risk-consulting firm, undertook a study of seven large U.S. banks and found that at least one—Morgan Guaranty Trust Company—believed that professional political analysts were unnecessary. "Politics is like sex," a Morgan executive was quoted as saying. "You don't need training to get the job done."[9]

Criticism of faulty reporting by private banks and government agencies usually provokes the retort that the critic's data are exaggerated, although often these institutions can produce no figures of their own. The U.S. Treasury Department, for example, claims to be "on top of" the Eurodollar situation but does not know how many Eurodollars are in circulation. At one point Citibank and Continental Illinois were both saying that there was no reason to worry about the soundness of loans to non-oil developing countries because half were guaranteed by entities outside the borrowing country, such as a U.S. government agency or the parent company of a multinational subsidiary. A subsequent investigation by the Federal Reserve showed that only 11 percent of U.S. bank loans to those countries were so guaranteed. Until the Fed upset the bankers' figures, the financial community took the claims as gospel. Thus faith in "market" gossip can become more important than real factors like employment, output, and incomes, adding to the uncertainties of a market famous for its hysteria.

Citibank Chairman Wriston harks back to the eighteenth and nineteenth centuries when the developing countries of the time had "one significant advantage over those of today: there were no balance of payments crises because there were no balance of payments statistics." Wriston thinks Americans take their "economic blood pressure" too often. But that is not the view of the government Export-Import Bank, which concluded that the risk evaluation systems of thirty-seven banks were miserably inadequate. Nor is it the opinion of H. Johannes Witteveen, former director of the IMF, who said the banks were in such a rush to lend to the poor countries that they did not maintain adequate standards for credit worthiness.[10] One result of the failure to get as wide and accurate a picture as possible is a situation where bankers mistake the temporary rallying of a terminally sick economy for permanent recovery. Rescheduling of debt payments may give a country some respite, but it does not address the fundamental problems of underdevelopment. Hence such countries as Peru and Turkey are constantly in and out of intensive care.

The Federal Reserve depends for its assessment of bank exposure on reports from private banks, supplemented by statistical tables on foreign debt compiled by the World Bank, Europe's Organization for Economic Cooperation and Development, and Switzerland's Bank for International Settlements. None are accurate. Of the three, the World Bank debt tables, which are cited most commonly, are nearly three years out of date and omit a number of countries, some of them significant debtors. Nor do they include debts not guaranteed by governments or short-term debts. Consequently the tables usually underestimate a country's foreign debt by 30 to 50 percent. The U.S. Treasury Department's debt survey, based primarily on World Bank statistics, is also three years out of date; but, says a Treasury official, "we do not feel that we are suffering from a lack of information."

The principal reason for the lack of data is that the banks and the borrowing governments do not want to advertise the size of the debt. Governments often have political reasons for keeping secret the amount and location of deposits. For example, congressional investigations showed that the Federal Reserve deliberately disguised the origin and size of OPEC deposits in U.S. banks because Arab rulers did not want their people to know that so much oil money was in the hands of the Americans. Economists and accountants agree that the only useful measure of debt figures is a breakdown by terms, type of recipient, and guarantor for a bank's individual loans to a given country. However, this information is not available to the public or to Congress, which must estimate the depth of exposure from aggregate figures that are frequently rigged for political motives.

In some countries the deception is chronic and massive. Brazil and Peru are both notorious for cooking the books. The IMF has caught Brazil's economic czar, Antonio Delfim Neto, tampering with inflation figures; since 1981 his government has been underreporting the foreign debt, so that it remained stationary at $60 billion when the true figure had risen to nearly $100 billion. Similar sleight-of-hand was used to disguise the sudden fall in foreign reserves in late 1982.[11]

If bankers lack the means to measure risk, why do they risk so much? Obviously because the profits are enormous. In Brazil, for example, where real interest rates were running at 200 percent, foreign banks earned up to 150 percent in profits. Citibank earned 21.7 percent of its worldwide profits for 1981 in Brazil alone. U.S. bankers, who are happy with a return of 13 to 14 percent at home, expect three times as much in Latin America.[12]

U.S. banking regulations forbid banks to lend more than 15 percent of their total portfolios to any one country, but the Comptroller of the Currency admitted that a number of banks had exceeded that limit, particularly in Mexico and Brazil, because of the lure of high profits. A Securities and Exchange Commission investigation and hearings by the House Subcommittee on Oversight and Investigations established that Citibank had disguised its loans to Latin America to circumvent such regulations, although the very purpose of the rules is to protect banks from the sort of trap that Citibank has set for itself in Brazil.‡

‡ See Chapter 3, pp. 29–39.

Chairman Wriston's Olympian attitude toward sound banking procedures is similar in many respects to the sense of invincibility that trapped Sindona in the Franklin National Bank.*

Just how unethical bankers have become in their drive for profit is illustrated by the case of Costa Rica, where commercial bankers attempted to coerce the government into an illegal action. As revealed in a detailed account of the country's loan-rescheduling problems published in *Euromoney*, which had access to the minutes of the bankers' meetings, a ten-bank steering committee led by Bank of America did everything it could to make Costa Rica deny the precedence given by legal contract and tradition to holders of its bonds and notes. When Costa Rica was unable to repay its $3.5 billion debt in late 1980, its creditors immediately fell to squabbling over the small amount of foreign exchange available for debt payment. International law grants precedence to bonds or notes backing the financial reputation of a country, but Bank of America, Citibank, and other commercial banks that held syndicated loans tried to use the small Central American nation as a test case to overthrow that legal tradition. At no time did Costa Rica want or request a rescheduling of its bonds; and it continued to pay interest and principal on publicly issued securities even when it could not pay interest on commercial loans. Had it suspended all bond payments, Costa Rica's reputation would have been permanently damaged. Moreover, the European banks that managed the bond issues told the Costa Rican Government that if it gave into the commercial banks on the matter, they would "campaign vigorously to ensure that you become ineligible for any financing from the multilateral institutions"—meaning the IMF. The threat was particularly serious because commerical debt negotiations with Bank of America and the others depended on the successful conclusion of a loan agreement between Costa Rica and the IMF. Attempting to bully Costa Rica into a dishonorable course of action, said the Europeans, demonstrated a lack of probity among the commercial banks.[13]

Nevertheless, the commercial bankers continued to pressure Costa Rica, repeatedly threatening to suspend all negotiations

---

* See Chapter 9, pp. 183–84.

unless the credit status of its bonds was downgraded. This seesaw activity went on for months, locking Costa Rica into a downward spiral. As a consequence, in late 1981 the country defaulted on a $10 million bond. A year later it still had not concluded loan negotiations with the IMF.[14]

Bank of America would never have tried such a stunt with a European country, but it is easy to push the small Central American nations around, and Bank of America has plenty of muscle. One of the biggest foreign lenders in the region, especially for agribusiness projects, the bank is particularly active in Guatemala, where it ranks second only to the Guatemalan Government as a source of capital for the agro-export sector, the mainstay of that country's economy. But recently Bank of America has come under criticism from shareholders in the United States because its clientele in Guatemala is drawn largely from the right-wing military/civilian establishment that has controlled the country since 1954, when a CIA-engineered coup toppled a democratically elected, mildly left-of-center government.[15]

Amnesty International cites Guatemala as one of the world's worst human rights violators. The record is gruesome: More than eighty-three thousand people have been killed since 1954 in Guatemala's political violence, the vast majority of them Indian peasants slain by the army. In the latest round of killing, following a change of dictators in 1982, some three thousand Indian peasants were massacred.[16] The United Church Board for World Ministries, which owns shares in Bank of America, questioned the bank's heavy support for "one of the most brutal regimes in Latin America." But while the bank was unhappy about the bad publicity arising from such charges, it dismissed the United Church Board's complaint as a nuisance because its members owned only eleven thousand shares. However, the California State Teachers Retirement System and the Public Employment Retirement System, which owned more than 1 percent of the bank's common stock, also complained of the bank's activities in Guatemala. Though primarily concerned with the riskiness of Guatemalan loans because of the political instability there, the pension funds also told Bank of America that they did not want to "subsidize the abuse of human rights," and felt that the bank had "social responsibilities to conform to the highest ethical standards."[17]

Far from honoring ethical standards, the bank's Guatemalan clients were champions of the death squads. Such, at least, was the position of Fred Sherwood, former president of the American Chamber of Commerce in Guatemala and the manager of PROKESA, a local corporation and client of Bank of America. In the first half of 1980, according to the Guatemalan press, six people were killed at PROKESA for labor-organizing activities. But Sherwood told CBS reporters that there was no reason to worry about death squads. "They're bumping off the Commies, our enemies . . . I'm all for it."[18] Another Bank of America client was former dictator General Romeo Lucas García, during whose time in office up to twenty thousand civilians were murdered, as documented by Amnesty International. García received a $750,000 loan from the bank to finance a ranch he had bought. The bank also provided financing for a military housing project. Still other prominent bank clients included a sugar plantation where at least a dozen workers had been killed; a luxury hotel where the leader of labor-organizing activities had been murdered; and an agro-industrial corporation whose owner was one of the founders of the White Hand, Guatemala's most feared death squad. But perhaps the most damaging connection was the membership of Bank of America executives in a notorious right-wing Guatemalan lobby called Amigos del País (Friends of the Country), some of whose supporters were directly linked to the financing of death squads. In response to charges of bank involvement with the organization, Bank of America said that it "cannot control the personal actions of its officers," a claim that any New York bank vice president responsible for personnel would deride.[19]

Bank of America is by no means the only financial institution that favors strong-arm governments, as is illustrated by Chase Manhattan's close relationship with the Shah of Iran and the U.S. banking community's preference for a Soviet takeover of Poland—since the Soviet Union would be in a stronger position to pay Poland's debts.[20] Indeed, the significance of the Guatemalan story is that it is so typical. It also underlines the connection between the lack of ethics abroad and shady dealing at home. As documented by Congress and the Securities and Exchange Commission,† Citibank endangered the U.S. financial system by recklessly circumventing U.S. laws on foreign lending to Brazil; Citibank has also been one of the strongest supporters of that country's hard-line military regimes. And at the same time that Bank of America was providing loans to some of the most ruthless repressers of the Guatemalan people, it was also "deceitfully" cheating 170,000 California mortgage holders on tax and insurance prepayments. According to San Francisco Superior Court Judge John Dearman, Bank of America was "guilty of willful, calculated and deceitful conduct" in illegally lending out prepaid trust-fund money for the bank's profit. "Malicious, fraudulent and oppressive" were the terms used by Judge Dearman in ruling that Bank of America must pay $101 million to California mortgage holders.[21]

The possibility that the Guatemalan people might make the same charges if they ever overthrew the country's military regime worried the California pension funds, particularly since a full-scale rebellion was in progress in Guatemala. Primarily interested in protecting their members' investment, the funds recognized the impossibility of separating financial questions in the Third World from the broader issue of human rights. Though a small beginning, that recognition goes to the heart of the controversy over foreign debt in the developing world, where many countries, particularly Brazil, are beginning to rebel against the equivalent of nineteenth-century debt peonage. The question is important to Americans on economic as well as moral grounds. By becoming so deeply involved in Latin America, the banks have succeeded in doing what no human rights organization has achieved, namely, they have tied the economic aspirations of Americans to the political fortunes of their neighbors.

Bankers have traditionally argued that countries cannot go bust, but the argument ignores the possibility that governments responsible for the debt mess may be overthrown or may decide that the only way to survive is to repudiate the debt. (In the past both England and the United States have repudiated their debts,

† See Chapter 3, pp. 29, 39.

so neither is in a position to play holier-than-thou.‡) During the 1930s many Latin-American governments fell because of economic pressures, and they are liable to fall again for the same reason. If the banks had their choice, there would be no liberalization in Brazil or elsewhere in Latin America, because the political opposition is always the most vociferous critic of the debt trap. The Brazilian Government already has gone some way to meet the opposition's demands by seeking renegotiation of the foreign debt despite threats from U.S. bankers. "The first step that the banks would take after a renegotiation would be to freeze their lending limits for Brazil," said a spokesman for Bank of America. "There is no way in which they could justify further loans to a country with serious financial problems."

But after the recent experience of Mexico, such threats seem ludicrous. In any case, loans to Brazil dried up *before* it sought renegotiation. The threats also ignore the fact that U.S. banks are so deeply involved in countries like Brazil and Mexico that they cannot get out. Or, to paraphrase economist John Maynard Keynes, "If you owe your bank $1 million, you are in trouble. If you owe your bank $1 billion, your bank is in trouble. And if you owe the bank $100 billion, then the whole world is in trouble."

Such knowledge has encouraged tough talk in Brazil. "We'll give you an arm and a leg this year," a Brazilian Government official told a U.S. banker by way of describing the austerity measures imposed by the Brazilian Government to service its debt in 1983. "But," he warned, "we're not going to give you another arm and leg next year." Ulisses Guimarães, the head of the principal opposition party in Brazil, went even further, proposing a common front with Argentina, Mexico, and other Third World debtors in negotiations with First World bankers. The Ecuadorian Government seconded the idea by formally proposing a debt cartel during a meeting of Latin-American bankers in early 1983. Some Venezuelan political leaders were also privately talk-

‡ Mississippi, one of the many states that defaulted in the nineteenth century, passed a constitutional amendment in 1875 disclaiming its responsibilities. More than a century later, London bankers were still trying to recover their money (Anthony Sampson, *The Money Lenders* [New York: Viking, 1982], p. 50).

ing of a common default. "The idea of a debtors' cartel is so logical that there may well be diplomats from one of the big debtors running around the Third World already trying to put such a cartel together," said U.S. economist Lestor C. Thurow. Still, the likelihood of such a cartel has little basis in history, since the Third World has never been able to act together on any issue. To organize such a group would take months, years, possibly an eternity. A more likely development, say U.S. economists, is a series of *de facto* defaults and debt moratoriums, as in the case of Poland, which in 1980 effectively stopped paying anything on its $25 billion debt, and of Bolivia, which told bankers they would not see their money for many years. "The world debt crisis isn't as great as our own internal crisis," explained a Bolivian cabinet minister. With the economy in shambles, an inflation rate of 220 percent, and almost nothing in the government cupboard, the merit of such a statement was unarguable. Like many Latin-American countries, Bolivia would have had to use two thirds of its export earnings to service its $2.5 billion debt, and the democratic government of Hernán Siles Zuazo* was not prepared to make that sacrifice at the cost of starving its people, even if Bolivia were reduced to barter status for vital inputs like seed and fertilizer.[22]

If a debt cartel seems unrealistic, the international bankers have no better ideas. They have already tried running indebted governments (e.g., in Peru and Zaire during the 1970s) and were badly burned for their political meddling. The Calvi/Gelli solution of reimposing world order by terror may appeal to some radical conservatives, but it proved an economic disaster in Argentina and a political nightmare in Italy. David Rockefeller's Trilateral Commission similarly aimed for a world order, only his was to have been controlled by multinational corporations and banks; but the interests of the commission's members were too diverse to allow them to agree on a common policy. Moreover, there was always a glaring fallacy in these proposals: Bankers are not elected or trained to be politicians, and every time they assume political responsibilities they put their foot in it, as with the American hostage crisis in Iran, which was brought on by.

* See Chapter 9, p. 176.

Rockefeller's international meddling on behalf of the Shah. And while Rockefeller was touring South America, telling the generals how to run their economies, his bank in New York was sinking into the quicksands of the Drysdale and Penn Square debacles.† As to his advice to the Latin Americans, they would have been better off without it, to judge by the mess they got themselves into by borrowing excessively from banks like Chase.

The overriding danger, of course, is that banks may end up setting U.S. foreign policy now that they have been sucked into Third World politics. A case in point is Chile, where in 1976 a military regime could ignore international condemnation and a congressional cutoff of U.S. aid thanks to $927 million in loans from Chase Manhattan, Citibank, Morgan Guaranty Trust, and other U.S. banks. The banks' loans nullified congressional action designed to persuade the Chilean Government that it should stop killing its people and, in effect, made U.S. bankers a higher authority than the elected representatives of the American people. Quite apart from the issues of ethics and foreign policy raised by the banks' action, it can be questioned solely on economic grounds. By borrowing excessively from its American banker friends, the Chilean regime ran up an $18.2 billion foreign debt, the highest per capita in South America. Chile has already lined up at the IMF trough and, like Brazil and Argentina, is seeking a rescheduling of its debts.[23]

Although the debt crisis has been looming for some time, the State Department has completely ignored its impact on the United States' foreign relations. Thus policy decisions in this area have fallen to the Treasury Department, where the banks have more influence, though the Treasury, too, has been extraordinarily slow in recognizing that a debt problem exists. Even after the near-defaults of Mexico, Argentina, and Brazil, the Reagan administration lacked any policy-making apparatus to deal effectively with the issue. Nobody in the White House—or Wall Street, for that matter—seems to have figured out how the developing countries can be persuaded to reverse the flow of money to which they have become accustomed since 1973. According to World Bank projections, four fifths of *all* new loans received by

† See Chapter 1.

the developing countries in 1985 will go to pay old ones; by 1990 the figure will be 95 percent! In effect, this means that there must be a net flow back to the banks from the developing countries at an average rate of $150 billion a year; and because of the international financial situation there will be very little in the way of development funds returning to the Third World.

Argentina, for example, has a debt of $43 billion. To meet amortization and short-term debt obligations in 1982, the government would have needed 135 percent of the country's export earnings, and even Argentine generals cannot pull money out of a top hat. Put another way, every worker in Latin America's 112 million-strong labor force is in hock for $2,525 to the foreign banks, yet most earn less than $1,200 a year. The figures describe a Kafkaesque world in which illiterate, undernourished peasants are somehow supposed to come up with $1 trillion, which will be the developing world's debt by 1986.[24]

"Apocalypse tomorrow is better than Apocalypse today," was how The Economist summed up the bankers' frantic efforts to repair the damage, with help from the IMF. But "Apocalypse tomorrow" means that the bankers must pour good money after bad, increasing their exposure and the probability that none of the loans will ever be repaid. "Apocalypse now" is to stop lending, thereby causing a string of defaults and a world financial crisis in what a Chase vice president described as a self-fulfilling prophecy of doom. IMF director Jacques de Larosière bluntly told the big U.S. banks that they would have to write off Mexico unless they came up with $6.5 billion in new loans and rescheduled another $15.5 billion in short-term debt, which meant the bankers would not see their money until 1987 at the earliest. Larosière made it clear that the IMF could not bail out the banks in Mexico because it had too many other sick countries on its hands. If the bankers wanted the IMF to loan Mexico $3.8 billion, they would have to come up with nearly twice as much. It was a sobering proposition. As one glum banker observed, the banks were being asked to lend billions of dollars on a "vague" letter to the IMF of Mexico's fiscal good intentions. "Is that sound banking today? I don't know. Has Mexico been helpful? No. Do we know who'll implement the IMF program? No. Does the IMF know what it's doing? Not totally. Is this better than nothing? Yes."[25]

Mexico epitomizes the problems facing both the big U.S. banks and the IMF. With the Europeans and Japanese rushing for cover in 1982, the U.S. banks accounted for nearly all new loans to the developing countries. After the Mexican debacle, regional and small U.S. banks tried to slam the door on Latin America. "You don't have to convince Chase and Bank of America to stay in this thing," said one banker of Larosière's ultimatum on Mexico. "They've no place to run." But the smaller U.S. banks were being dragged back into the fray. If they did not ante up and the Europeans continued to regard the Latin-American debt as a U.S. problem, the whole show would fold. "The biggies can't pick it all up; it's too much," warned a U.S. banker.[26]

It was also too much for the IMF, which was running out of money and was forced to borrow from commercial banks, thus setting yet another debt trap. The IMF's 1982 reserves were just sufficient to cover the needs of Mexico, Argentina, and Brazil, with nothing left over for the rest of the world. In a panicked about-face from its earlier position of "no free lunches for the Third World," the Reagan administration agreed with central bankers from France, West Germany, Great Britain, and Japan to seek a 50 percent boost in IMF quotas to increase its lending reserves. But even if the increase were approved by the IMF's members—a complicated process that also involves changing the ratio of quotas and hence the voting influence—the earliest that new funds could be available would be the end of 1984, which would perhaps be too late for some emergency cases.[27]

Finding the money is just the start of the problem, because IMF programs are designed to brake an economy's growth, and it is therefore an open question whether the medicine administered in return for IMF loans will not kill the patient. Most Latin-American nations were experiencing zero growth rates when they went to the IMF, and its tough austerity measures could only worsen their economic condition. Quite apart from the suffering they impose on the people, such programs usually don't work. By the IMF's own reckoning, fewer than one third of the twenty-one countries that followed its dictates between 1973 and 1975 achieved their monetary goals, and then only "with some qualifications." Seventeen countries suffered worse inflation. Specific fund recommendations suggest why. In its report on Haiti, the poorest nation in the Western Hemisphere, the IMF "staff welcome[d] the decision to eliminate promptly restrictions on luxury model [automobiles]" because that move somehow conformed to the IMF's ideas on free trade.[28]

Money was only part of the IMF's problems. As has been pointed out by many economists, the IMF lacks the breadth of vision necessary to deal with a global problem. While its economic formulas are always the same, be the country in Latin America, Asia, or Africa, the IMF treats each sick client separately, thus hastening contagion. For example, its insistence that Argentina reduce its imports contributed to Bolivia's failure to pay foreign bankers, since Bolivia depends on Argentina to buy its natural gas exports. Similarly, Mexico's austerity program caused a $6 billion cutback in U.S. imports in 1982, costing an estimated 150,000 jobs in the United States, according to Wharton Econometric Forecasting Associates, Inc. Moreover, many insolvent countries are themselves creditors of debt-ridden nations, as in the case of Brazil, which is owed money by bankrupt Poland.[29]

Not only is the IMF's economic vision flawed, but it also fails to consider the political consequences of its acts. In Mexico agricultural development programs established to prevent recurrent land takeovers by peasants were cut back under pressure of IMF-imposed budget-cutting. In Chile the IMF was pressing its demands for a 50 percent cut in public spending even though that country's unemployment rate had shot up from 4 to 26 percent. And in Argentina the IMF was forcing the government to reduce its deficit spending by almost two thirds in the face of an unemployment rate that had tripled between 1981 and 1983. There were riots in Argentina, Bolivia, Chile, and Brazil, all of which were suffering from a double squeeze of growing unemployment and declining wages. Political and economic observers predicted more turmoil, because none of these nations has unemployment insurance or welfare benefits to cushion the effects of austerity. "The IMF has destroyed more governments than communism by imposing measures which are technically perfect but politically impossible," said a Chilean business leader.[30]

With foreign debt becoming front-page news in the United States as well as Brazil, bankers pored over balance sheets seeking ways to hide their plight. As admitted by one investment banker, Felix G. Rohatyn of Lazard Freres & Company, most of the money lent to the developing countries would either "never come back" or come back only over a very long time. Most of the big U.S. banks showed a reduction in 1982 earnings: Those that were not caught early in the year (e.g., by the Penn Square panic), were hit by the Mexican default. The big questions posed by the debt disaster were: how much of their capital banks would be forced to set aside for potential losses as an insurance for depositors and shareholders; and how many loans would have to be placed in the nonperforming category, reducing the amount of interest that could be reported. European central bankers took a prudent attitude in encouraging their banks to increase bad-debt reserves—and a number did so. Lloyds Bank International more than doubled its reserves because of its large exposure in Latin America. Similar action was taken by West German, British, Dutch, and Scandinavian banks. But performance-oriented U.S. bankers did not want to make such concessions to risk, and the Federal Reserve apparently was willing to go along with them. While the Mexican loans would be classified as substandard in anyone's portfolio, the Fed decided to look the other way, leaving Mexico to fall into a "special comment" category. George J. Clark, an executive vice president at Citibank, explained that it really wasn't necessary to increase loss reserves "because the likelihood that the developing world would not service its obligations is low." Yet at the start of 1983 the number of countries that could not service their obligations had swollen from 20 to 35.[31]

***

In December 1982 Ronald Reagan flew down to Brazil with a $1.2 billion Christmas present from U.S. taxpayers. Actually the present wasn't for the Brazilians but for Citibank, Chase Manhattan, and the like, since they could collect from the Brazilians only if the U.S. Treasury gave them the money. The handout came on top of a $3.8 billion rescue of U.S. banks in Mexico, and there was talk of another $2 billion for Mexico's Christmas stocking. The Treasury Department was also pressing Congress to increase the U.S. contribution to the IMF by $8.4 billion to enable it to expand its lending to these countries so that they could pay back the banks. Unlike European and Japanese central bankers, who were telling their banks to tighten lending procedures because there ..as no lender of last resort to bail them out, the "New Right" administration of Ronald Reagan was putting taxpayers in hock for the follies of U.S. banks. (This was the administration that came to power on a promise "to get the government off the backs of the American people.")[32]

It was all perfectly legal. Unbeknownst to most of its members, in March 1980 Congress voted a bank bailout into law when it approved the Depository Institutions Deregulation and Monetary Control Act. The main purpose of the eighty-five-page act had been to require banks to belong to the Federal Reserve system and to allow commercial banks to accept Negotiated Order of Withdrawal (NOW) accounts. However, just before the bill was approved by a joint House-Senate committee six lines were added at the request of the Federal Reserve Board. It is estimated that no more than ten congressmen were even aware of the insert that gave the Federal Reserve the right to buy securities of foreign governments just as it buys securities issued by the U.S. Treasury, thereby allowing the Fed to prop up U.S. banks by covering the deficits of foreign governments. According to congressional and Federal Reserve sources, the inspiration for the insert came from Fed Chairman Paul A. Volcker, an alumnus of Chase Manhattan, which, with other major U.S. banks, stood to gain most from the authorization.[33]

The never-publicized legislation explains why U.S. banks continued to lend to countries like Mexico long after the Europeans took fright. They knew they had a safety net despite warnings by central bankers in the Basle Concordat, after the Ambrosiano debacle,‡ that private banks were on their own. Third World governments also knew that the last-minute postscript offered U.S. banks a financial life jacket. The dean of a Chicago college of business administration said that he learned about it from officials of Third World nations with severe debt problems. "In some cases," he said, "it was the agriculture minister of a particular

‡ See Chapter 10, pp. 220–21.

government who spoke to me . . . When it is an agriculture minister who is aware of the change, not just finance ministers, you know that such talk is pretty widespread."[34]

The last to know were the people who would pay. U.S. taxpayers learned that they had been sucked into the debt trap only after President Reagan visited Brazil to confirm the swap arrangement between the U.S. and Brazilian treasuries, whereby dollars were exchanged for bad Brazilian paper held by U.S. banks. The deal had been worked out secretly two months earlier but was not made public until the details were leaked in Brazil.[35]

The bank bailout made a mockery of Reaganomics since it undercut the administration's fight against inflation. By buying up defaulted loans with dollars, the Federal Reserve was increasing the money supply around the world while simultaneously undermining the drive to control the federal budget. One argument for pushing toward a balanced budget is that if the federal government stopped running deficits the Fed wouldn't have to increase the money supply to cover them. But with the Fed in the business of monetarizing foreign as well as domestic debt, there is no point in balancing just the U.S. budget. "It is bad enough when the U. S. Treasury repays its own obligations by issuing new ones," complained William E. Simon, former Secretary of the Treasury, "but to do this for the likes of Tanzania, Rumania and oil-rich Mexico indicates that we have taken leave of our senses."[36]

The bank rescue also made nonsense of the Fed's tight monetary policies and Volcker's unyielding stand on high interest rates. While such rates had proved profitable for the banks, they were one of the primary causes of the developing countries' inability to service their loans. Since most of the Third World's debt is in dollars, the cost of repayment in depreciated local currencies added greatly to the burden. Indeed, every time U.S. interest rates increased by one point, it cost a country like Brazil or Mexico $750 million more a year in debt service. As the Brazilians and Mexicans were quick to point out, a sizable portion of their debt was unreal—money they never received, in the form of unconscionable interest that had piled up because of an experiment with the free-market theories of economist Milton Friedman. Volcker's tight-money policies also contributed to a prolongation of the recession in the United States, which, in turn, deepened the world recession. "The Reagan administration . . . may have [made] the gravest policy mistake of this century," wrote Princeton economist Peter B. Kenen. "Beguiled by the doctrines of economists whose contempt for evidence was exceeded only by their craving for publicity, it brewed a mix of fiscal and monetary policies that poisoned the world economy."[37]

Rephrasing General Motors' famous boast, Volcker and Treasury Secretary Donald Regan, also an alumnus of the financial world, were proclaiming, "What's good for the banks is good for the United States"—though, one should add, only certain kinds of banks. The Federal Reserve is willing enough for small and regional banks to take their lumps, but the large banks can rely on their special relationship with the Fed to save them from disaster. And Volcker had earlier shown his preference for the big gamblers by saving the billionaire Hunt Brothers of Texas after their costly 1980 adventure in silver speculation.*

While U.S. bankers frankly admitted that the taxpayer was providing a bailout for their Latin-American ventures, they claimed that there was no alternative. After all, they said, Washington could not set off a worldwide depression by allowing the banks to fail, nor could it risk triggering a revolution in Mexico or Brazil by letting their economies collapse. The arguments had some validity, but, as pointed out by U.S. critics, the problem was that American taxpayers were footing the bill for the mess, not the bankers who were responsible for it.[38]

---

* W. Herbert and Nelson Bunker Hunt had succeeded in cornering two thirds of the world's silver market, but when silver prices suddenly dived from $50 to $10 per ounce in March 1980, the Hunts faced the prospect of losing their fortune. Although the brothers guessed wrong on a dangerous, high-stakes gamble, they did not have to liquidate their assets because Volcker came to their rescue. Congressman Fernand St. Germain, chairman of the House Banking Committee, said that his action showed that when big speculators lose money they turn to Volcker for "a quick fix" (Time [May 12, 1980]; Business Week [May 19, 1980]).

Chapter 12

Conclusion

Throughout their history Americans have been ambivalent about banks, distrusting yet needing them. Imbued with a deep suspicion of privilege and monopoly, the colonists, while hostile to any form of concentrated wealth, depended on Robert Morris of Philadelphia and other bankers to finance the American Revolution. Thomas Jefferson, typifying the young nation's ambiguous feelings, feared the banks' power yet was glad to profit from them. Andrew Jackson, reelected on a promise to do away with Philadelphia's giant Bank of the United States (a short-lived predecessor of the Federal Reserve), in the end merely shifted financial power to New York City. The banking dispute reflected a deeper conflict over how the United States should develop—as a society of monied interests or as a democracy—and posed the question, still unsettled, of who should control the banks and how they should lend money. Farmers and ranchers saw themselves as defenders of democracy in a battle with merchant traders and bankers; Westerners' suspicion of banks was so deep-rooted that several states, including California, banned them altogether. In the 1890s the farmer-backed Populist movement wanted a complete restructuring of the banking system, and at the turn of the century bankers were still under siege: J. P. Morgan, the symbol of American money to the aristocrats of New York and Europe, was known to the workers as "the great financial Gorgon." Yet throughout the period banks were essential to underwrite the young nation's expanding trade and industry and to finance its wars. (During the Civil War Citibank's forerunner supplied Lincoln with gold.)

Bankers were never as villainous as portrayed in the popular imagination nor as virtuous as they claimed. Rather, they have tended to reflect the economic pressures and social mores of the times. In the 1890s and the first decade of the twentieth century, when philanthropy was considered good business, the House of Morgan reaped profits while also serving the country's interests —by saving Grover Cleveland's administration from bankruptcy, for example, and by staving off a bank crash in 1907. And when the federal government sought means to revive Europe after World War I, it turned to American bankers.

When asked if a borrower should be judged on the basis of money and property, Morgan replied, "No sir: the first thing is character." In the 1920s, as again in the 1970s and 1980s, when society tended to place less value on "character" or integrity than on fast bucks, bankers went with the tide. Then, as now, many Americans were convinced that making money was the only goal in life, and leading bankers, businessmen, and economists encouraged them in their folly. "Everybody Ought to Be Rich" was the title of an article by a General Motors executive in a 1928 issue of the *Ladies' Home Journal* that could have been an advertisement for a money market fund today. Indeed, the clearest parallel between the two periods is the atmosphere of financial speculation and wheeling-dealing that has led to widespread fraud and the growth of organized crime.

As shown by congressional hearings in the 1930s, some of the country's leading bankers were guilty of serious malpractice. Charles E. "Sunshine Charlie" Mitchell, chairman of Citibank's predecessor, resigned after it was shown that he had sold bank stock to his wife at a loss in order to avoid paying taxes. He was successfully sued for $1 million in taxes. Albert H. Wiggin, president of Chase, followed Mitchell into early retirement when he was found to have sold short 42,506 shares of his own bank, at a profit of $4 million. Other bankers suffered public disgrace or saw their institutions ruined: More than nine thousand banks collapsed between 1929 and 1933. The bank crash of 1929, said Bernard Baruch, "shattered the stereotype of bankers as conservative, careful, prudent individuals." Years later, with the banking community reeling from the shocks of Drysdale, Penn

Square, and the near-default of Mexico, bank analysts were making similar observations.[1]*

Like some bankers today, Mitchell shrugged off his public responsibilities by telling Congress that it wasn't his lookout if a lot
of Americans wanted to invest their money in worthless bonds
and stocks. We were just supplying what the customer wanted, he
said. Yet it was "Sunshine Charlie" who had urged the public to
go on buying even as the stock market was collapsing.[2] Appropri-
ately, the chief huckster for the banking sector today is Mitchell's
successor at Citibank, chairman Walter Wriston, who claims that
the Third World's debt problems have been greatly exaggerated.
Like so many bankers who rose to power after World War II,
Wriston has never had to deal with a truly sick economy. In the
words of *Business Week,* these men "took their ability to survive
the minor economic disturbances . . . as proof they could survive anything."[3]

The belief of Mitchell and other bankers in unending prosperity points up another parallel with the recent past. Stuffed with
money after World War I, American bankers embarked on a
lending spree, pushing loans on any who would take them. As in
the 1970s, when banks recycled Arab money to the developing
countries to pay for imported oil,† bankers in the 1920s sold
German bonds to the American public to enable Germany to pay
war reparations to France and England, so that they, in turn,
could repay their war debts to the U.S. Treasury. The recycling
scheme was so successful that a second wave of German bonds
was floated to pay interest on the old ones. By 1929 Americans
were contributing 80 percent of the capital borrowed by German
credit institutions—75 percent of it to local governments and 5
percent in loans to large corporations. Not satisfied with selling
German bonds, bankers were soon peddling to the American
public the bonds of Argentina, Bolivia, Brazil, Bulgaria, Chile,
Costa Rica, Ecuador, Mexico, Peru, and Rumania. At one time
representatives of twenty-nine financial houses were in Colombia
competing for clients, and a hamlet in Bavaria that wanted to
borrow $125,000 was eventually persuaded to take $3 million. As

* See Chapters 1, 2, and 11.
† See Chapter 11, p. 229.

with Reagan's Great Bank Bailout, the bonds sold to U.S. investors turned into gifts from the public: By 1933 $25 billion in bonds were in default.⁴‡

The recycling game did not come about by chance in the 1920s, any more than it did in the 1970s. In both cases Washington took an active role in promoting trade for U.S. corporations and encouraging U.S. banks to back bonds and, later, loans for foreign countries. Indeed, the German bond market might never have prospered had the State Department not pressured the reluctant House of Morgan to sell German bonds on the American market in 1924. Five years later, when the alarmed Hoover administration attempted to slow the bond deluge by "jawboning" bankers about the dangers of speculation, it was too late to stop the frenzy: Like their modern-day successors, Mitchell and other bankers easily ignored the government's plea "not to do it any more."* American bankers received similarly encouraging signals from the Carter administration, and later, under Reagan, from Federal Reserve chairman Paul Volcker, who advised the banks that they should go on lending to countries like Mexico and Brazil.⁵†

Poland offers a good example of how banks step into traps abroad for reasons of foreign policy. In the late 1920s the Treasury Department was closely involved with the financial projects of a Polish dictator, even sending a former Treasury official to serve as his chief economic planner. Several decades later, when Washington was trying to wean Poland from Soviet influence, U.S. banks were again encouraged to lend. When Poland could not service its debt, Reagan's Treasury Department paid off the banks to prevent them from foreclosing.⁶ Now, as before, such lending policies bring banks into the governmental sphere, confusing private goals with the broader public interest. Such confusion has also obscured an essential problem in the historical debate over banking, namely, how a government can persuade

---

‡ Shades of the 1920s: The $15.5 billion in bonds issued by Third World and East European countries looked "precarious" in 1983 *(The Banker* [April 1983]).

* See Chapter 2.

† See Chapter 11.

banks to act for the public good without, at the same time, giving them a position of privilege in which the government serves as their protector.

***

The banking reforms of the 1930s were designed to guard the public interest by separating commercial banking (taking deposits and making loans) from investment banking (underwriting and dealing in securities). Until the law was changed, bankers had participated in nearly two thirds of all new stock and bond issues—sometimes for dubious reasons. Congressional hearings showed that Chase had absorbed $10 million in securities of doubtful quality to aid its securities affiliate, and Citibank (then known as National City) apparently sold its subsidiary about $25 million in speculative loans that were paid out of new stock issues. So great was the public outcry following such revelations that even before Congress passed the Glass-Steagall reforms in 1933, many banks had already spun off their investment subsidiaries. Ironically, the most controversial aspect of the Glass-Steagall Act—the establishment of federal bank insurance—was to prove a boon to bankers, but at the time the American Bankers Association held it to be "unsound, unscientific, unjust and dangerous."[7]

The effects of Roosevelt's New Deal legislation were long-lasting, and it was only in the late 1950s, after World War II and a decade of prosperity, that bankers began to emerge from their somnolence to reassert their financial power. The first hole in the legislative dike was the 1956 Bank Holding Act. Intended only for small-town bankers who also owned a local gas station or hardware store, the act was interpreted by the large banks as giving them permission to engage in extensive nonbanking activities and to cross geographical borders otherwise closed to them. Citibank was the first to create a major bank holding company, Citicorp, and other large banks soon followed. Through their holding companies, and undeterred by Congress or any regulatory agency, the banks were soon deeply engaged in insurance, travel services, credit cards, the leasing of industrial equipment, real estate, data processing, certain types of mutual funds, and commercial paper. But while deregulation and the expansion into new pursuits increased bank profitability, they also encouraged bankers to push into unknown territory, as for example, into real estate speculation, which cost Chase, Citibank and other large banks substantial losses in the mid-1970s.‡

Deregulation also changed the way a banker ran his business. "Before, bankers sat in their offices and waited for customers to come to them," said the vice chairman of a large regional bank. "Now bankers have to go out and compete." The pressure of the marketplace has been intense, since U.S. banks are not only expected to increase profits but also to keep high their stock valuations and multiply their equity. In such circumstances it is not surprising that they have cut corners, as in the Drysdale debacle,* or ignored laws designed to protect their depositors. Speculation by banks has been particularly evident in loans to the developing countries, where volume has become more important than quality. "Bankers should stop selling loans like cans of beans," commented *The Economist.* They should "return to first principles and reward bank lending officers for not making bad loans as highly as for making a good loan."[8]

A familiar hazard of gambling is not knowing when to stop, and it is the rare bank that heeds prudent advice when the pressure is on for profits. Although Arthur Burns, Volcker's predecessor at the Fed, several times chastized the banks for their wild lending to the Third World, they continued as though the game would never end. Warnings from the Comptroller of the Currency and the IMF were also ignored. And, as shown by Citibank's attitude toward lending limits,† the admonishments of regulatory agencies have proved utterly ineffective. Since 1977 not a few economists have urged more stringent regulations on foreign lending, but only after the Latin-American defaults did it become clear that "the present framework for regulating and supervising international banking invites circumvention," as Richard S. Dale, an authority on international banking, told Congress. While warding off imminent financial disaster, Reagan's Latin-American largesse did nothing to prevent such circumven-

‡ See Introduction p. 1, and Chapter 1, p. 4.
* See Chapter 1, pp. 7–10.
† See Chapter 2, pp. 29–39.

tion in the future. On the contrary, rescuing the banks from their folly without demanding complementary controls for the future was an invitation to gamble with taxpayers' money. "That emphasis is wrong," said *The Economist*. "Better to work on a system that allows banks which deserve to go bust to do so without busting everybody else."[9]

***

In the spring of 1983, when Congress was debating the Reagan administration's request for an $8.4 billion contribution to the IMF amidst daily reports of new banking excesses, history's pendulum swung again, hitting the bankers with the double whammy of more competition and broader disclosures. The failure of forty-two banks in 1982—the most since 1940—had been bad enough, but when congressmen learned that the country's nine largest banks had 112.5 percent of their combined capital on loan to just three countries (Mexico, Brazil, and Argentina) they were outraged. "You want assistance? Fine," Fernand J. St. Germain, the House Banking Committee chairman, warned bankers. "But, by cracky, you are going to have to mend your ways." Even the Reagan administration fumed at the banks. Treasury Secretary Donald Regan complained that they were keeping domestic interest rates high in order to recoup losses from unsound loans, and President Reagan said he was up to his "keister with the bankers in this country . . . for their distortion and outright false information" in their lobbying efforts to repeal withholding taxes on bank interest and dividends. The nation's bankers were "a selfish special interest group," said President Reagan. And the Secretary of the Treasury asserted that banks "pay little taxes themselves but want others to pay more taxes rather than collect those already owed." The administration's ire was matched by that of Kansas Republican Robert Dole, chairman of the powerful Senate Finance Committee and a former ally of the banks. Dole said that a congressional study of the twenty largest banks had revealed that they paid an average income tax of only 2.7 percent in 1981, compared to 20 percent for individuals and 30 percent for many industries. Some, such as the giant Bank of America, not only paid no taxes but also received $18 million in tax refunds.[10]

Spurred by a flood of letters from angry constituents, congressmen were demanding an end to secrecy, more regulation, and new accounting procedures. As one legislator put it, "Money is a commodity, and if the banks are exporting it to other countries, we ought to know where and who." A small step in that direction was taken by the Securities and Exchange Commission in the fall of 1982, when it required bank holding companies to reveal more information about problem loans to foreign countries, and as of mid-1983 federal regulators were also requiring disclosure on troubled domestic loans. After the brouhaha in Congress, bank regulators agreed to demand quarterly reports on foreign lending, with more details on risk whenever loans to an individual country exceed 1 percent of a bank's assets. Prudent bankers said they had no argument with the disclosure requirements, but others complained the "undressing in public" would cause a loss of investor confidence. "How can you lend in the face of this?" wondered one banker. "In the end, you'll have to admit you've been lending to someone who can't pay you back."[11]

Such lending practices moved William Isaac, chairman of the Federal Deposit Insurance Corporation (FDIC), to propose a sweeping overhaul of government bank insurance to force risk-taking banks to pay a higher premium in insurance and public exposure. While Isaac's plan would not affect "little people" with deposits of less than $100,000, it would force big depositors to pay closer attention to how banks are managed by reducing the amount of effective coverage over $100,000 to seventy-five cents on the dollar.‡ Under the current system deposits over the $100,000 limit are at risk only if the FDIC is unable to find a merger partner, as in Penn Square's case.* A more common course is for the FDIC to underwrite the merger of a sick bank with a stronger one, which assumes responsibility for deposits both under and over $100,000, thus eliminating any penalty to large depositors for banking with high flyers. To help uninsured depositors the FDIC was developing a disclosure form that

‡ Banks, savings and loan associations, and credit unions have about $988 billion worth of insured deposits and approximately $420 billion in uninsured money.
* See Chapter 1, pp. 12–13.

would make it easier to assess a bank's financial condition; the FDIC said it would penalize uncooperative banks by recommending that depositors take their money elsewhere. The Isaac plan also aimed to discipline reckless banks by charging higher insurance premiums for those classified as high or medium risk.[12]

The FDIC had good reasons for such proposals. In relatively properous times America's banking system can survive the ups and downs of temporary crisis, like the real estate and foreign-currency losses of the 1970s; and if a bank goes under, as Sindona's Franklin National did,† the FDIC will come to the rescue. Problems arise in abnormal times when banks lose the public's confidence; surveys in 1982 showed that nearly 90 percent of Americans questioned were concerned about the stability of U.S. financial institutions. The FDIC can handle one, two, perhaps a half dozen Penn Squares, but it does not have the resources to cover deposits or claims in a general bank panic. Bank regulators said they expect more failures because of the "explosive" changes in banking that set financial institutions at each other's throats in the competition for loans, deposits, and the highest interest rates. "Our regulatory and insurance systems weren't designed to deal with the financial system as we know it today," Isaac told Congress. "They are in need of a major overhaul."[13]

As the regulators admitted, banks face a painful dilemma: On the one hand, they chafe against regulatory restrictions, wanting to be free to engage in new, riskier activities; on the other, they are reluctant to forego the government protection that comes with regulation. "They can't have it both ways," warned Comptroller C. Todd Conover. "In a deregulated environment there will be more risks for banks. Banks can't take on that increased risk without accepting ultimate responsibility for their own mistakes."[14]

Many bankers were stunned by the options. If Congress were to approve the Isaac plan, for example, some of the country's biggest banks could end up in the FDIC's high- and medium-risk categories. As defined by the FDIC, such risks include capital of less than 5 percent to support total loans, a high percentage of problem loans, and/or a high degree of exposure to possible

† See Chapter 9, pp. 183–84.

losses from interest-rate fluctuations. According to an analysis of the country's strongest and weakest banks by T. J. Holt and Company of Westport, Connecticut, which based its findings on material submitted by the banks to the Federal Reserve, many of the largest U.S. banks had a capital cushion of less than 5 percent and a high percentage of loans in such vulnerable areas as the developing countries, commercial and industrial credits (an important factor given the rising number of corporate bankruptcies), and real estate. (U.S. and Canadian bankers who financed $100 billion in U.S. office construction are "terrified" that the sharp downturn in commercial real estate may leave them holding the bag, reported *Business Week.* [15]) Among T. J. Holt's twenty-five "weakest banks" were Bank of America, Continental Illinois, Chase, and Citibank. Conversely, the strongest banks were the small to medium ones, such as Morgan Bank (Delaware), First Blair City National Bank (Pennsylvania), First Union Bank (Ohio), and McDowell County National Bank (West Virginia). None had loans to the developing countries; their real estate loans averaged only 1.1 percent of total portfolios; loan-loss reserves were 2.2 percent of total loans (0.9 percent for the big banks); and their capital cushion was 16.5 percent, in contrast to 4.1 percent for the weakest banks. In effect, if the assets of the latter declined by 4 percent, because of defaulted mortgages or uncollectable loans, their net worth would be reduced to nearly zero. But a strong bank with a 16.5 percent ratio would survive. [16]

Many bankers would—and did—argue that such statistics gave only a partial picture, but in a period of prolonged recession, with personal and corporate bankruptcies reaching Depression highs, conservative bankers looked a lot smarter than growth-oriented ones. Such, at least, was the market's assessment. Share prices of big New York banks like Chase and Chemical dropped precipitously, to an average of only four times earnings, roughly the same price-earnings ratio of the severely depressed oil-drilling industry. As noted by *The Economist,* any bank can be hit by a liquidity crisis if a rumor sets off a run, but solvency problems, while less dramatic, can prove just as destructive. "As its bad debts (or loans on which it is never going to be repaid) increase, they have to be written off against the bank's capital and reserves. Since capital and reserves amount to about 5 percent of a bank's total assets, a few bad loans can make a bank insolvent." [17]

***

"What you don't know can't hurt you" has long been a banking maxim; in fact, secrecy can hurt bankers as much as the public, Penn Square being a case in point.‡ Had bank accounting procedures been less devious, banks like Chase and Continental might have been alerted to Penn Square's problems, but because of the peculiar way in which assets are listed, financial institutions can carry problem loans at a value higher than their real worth. Nor are banks required to reserve commensurately against possible loan losses or to start writing them down. Moreover, it is standard accounting practice to show interest from old loans as income even when new loans have been made so that old loan interest payments can be met. Banks are also allowed to show fees charged for making those new loans as immediate earnings instead of spreading them over the life of the loans. Consequently a sick bank can look perfectly healthy in its annual report, and neither the public nor other banks will be the wiser. Indeed, one reason some banks may have been so sanguine about the Third World's foreign debt is that fees for debt rescheduling have increased their short-term income. Mexico, for example, paid a $262.5 million fee to the banks to reschedule $20 billion of its debts. Congressional critics charged that by classifying fees as "current income" banks were benefiting temporarily by renegotiating loans that were probably imprudent in the first place. [18]

The accounting profession has also contributed to dubious practices thanks to the cozy relationship between accountants and their bank clients. Peat, Marwick, Mitchell & Company, for example, approved Penn Square's accounts for public consumption, yet it noted fourteen internal problems in a confidential letter to the bank's management. Ernst & Whinney, another of the nation's "Big Eight" accounting firms, gave the United American Bank of Knoxville, Tennessee, unqualified approval three weeks before the FDIC declared the bank insolvent because of massive insider loans.* How Ernst & Whinney's auditing team missed

‡ See Chapters 1, pp. 10–19, and 2, pp. 21–28.
* See Chapter 2, p. 22.

what was going on is a mystery, since United American and its branches were swarming with FDIC investigators at the time. The auditors' excuse for not seeking the regulators' opinion was that the firm did not believe the FDIC would share its findings, a claim that the FDIC said was utter nonsense. "In no instance would access to the findings have been refused," said an FDIC spokesman. Ernst & Whinney's track record also raised doubts about the thoroughness of its accounting procedures: As the auditors of Sindona's Franklin National Bank, it had found nothing to criticize before the bank failed in 1974.† The FDIC subsequently sued the firm for failing to provide "correct opinions" on Franklin's financial status and won an out-of-court settlement.[19]

In discussions with the Office of the Comptroller of the Currency, representatives of the accounting profession stated that they were unwilling or unable to assume responsibility for monitoring bank compliance with such laws as truth-in-lending since the bank client might object to whistle-blowing. But it is precisely the immunity to whistle-blowing that has made banking so risky. Indeed, bankers' resistance to telling regulators the truth about illegal activities in their own or other banks reveals a lot about the state of the industry. The few who did talk, like David Edwards at Citibank and John Marcilla at Chase, paid with their jobs and their reputations.‡ Marcilla was falsely accused of mental illness and Edwards of incompetence. Amply vindicated by the Securities and Exchange Commission's investigation of Citibank, Edwards later said, "My job was to say it was wrong. Period."[20]

While bankers might dispute that assertion on the grounds of loyalty to the employer, the law clearly states that it is the regulators' job to speak out when something is wrong at a bank; yet the regulators have often refused to say or do anything, even when possessed of overwhelming evidence. Such was the record of the Office of the Comptroller of the Currency in the Penn Square and Franklin National failures, when its inaction allowed those banks to collapse.* Such has also been the record of the Federal Re-

† See Chapter 9, pp. 183–85.
‡ See Chapters 2, pp. 29, 32; and 7, pp. 138–39.
* See Chapters 2, pp. 26–28, and 9, pp. 183–84.

serve, which has enabled—indeed, encouraged—U.S. banks to go on lending to the debt-ridden developing countries. As noted by Robert A. Mullin, a former deputy comptroller of the currency for special surveillance, "The comptroller's attempts to reduce or eliminate these loans were thwarted by a Federal Reserve Board that contended that loans to foreign countries should not be criticized and by bank executives who argued that such countries could not go bankrupt or fail to exist. In view of the current situation, the Fed and the bankers should remember that they were told that even in lower Manhattan the chickens would come home to roost."[21]

Nor has the Fed shown any interest in restraining the acquisition of banks by criminals. On the contrary, it has approved applications of questionable or crooked foreign interests, as in the case of the Colombian speculator Felix Correa and his banker associate Jaime Mosquera, who was due to receive Federal Reserve approval for the purchase of a Georgia bank in the very same week the Colombian authorities jailed him on charges of bank fraud![22]†

While many recognize the need to overhaul the international financial system, there is no point in more regulations if they are not to be enforced. For example, the Office of the Comptroller of the Currency knew that Citibank was engaged in illegal currency dealings but did nothing to stop it from further follies in Latin America. Whereupon the bank continued to gamble, knowing that Uncle Sam would come to its rescue. The result of such slackness is that everybody scurries about trying to stem the tide after the dike has ruptured in places like Mexico and Brazil. Former White House economist Alan Greenspan feels that "the chances of a dangerous breakdown are the greatest in a half century," yet the regulators have no plan to handle a world banking crisis. Because there is none, said Senator Bill Bradley (D-N.J.), a member of the Senate Finance Committee, the system "is like a string that you pull and unravel the whole blanket." Thus, if some country or bank pulls the string in the Cayman Islands or Luxembourg—where there are no central banks—the entire international banking system could unravel, since many banks use

† See Chapter 5, pp. 95–99, and 8, pp. 161–63.

such offshore havens to lend money to governments and corporations. And if one large bank went under in Europe, it could pull down all the rest, because banks depend on one another for two thirds of their funds. The Italian authorities moved swiftly to save Calvi's Ambrosiano Bank in Milan, even though they passed the buck for its Luxembourg company to the Vatican Bank.‡ But what if they had held off too long or waited for some other participant to bear the primary risk? During the delay there would have been a run on other banks with loans to Ambrosiano, and they might also have collapsed.[23]

Such panic reactions have become all too real in countries like Argentina and Chile, where the collapse of one bank set off a string of failures. In Canada the Bank of Nova Scotia (with assets of more than $52 billion) felt compelled to announce that "rumors about [our] stability are completely unfounded," after Newfoundland depositors besieged its branches to withdraw their money. In hypersensitive Hong Kong, itself a banking haven, a bus queue that took shelter in a bank entrance led a nervous broker across the street to conclude there was a run on the bank. There wasn't, but the local stock market took a dive before the truth was out. Meanwhile, in Texas depositors withdrew nearly one eighth of an Abilene bank's deposits when a newspaper compared it to Penn Square.[24]

Obviously international finance markets would be less subject to rumor if ther were clear ground rules for bank responsibility, particularly on the crucial issue of lender of last resort. But to be effective, cautioned Johannes Witteveen, the former managing director of the IMF, "monetary authorities [must] develop effective instruments to influence and if necessary to contain" foreign lending in a complementary if not identical system of regulation. To work effectively such a system would necessarily eliminate much of the secrecy that shrouds international banking, enabling U.S. regulators, for instance, to examine the books of foreign branches of U.S. banks, a right of access that American bankers have fought tooth and nail. Such a system also presupposes that the regulators are not captives of the industry they are supposed to regulate, as the Federal Reserve appears to be under chairman

‡ See Chapter 10, pp. 217–22.

Volcker, who has made no attempt to rein in the large banks. On the contrary, he has proposed that their bad loans to the developing countries be exempted from the normal "supervisory criticism" of bank regulators.[25]

***

Congressman John Dingell's complaint that the banks have become a law unto themselves* was probably best demonstrated in the Securities and Exchange Commission's investigation of Citibank, but the "Rogues' Gallery" preceding each chapter clearly shows that chairman Wriston and his executives are hardly the only people to have used a financial institution for questionable gain. And since there are probably just as many rogues in other industries, why pick on bankers? Two decades ago it might have been harder to answer that question, because bankers did not dominate the world stage as they do now, with international debt hanging like a sword of Damocles over world trade. Nor were banks as essential to criminal industries such as the drug traffic and the clandestine arms trade, since the volume of money so generated was still relatively small. Mobsters used banks, of course, but they rarely owned them. Only in the 1970s did they grasp the importance of ownership: hence the arrival of criminals like Sindona on the international finance scene. In an earlier incarnation Sindona might have dealt in stolen cars; in the 1970s banks offered a better vehicle to power and wealth.

In cases like the Nugan Hand Bank in Australia, the World Finance Corporation (WFC) in Miami, and the Abrosiano-Vatican imbroglio in Italy and Latin America, it is difficult to separate those two driving motives, since the banks were used both to advance political ambitions and to enrich the people who controlled them. If the CIA is to be believed, it had nothing whatsoever to do with Nugan Hand, which means that all the generals and CIA types were in it only for the money. That they did not know of the bank's drug connections or its dealings with arms trafficker Edwin Wilson is possible, though improbable, in view of the rush to shred bank files after Frank Nugan's death, a cover-up in which Rear Admiral Yates and other directors par-

---

* See Chapter 2, p. 36.

ticipated. And if they didn't know, they should not have been in the banking business, since it was precisely their presence that convinced gullible American depositors to entrust their savings to the bank. On the other hand, if the CIA was involved—and there is strong circumstantial evidence to that effect—the affair was the more reprehensible, since it meant that the agency was still in the heroin traffic in Southeast Asia.

At least one issue was clear in both the Nugan Hand and WFC cases: The CIA's former employees have run amok. That should come as no surprise after the CIA's record of collaboration with gangsters like "Lucky" Luciano and Santo Trafficante, or the role of CIA agents in Watergate and the Chilean coup, to cite but a few such "adventures." "I'm Glad the CIA Is Immoral" was the title of the confessions of one ex-CIA agent, who wrote a cold war justification of the agency's methods in Europe.[26] But when people are schooled in immorality, they don't suddenly turn moral when they leave the agency, and that may explain why so many former agents were mixed up with Nugan Hand and WFC. Paul Helliwell, the former OSS intelligence officer who specialized in Florida banks and Caribbean tax havens, was a good example of the breed—a man who knew how to exploit his connections with the CIA long after leaving its employ.

The Vatican is the only other organization with an intelligence network in the West comparable to the CIA's that has hobnobbed with the likes of Nugan Hand, and even the CIA might have had trouble swallowing such a foursome as Sindona, Calvi, Gelli, and Count Ortolani. Yet Archbishop Marcinkus fell for their wiles—unknowingly, he said, just as the Pentagon brass denied any knowledge of Nugan Hand's illegal doings. But the denial could not undo the financial losses suffered by the Vatican Bank—or the loss of confidence among Catholics in the Vatican's handling of their dutiful offerings.

Another thread that runs throughout these stories is drugs and right-wing terrorism. Thus Italian terrorist Stefano Delle Chiaie worked with Gelli's P-2 and the Chilean secret police, who in turn worked with the CIA and Cuban exile terrorists. The Vatican's Panamanian companies financed the P-2's neofascist activities, through Calvi's Ambrosiano Bank, while Hernández Cartaya's WFC looked after the financial needs of exile Cubans with a similar ideological outlook. That is not to say there was a connection between Ambrosiano and WFC, but rather that extremist politics find a natural partner in such criminal activities as drugs.

Banks are crucial to such activities because they launder illegal gains and provide financing for criminal projects. In places where such activities are widely accepted, such as southern Florida, even honest bankers have difficulty resisting the enormous profits, as shown by Miami banker Orlando Arrebola, who was indicted for "furthering the business of the bank" by accepting large drug deposits.† Occasionally a strong bank will try to resist an unfriendly takeover by questionable investors. That happened in the case of Florida's Southeast Bank, which went to court, but lost in its attempt to stop a real estate manipulator from buying more of its stock. Robert Marlin, the lead investor, had frequently been cited by Florida authorities for improper real estate dealings in the 1970s, but in the 1980s his interest shifted to banks, perhaps because they had become the hottest speculative item on the market.‡ When one third of the banks in a large metropolitan area are suspected of laundering drug money, they reflect the mores of the community as well as those of the banking profession. As observed by a Florida grand jury that studied Miami's crime problems, it is "clearly a costly hypocrisy" to pretend that a commitment exists to eradicate narcotics when "our local economy apparently has benefited enormously and our culture has become tolerant of marijuana and even of cocaine."*

But that sort of tolerance encourages crime, as illustrated by Miami's Great American Bank, which adopted a laissez-faire attitude toward drug deposits that ended in the bank's indictment. Shortcuts to big profits can also encourage gross negligence; as the deputy comptroller warned (see p. 262), the "chickens have now come home to roost" in some of the country's biggest banks. Chase Manhattan, which lost $542 million on the Drysdale, Lombard-Wall, and Penn Square debacles, was sued by a Chase shareholder who charged that the bank, in an effort to increase

† See Chapter 7, p. 132–34.
‡ See Chapter 3, pp. 46–48.
* See Chapter 6, pp. 116–17.

its loan portfolio, took on business that was "inferior, risky and imprudent." Among the twenty-eight bank officers and directors named in the suit was chairman Willard Butcher. Penn Square's auditors—Peat, Marwick, Mitchell & Company—were also being sued on charges that the firm "breached its contractual duty . . . by rendering unqualified opinions" on the bank's financial statements. Meanwhile, the chairman of Drysdale Securities Corporation—who was also a director of the failed Drysdale Government Securities—pleaded guilty to federal charges that he had made fraudulent reports, thereby inflating the value of investment accounts involving several million dollars.[27]

Continental Illinois, also being sued for its involvement in the Penn Square debacle, found itself under investigation by the Securities and Exchange Commission (SEC) for possible violations in disclosure requirements on its financial condition. The SEC was also looking into charges that a Continental executive vice president took advantage of inside knowledge of the bank's troubles to sell Continental stock at "considerable financial gain" a month before the Penn Square scandal erupted. As for Citibank, an irate shareholder took the bank's top fifteen executives to court, including chairman Wriston, to ask that the bank recover money lost in fines for evading taxes† and that Wriston and the others be fined for incurring a drain on profits.[28]

Sindona's Franklin National hit the headlines again when it was disclosed that European American Bank & Trust Company, Franklin's new name, had nearly $300 million in problem loans at the end of 1982. Absorbed by a group of European banks, the Long Island institution was back on the problem list of the Comptroller of the Currency, this time for excessive lending to Mexico, Argentina, and other Latin-American countries.[29] But perhaps the most dramatic example of the costs of gambling was Seattle-First National Bank, where massive dismissals and a complete new management could not rescue it from the hole it had dug for itself with the help of a small bank in an Oklahoma shopping center. No longer touting high-profit gains far from home, bank executives have been returning to basics, as in financing the Pacific coast fishing industries that had helped build the

† See Chapter 2, pp. 29–39.

bank in the first place. But the lesson of making sound loans for productive local investments came too late for Seattle-First: Due to losses incurred from Penn Square, its management was forced to open negotiations for its acquisition by Bank of America. At the same time a federal grand jury and the Securities and Exchange Commission began a major probe into possible bank fraud and misapplication of funds in the Seattle bank's dealings with Penn Square.[30]

Parallels abounded throughout the United States, particularly in the depressed Northeast, where banks had ignored the needs of their own communities and industries in order to lend to countries like Brazil and Mexico, where the short-term profits were much higher. But when the bottom fell out of the Latin-American market, bankers turned for help to the same Americans they had earlier spurned. The bankers were not wholly responsible for the situation, there being plenty of others who encouraged them in their greed, including OPEC oil ministers and Latin-American dictators. Indeed, when it comes to sharing the blame, the federal government and its central bank, the Federal Reserve, must bear the largest responsibility, not only for promoting the money-recycling game of the 1970s but also for refusing to stop the money-go-round after it spun out of control.

GLOSSARY OF BANKING TERMS

ASSETS: bank loans.

CERTIFICATE OF DEPOSIT (commonly called a CD): a certificate for money deposited in a commercial bank for a specified period of time and earning a specified rate of return; a negotiable instrument.

COMMERCIAL PAPER: unsecured promissory notes of well-known business concerns with a high credit rating.

COOK THE BOOKS: colloquialism for falsifying records and accounts.

DEFAULT: failure by a government or private borrower to meet scheduled payments on the interest and principal of a debt.

EDGE ACT BANK: a bank established under a 1919 act allowing holding companies to set up banks outside their home states devoted exclusively to foreign business.

EQUITY CAPITAL: the total investment in a business or bank by all its owners; investors supply equity capital when they buy shares of stock; they are not promised a fixed rate of interest but participate in the profits.

EUROCURRENCY MARKET: came into being during the cold war, when the Soviet Union placed dollar deposits with banks in London, beyond the reach of the U.S. Government. Eurodollars and, later, Eurofrancs and Europounds (Eurocurrency) became a common source of financing for corporations and banks. Because the market was uncontrolled, it grew exponentially to about $1.8 trillion in 1982. Eurocurrencies are not really money in the traditional sense but entries in the ledgers of banks located outside the geographical and regulatory boundaries of the country of a particular currency (e.g., Eurodollar deposits in European banks).

Billions of Eurodollars are shifted across the world with a single telex message on an around-the-clock basis through a network of bank branches in different time zones.

FEDERAL FUNDS: having nothing to do with government spending, they are funds that banks lend each other overnight in order to meet Federal Reserve requirements that a certain amount of capital be retained for contingencies; prices change daily.

INSIDER LOANS: loans made by a bank to its officers or shareholders; theoretically U.S. regulations place strict limits on such loans, but many financial institutions ignore them.

LETTER OF CREDIT: a letter, issued by a bank, instructing a correspondent bank to advance a certain sum of money to a third person; the issuing bank guarantees the reimbursement of the money advanced by the correspondent bank; commonly used in commercial transactions and foreign trade.

LIABILITIES: bank deposits.

LIQUIDITY: having assets either in cash or readily convertible to cash; the ratio of loans to deposits is the most commonly used measure of bank liquidity.

LOAN LOSS RESERVE: capital set aside by a bank to cover losses on bad loans.

MONETARIZATION OF THE DEBT: the process of increasing currency in circulation by increasing the public debt; the debt becomes monetized when new securities issued by the government are purchased by the banking system to expand reserves.

MONEY BROKERS: free-lance salesmen who receive fees from banks for finding deposits of more than $100,000, which are usually attracted by higher interest rates.

NONPERFORMING LOANS: bad loans unlikely to be repaid.

OFFSHORE HAVENS: countries that provide special advantages to individuals, corporations, and banks, including strict secrecy laws, little or no regulation, or low tax rates.

PARKING: an accounting procedure shifting, on paper, the profits from the sale or purchase of some currency from a high tax jurisdiction (e.g., Europe) to a tax haven (e.g., the Bahamas).

PORTFOLIO: a bank's itemized account of loans, securities, etc.

PRICE-EARNINGS RATIO: the current market value of a company's stock expressed as a multiple of the company's per-share earnings; computed by dividing the market value of the stock by the annual per-share earnings.

RECYCLING: a process whereby banks lend money from wealthy depositors to borrowers in need of capital; identified with the recycling of petrodollars from the oil-exporting nations to the developing countries after the 1973 increase in world oil prices.

REITS: real estate investment trusts used by banks, mainly in the 1970s, to invest in real estate.

REPOS: repurchase agreements used by government-securities dealers to borrow short-term money by selling securities and simultaneously agreeing to repurchase them in a few days.

REPRESENTATIVE OFFICE: an office of a foreign bank engaged in recruiting business; all deals must be referred to a branch or home office of the parent bank since the office cannot do any banking business.

REQUIRED RESERVES: a percentage of deposits that U.S. commercial banks are required to set aside as reserves with their regional Federal Reserve bank or as cash in their vaults; reserve requirements vary according to the category of bank.

RESCHEDULING: a procedure for postponing debt payments by establishing a new deadline for repayment of interest and principal; the penalty is higher interest rates.

SWAP ARRANGEMENT: an official arrangement between the central banks of two countries to exchange holdings of each other's currencies.

SYNDICATED LOAN: a loan in which several banks participate.

VOTING TRUST: a stockholders' agreement to vote their shares as a single bloc, thus giving them more power collectively.

Sources: Dictionary of Modern Economics (New York: McGraw-Hill, 1973); "The Eurocurrency Market Control Act of 1979," Hearings before the Subcommittee on Domestic Monetary Policy and the Subcommittee on International Trade, Investment and Monetary Policy of the Committee on Banking, Finance, and Urban Affairs, House of Representatives, June 26, 27 and July 17, 1979 (Washington, D.C.: U.S. Government Printing Office, 1979).

NOTES

Chapter 1

1. Alena Wells, "Chase after Drysdale," *The Banker*, July 1982, pp. 25–28; See *Newsweek*, May 31, 1982, pp. 46–49, and Anthony Sampson, *The Money Lenders* (New York: Viking, 1982), p. 139, for Chase's problems in the 1970s.
2. *Newsweek*, May 31, 1982, pp. 46–49.
3. Sampson, *Money Lenders*, p. 252.
4. Michael J. Crozier, Samuel P. Huntington, and Joji Watanuki, *The Crisis of Democracy* (New York: New York University Press, 1975).
5. *The Nation*, Nov. 29, 1980, p. 561.
6. *Newsweek*, May 31, 1982, p. 49; New York *Times*, April 5, 1981.
7. New York *Times*, July 25, 1982.
8. *The Wall Street Journal*, June 11, 1982.
9. *The Banker*, July 1982, p 25.
10. *Newsweek*, May 31, 1982, pp. 46–49.
11. Ibid.
12. New York *Times*, July 25, 1982.
13. *The Wall Street Journal*, June 11, 1982.
14. *Newsweek*, May 31, 1982, pp. 46–49.
15. *The Wall Street Journal*, June 11, 1982.
16. *The Wall Street Journal*, Aug. 13 and 16, 1982.
17. New York *Times*, July 25, 1982.
18. *The Wall Street Journal*, July 23, 1982.
19. *The Wall Street Journal*, Aug. 27, 1982.
20. Ibid.; *Fortune*, Aug. 23, 1982.
21. *The Wall Street Journal*, Aug. 17 and 27, 1982; *Fortune*, Aug. 23, 1982.
22. New York *Times*, July 19, 1982.
23. *The Economist*, Aug. 21, 1982, pp. 68–69.
24. *Business Week*, Aug. 2, 1982, pp. 40–42.
25. *The Wall Street Journal*, July 27, 1982.
26. Ibid.
27. New York *Times*, July 19, 1982.
28. *Business Week*, Aug. 2, 1982, pp. 40–42.
29. New York *Times*, Aug. 14, 1982.
30. Ibid.

31. Ibid.; *The Wall Street Journal,* Nov. 22, 1982.
32. Ibid.
33. New York *Times,* July 19, 1982; *The Wall Street Journal,* July 27, 1982.
34. *The Wall Street Journal,* Aug. 17, 1982; *Business Week,* Aug. 2, 1982, pp. 40–42.
35. Ibid.
36. New York *Times,* Aug. 4, 1982.
37. New York *Times,* July 25, 1982.
38. New York *Times,* Aug. 6, 1982.
39. Ibid.
40. Michael M. Thomas, *Someone Else's Money* (New York: Simon & Schuster, 1982).
41. *Newsweek,* Aug. 2, 1982, pp. 51–52.

Chapter 2

1. *Barron's,* Sept. 26, 1977.
2. *Fortune,* Aug. 23, 1982.
3. Ibid.
4. See Joan Edelman Spero, *The Failure of the Franklin National Bank* (New York: Columbia University Press, 1980), for a detailed description of the guerrilla war between the Federal Reserve and the Office of the Comptroller of the Currency.
5. New York *Times,* July 23, 1982.
6. *The Wall Street Journal,* July 23, 1982.
7. Ibid.
8. New York *Times,* Aug. 20, 1982.
9. *The Wall Street Journal,* Aug. 20, 1982.
10. New York *Times,* Aug. 20, 1982.
11. New York *Times,* July 17, 1982.
12. *The Wall Street Journal,* July 29, 1982.
13. New York *Times,* July 23, 1982.
14. *The Wall Street Journal,* July 27, 1982.
15. "The Eurocurrency Market Control Act of 1979," Hearing before the Subcommittee on Domestic Monetary Policy and the Subcommittee on International Trade, Investment and Monetary Policy of the Committee on Banking, Finance and Urban Affairs, House of Representatives, 96th Cong., June 26, 27, and July 12, 1979 (Washington D.C.: Government Printing Office, 1979); "Foreign Indebtedness to the United States," Hearing before the Subcommittee on Taxation and Debt Management Generally of the Committee on Finance, U.S. Senate, 95th Cong. (Washington, D.C.: Government Printing Office, Jan. 23, 1978).

16. *National Catholic Reporter,* Jan. 25, 1980.
17 *National Catholic Reporter,* Feb. 29, 1980.
18. Ibid.
19. New York *Times,* Sept. 13, 1982.
20. *The Nation,* Nov. 25, 1978, pp. 572–74; New York *Times,* Feb. 18, 1982; *Fortune,* Jan. 10, 1983, pp. 46–56.
21. New York *Times,* Sept. 13, 1982.
22. New York *Times,* Feb. 18, 1982.
23. Ibid.
24. Matthew Rothschild, "Part I: 'Rinky-dink' Lending," *Multinational Monitor,* October 1982, pp. 9–15.
25. *The Wall Street Journal,* Feb. 4, 1983; *Current Biography* (New York: H. W Wilson, 1977), pp. 443–46.
26. *Current Biography,* pp. 443–46.
27. *Multinational Monitor,* October 1982, pp. 9–15.
28. *Fortune,* Jan. 10, 1983, pp. 46–56.
29. Ibid.
30. *Current Biography,* pp. 443–46.
31. *The Wall Street Journal,* Sept. 14, 1982.
32. Ibid.
33. *The Nation,* Nov. 25, 1978, pp. 572–74.
34. New York *Times,* Feb. 18, 1982.
35. New York *Times,* Sept. 13, 1982.
36. Ibid.
37. Ibid.
38. Ibid.
39. *Latin America Weekly Report,* Sept. 24, 1982.
40. *Multinational Monitor,* October 1982, pp. 9–15.
41. Ibid.
42. *Sojourners,* April 1982, p. 9.
43. New York *Times,* Feb. 18, 1982.
44. *Multinational Monitor,* October 1982, pp. 9–15.
45. *Business Week,* March 8, 1982, p. 42.
46. *Business Week,* Feb. 22, 1982, p. 54; *The New Republic,* Aug. 16 & 23, 1982, pp. 19–23.
47. *The New Republic,* Aug. 16 & 23, 1982, pp. 19–23.
48. Interview, Organized Crime Bureau, Miami, Aug. 18, 1982.

Chapter 3

1. Miami *Herald,* April 6, 1979.
2. Ibid.

3. Ibid.

4. Ibid.

5. Miami *Herald,* April 24, 1980.

6. Case No. 81–434–CR–JLK, U.S. District Court, Miami; Miami *Herald,* April 6, 1979.

7. Ibid.

8. *American Banker,* Sept. 8, 1975.

9. Staten Island *Advance,* May 22, 1980.

10. Washington *Post,* March 29, 1982.

11. *The Wall Street Journal,* May 21, 1981.

12. Ibid.

13. Ibid.

14. *The Wall Street Journal,* March 27, 1982; Miami *Herald,* May 18, 1983; Fort Lauderdale *News,* Nov. 18, 1982; Columbus *Dispatch,* May 21, 1982.

15. See note 6.

16. Case No. 82–0885–CIV–JWK, U.S. District Court, Miami.

17. Mary Adelaide Mendelson, *Tender Loving Greed* (New York: Vintage Books, 1975), pp. 29, 49, 115–16, 123–55, 169, 170–74, 197, 218; Miami *Herald,* Dec. 24, 1980.

18. Case No. 82–2553, Eleventh Circuit Court, Dade County.

19. See note 16.

20. See note 16.

21. New York *Times,* June 26, 1982; *The Wall Street Journal,* Oct. 4 and Dec. 2, 1982; Miami *Herald,* Oct. 2, 1982; Case No. 82–0885–CIV–JWK, U.S. District Court, Miami.

22. New York *Times,* May 4, 1982.

23. See note 16.

24. Howard Kohn, "The Hughes-Nixon-Lansky Connection: The Secret Alliances of the CIA from World War II to Watergate," *Rolling Stone,* May 20, 1976; James Hougan, *Spooks* (New York: William Morrow, 1978), p. 212; Henrik Kruger, *The Great Heroin Coup* (Boston: South End Press, 1980), p. 90; Miami *Herald,* Feb. 10, 1981, March 4, and April 25, 1982; *Parapolitics,* Spring 1981, citing Miami *Herald,* March 13, 1981, *El Espectador,* May 25, 1983; interviews, Organized Crime Bureau, Aug. 18, 1982.

25. Philadelphia *Daily News,* April 8, 9, 10, 16, and 28, 1980.

26. Interviews, Organized Crime Bureau, Miami, Aug. 18, 1982; Dade County Court House Book 11282, pp. 446–49.

27. *El Tiempo,* June 5 and 7, 1983.

28. Interview anonymous, Bogotá, July 13, 1982; *El Tiempo,* Oct. 29, 1981, and June 5 and 12, 1983; *The Wall Street Journal,* June 22, 1983; Miami *Herald,* July 24, 1983.

29. Annetta Miller, *Florida Trend* (March 1982), pp. 35–38.

30. *Fortune,* May 19, 1980, pp. 134–38; New York *Times,* May 20 and June 25, 1983; *El Tiempo,* June 12, 13, and August 17 and 18, 1983; United Press

International [New York], May 13, 1983, and [Miami], May 20, 1983; Miami *Herald,* May 14 and 19, 1983; *The Wall Street Journal,* June 6, 1983; *El Espectador,* Aug. 18, 1983.

31. New York *Times,* June 25, 1983; *El Espectador,* June 6, 1983; *El Tiempo,* June 7 and 8, 1983; Miami *Herald,* July 24, 1983.

32. New York *Times,* June 25, 1983; Miami *Herald,* July 24, 1983; Miami *News,* May 27 and June 3, 1983; *El Espectador,* June 5, 1983.

33. Alberto Donadio, *Banqueros en el Banquillo* (Bogotá: El Ancora Editores, 1983), pp. 98–103, 142–45; *El Tiempo,* June 12, 1983; *Semana,* May 24, 1983; *El Espectador,* March 30, 1983.

34. *El Tiempo,* June 7 and 12, 1983; United Press International [Miami], July 24, 1983; *The Wall Street Journal,* June 2, 6, 13, and 27, 1983; *El Espectador,* June 9, 1983; AFP [Miami], May 24, 1983; Miami *Herald,* July 24, 1983.

35. New York *Times,* June 25, 1983; interviews, anonymous, Bogotá, June 1982.

36. *The Wall Street Journal,* May 20 and June 23 and 27, 1983; interview, James Drumwright, Aug. 21, 1982; New York *Times,* June 25, 1983; Miami *Herald,* March 21 and May 13, 1983; *El Tiempo,* June 7 and 19, 1983; AFP [Miami], May 23, 1983.

37. Interview, Federal Reserve official, Federal Reserve Board of Atlanta, Aug. 19, 1982.

38. Interview, anonymous, Miami, Aug. 12, 1982.

39. Interview, Florida State bank regulator, Miami, Aug. 2, 1982.

40. Interview, Wayne Dicky, Tallahassee, Aug. 20, 1982.

41. See note 37.

42. Miami *Herald,* Aug. 21, 1982; St. Petersburg *Times,* Aug. 21, 1982.

43. Interviews, Alexander McW. Wolfe, Jr., Miami, Aug. 17, 1982; Oakley Chaney, Miami, Aug. 12, 1982.

44. Interview, Alexander McW. Wolfe, Jr., Miami, Aug. 17, 1982.

Chapter 4

1. *The Wall Street Journal,* Aug. 24, 1982; *Maclean's,* Sept. 6, 1982, pp. 19–20.

2. *Covert Action,* March 1982, pp. 51–55.

3. Jonathan Marshall, "The Friends of Michael Hand," *Inquiry,* Nov. 24, 1980, pp. 9–12.

4. Ibid.; *Covert Action,* March 1982, pp. 51–55.

5. Alfred W. McCoy, *The Politics of Heroin in Southeast Asia* (New York: Harper & Row, 1972), pp. 7, 8.

6. *Covert Action,* March 1982, pp. 51–55.

7. *The Wall Street Journal,* Aug. 24, 1982.
8. *Maclean's,* Sept. 6, 1982, pp. 19–20.
9. McCoy, *Politics,* pp. 7, 8.
10. *The Wall Street Journal,* Aug. 26, 1982.
11. Ibid.; Marshall, "Friends"; *Maclean's,* Sept. 6, 1982, pp. 19–20.
12. Brian Toohey, *The National Times* [Australia], Jan. 4–10, 1981.
13. *The Wall Street Journal,* Aug. 24, 1982; *Maclean's,* Sept. 6, 1982, pp. 19–20.
14. Ibid.
15. *Covert Action,* March 1982, pp. 51–55.
16. McCoy, *Politics,* pp. 247, 263–64, 267, 269–71, 274–81, 283, 288, 292–93; New York *Times,* Nov. 13, 1982.
17. *Covert Action,* March 1982, pp. 51–55.
18. Marshall, "Friends."
19. *Covert Action,* March 1982, pp. 51–55.
20. Ibid.
21. *The Wall Street Journal,* Aug. 24, 1982.
22. Marshall, "Friends"; *Covert Action,* March 1982, pp. 51–55; *Parapolitics/ USA,* Oct. 31, 1981; *Newsweek,* May 23, 1983; *The Wall Street Journal,* Aug. 24, 1982.
23. Marshall, "Friends"; *The Wall Street Journal,* Aug. 24, 1982.
24. *The National Times,* Oct. 12–18, 1980; *Inquiry,* Nov. 23, 1981, pp. 11–13.
25. *The Wall Street Journal,* Aug. 25, 1982.
26. Ibid.
27. *Covert Action,* March 1982, pp. 51–55.
28. *The Wall Street Journal,* Aug. 26, 1982; *Inquiry,* Nov. 23, 1981, pp. 11–13.
29. Ibid.
30. *The Wall Street Journal,* Aug. 24, 1982; Marshall, "Friends."
31. McCoy, *Politics,* p. 6.

Chapter 5

1. *The Wall Street Journal,* April 18, 1980.
2. Ibid.; Alfred McCoy, *The Politics of Heroin in Southeast Asia* (New York: Harper & Row, 1972), pp. 130, 138, 141, 144; Henrik Kruger, *The Great Heroin Coup* (Boston: South End Press, 1980), pp. 15, 130–31.
3. Kruger, *Heroin,* p. 131; Peter D. Scott, *The War Conspiracy* (Indianapolis, Ind.: Bobbs-Merrill, 1972), pp. 210–12.
4. McCoy, *Politics,* pp. 136–40; Jonathan Marshall, "Opium and the Politics of Gangsterism in Nationalist China, 1927–1945," *Bulletin of Concerned Asian Scholars* (July–September 1976), pp. 19–48.
5. McCoy, *Politics,* pp. 226–27.

6. McCoy, *Politics*, pp. 16, 19, 20–24; Norman Lewis, *The Honored Society* (New York: Putnam, 1964), p. 18; Hank Messick, *Of Grass and Snow* (Englewood Cliffs, N.J.: Prentice-Hall, 1979), p. 13; "Special Issue—Nixon and the Election," *NACLA's Latin America & Empire Report* (Vol. VI, No. 8/October 1972), p. 14.

7. McCoy, *Politics*, pp. 7, 16; *Le Monde*, June 17–18, 1973.

8. McCoy, *Politics*, pp. 7, 22; Fred Hirsch, "An Analysis of Our AFL-CIO Role in Latin America" (San Jose, Calif.: Emergency Committee to Defend Democracy in Chile, 1974), pp. 14–16; Thomas Braden, "I'm Glad the CIA Is Immoral," *The Saturday Evening Post*, May 20, 1967.

9. McCoy, *Politics*, pp. 247, 263–64; Kruger, *Heroin Coup*, p. 136.

10. "Nixon and the Election," p. 7.

11. *The Wall Street Journal*, April 18, 1980; New York *Times*, Jan. 7, 1978; Los Angeles *Times*, May 28, 1976; Miami *Herald*, Oct. 13, 1975; interview, Richard Jaffe, Miami, Aug. 5, 1982.

12. Gigi Mahon, *The Company That Bought the Boardwalk* (New York: Random House, 1980); *Martindale-Hubbell Law Directory, 1977* (Summit, N.J.: Martindale-Hubbell, 1976).

13. Kruger, *Heroin Coup;* Scott, *War Conspiracy;* "Nixon and the Election."

14. "Oversight Hearings into the Operations of the IRS (Operation Trade winds, Project Haven, and Narcotics Traffickers Tax Program)," Hearings before a Subcommittee of the Committee on Government Operations, House of Representatives, 94th Cong., 1st sess., Oct. 6, Nov. 4 and 11, 1975 (Washington, D.C.: Government Printing Office, 1976), pp. 91, 140–41, 153, 929; transcript of "60 Minutes" TV program segment on "The Castle Bank Caper," Nov. 21, 1976; Cleveland *Press*, March 17, 1977; San Francisco *Examiner*, July 26, 1976.

15. "Oversight Hearings," p. 160.

16. Interview, Richard Jaffe, Miami, Aug. 5, 1982.

17. *The Wall Street Journal*, April 18, 1980; "Castle Bank Caper"; master list of Accounts of Castle Bank, March 27, 1972, Nassau; *Parapolitics*, Spring 1981.

18. Knut Royce, Kansas City *Times*, March 8, 9, and 10, 1982. (Royce's investigative series grew out of the 1981 tragedy at Kansas City's Hyatt Regency, where 114 people died when the hotel's sky walks collapsed.)

19. Ibid.

20. Ibid.

21. Interview, Richard Jaffe, Miami, Aug. 5, 1982; "Oversight Hearings," p. 153.

22. Interviews, Richard Jaffe, Miami, Nov. 5 and 8, 1982; interviews, Archimedes L. Patti, Florida, Nov. 8 and 16, 1982; Patti, *Why Viet Nam?* (Berkeley: University of California Press, 1980), pp. 265–70; Royce, Kansas City *Times*, March 8, 9, and 10, 1982; *The Wall Street Journal*, Feb. 17, 1981.

23. *Wall Street Journal*, May 23, 1977; Feb. 17, 1981; *Parapolitics, Spring 1981*.

24. Royce, Kansas City *Times*, March 8, 9, and 10, 1982; Los Angeles *Times*, April 25, 1976.

25. *John and Martha Fogerty* v. *Kanter et al.* Complaint before the Superior Court of the State of California in and for the County of Santa Barbara, March 20, 1978.

26. "Oversight Hearings," p. 149.

27. Ibid., pp. 79, 105, 231–34; Nassau *Guardian*, Dec. 8, 1975; Los Angeles *Times*, Jan. 28, 1976.

28. San Francisco *Examiner*, Oct. 31, 1976; Los Angeles *Times*, June 11, 1976.

29. "Oversight Hearings," p. 56.

30. Miami *Herald*, June 24, 1980.

31. Memo from Richard Jaffe to Congressman Sam Gibbons, Chairman, Oversight Subcommittee, House Ways and Means Committee, June 14, 1979.

32. New York *Times*, Aug. 3, 1981; *Soho Weekly News*, March 18, 1981.

33. New York *Times*, Aug. 3, 1981; *Soho Weekly News*, Nov. 17, 1981.

34. Ibid.; *The Wall Street Journal*, Aug. 16, 1982.

35. *The Wall Street Journal*, April 18, 1980; letter, Jim Drinkhall, July 13, 1981, and memorandum, July 13, 1980; letter, Burton Kanter, July 9, 1981.

36. Interview, William Losner, Miami, Aug. 3, 1982.

37. Ibid.

38. Drug Enforcement Administration (DEA) file, July 13, 1982; *Latin America Regional Reports/Andean Group* [London], June 19, 1981; *El Espectador* [Bogotá], July 12 and 14, 1982.

39. Ibid.; *Semana* [Bogotá], July 13, 1982.

40. *El Espectador*, July 9 and Oct. 22, 1982; *El Tiempo* [Bogotá], Aug. 2, 1982; New York *Times*, Dec. 25, 1982.

41. *El Espectador*, July 9, 11, and Sept. 2, 1982; *El Tiempo*, July 8, 10, 11, 16, 21, 29, and Sept. 1, 8, 1982.

42. File on Felix Correa in the Office of the Comptroller, State of Florida, Tallahassee; Florida International Bank Statement of Condition, Dec. 31, 1981; *El Tiempo*, Aug. 1, Sept. 11, Oct. 5, and Dec. 12 and 13, 1982; *El Espectador*, Sept. 15 and Oct. 2, 1982.

43. Correa file; interviews, Ken Meyers, Miami, Aug. 8 and 10, and Oct. 4 and 19, 1982; Alberto Donadio, *Banqueros en el Banquillo* (Bogotá: El Ancora Editores, 1983), pp. 53–54; interview, anonymous, Miami, Aug. 10, 1982.

Chapter 6

1. *Newsday*, April 28, 1982; Hank Messick, *Of Grass and Snow* (Englewood Cliffs, N.J.: Prentice-Hall, 1979), pp. 52–54.

2. Ibid.; Miami *Herald*, April 29, 1982; Miami *News*, April 28, 1982; *Caribbean Contact*, July 1982.

3. Miami *Herald,* April 29, 1982.

4. Ibid.; Messick, *Grass and Snow,* pp. 52–54.

5. *Time,* Nov. 23, 1981, pp. 22–32.

6. Peter Dale Scott, "Foreword," *The Great Heroin Coup* by Henrik Kruger (Boston: South End Press, 1980), p. 16.

7. Miami *Herald,* April 29, 1982.

8. St. Petersburg *Times,* May 30, 1982.

9. Interview, anonymous, Oct. 14, 1982.

10. Messick, *Grass and Snow,* p. 44.

11. Jeff Stein, "An Army in Exile," *New York* Magazine, Sept. 10, 1979.

12. Edward S. Herman, *The Real Terror Network* (Boston: South End Press, 1982), p. 68.

13. Miami *Herald,* April 29, 1982; Messick, *Grass and Snow,* pp. 52–54; Miami *News,* April 28, 1982; *Newsday,* April 28, 1982; "Special Report on the Miami Drug Traffic," *Parapolitics/USA,* Oct. 31, 1981, citing Miami *Herald,* Aug. 2, 1973, and Miami *News,* Aug. 2, 1977, and July 3, 1974.

14. Miami *Herald,* April 29, 1982; Kruger, *Heroin Coup,* pp. 147–48.

15. Kruger, *Heroin Coup,* pp. 147–48; Messick, *Grass and Snow,* pp. 171–80; "Special Report."

16. Alfred W. McCoy, *The Politics of Heroin in Southeast Asia* (New York: Harper & Row, 1972), pp. 27, 54–55.

17. Ibid., p. 55.

18. Kruger, *Heroin Coup,* pp. 56, 144.

19. James Hougan, *Spooks* (New York: William Morrow, 1978), pp. 114, 120, 195; Kruger, *Heroin Coup,* p. 144, citing U.S. Congress, Senate, Select Committee to Study Governmental Operations with Respect to Intelligence Activities, *Alleged Assassination Plots Involving Foreign Leaders,* Interim Report, 94th Cong., 1st Sess., Senate Report No. 94–463, 1975; Stephen Schlesinger and Stephen Kinzer, *Bitter Fruit* (New York: Doubleday, 1982), p. 145.

20. Kruger, *Heroin Coup,* p. 146; McCoy, *Politics,* pp. 56–57, 263–81.

21. *The Economist,* Oct. 16, 1982, pp. 18–19.

22. Messick, *Grass and Snow,* p. 87.

23. *Newsweek,* Oct. 25, 1982, pp. 60–64.

24. Miami *Herald,* Aug. 22, 1982.

25. Interview, anonymous, Miami, Aug. 12, 1982; *Time,* Nov. 23, 1981, pp. 22–32.

26. Interview, Michael Y. Cannon, president of Appraisal and Real Estate Economics Associates, Inc., Miami, Aug. 5, 1982. Testimony of Charles Kimball, real estate economist, House Select Committee on Narcotics Abuse and Control, Fort Lauderdale, Oct. 9, 1981.

27. *Inquiry,* May 17, 1982.

28. Interview, anonymous, Miami, Aug. 10, 1982.

29. Interview, anonymous, Miami, Aug. 10, 1982.

30. Interview, Lt. George Ray Havens, Criminal Investigative Division, State Attorney's Office, Miami, Aug. 5, 1982.
31. *Inquiry,* May 17, 1982.
32. *Time,* Nov. 23, 1981, pp. 22–32.
33. *Time,* Nov. 24, 1980, p. 37.
34. *Maclean's,* April 5, 1982, pp. 14–20.
35. Interview, Gov. Robert Graham, Tallahassee, Aug. 20, 1982; United Press International, May 29, 1980.
36. Miami *Herald,* Oct. 11, 1981.
37. Ibid.
38. "Asset Forfeiture—A Seldom Used Tool in Combatting Drug Trafficking," Report by the Comptroller General to the Honorable Joseph R. Biden, U.S. Senate (Washington, D.C.: General Accounting Office, April 10, 1981).
39. Interview, Havens, Miami, Aug. 5, 1982.
40. Miami *Herald,* Aug. 17 and 27, 1982; *El Tiempo* [Bogotá], June 13, 1982; transcript of "No Questions Asked" segment on "60 Minutes," Feb. 22, 1981.
41. "No Questions Asked."
42. *Maclean's,* April 5, 1982, pp. 14–20; United Press International, Feb. 7, 1982.
43. Final Report of the Grand Jury, in the Circuit Court of the Eleventh Judicial Circuit of Florida in and for the County of Dade, filed May 11, 1982.

Chapter 7

1. Interview, Richard H. Dailey, president, Dadeland Bank, Miami, Aug. 9, 1982; interview, Aristides Sastre, president, Republic National Bank, Miami, Aug. 10, 1982.
2. "Banks and Narcotics Money Flow in South Florida," Hearing before the Committee on Banking, Housing and Urban Affairs, U.S. Senate, 96th Cong., June 5 and 6, 1980 (Washington, D.C.: Government Printing Office, 1980), pp. 64–65.
3. *Time,* Nov. 23, 1981, pp. 22–32; "Banks and Narcotics Money Flow," p. 207.
4. *Latin America Weekly Report* [London], May 15, 1981.
5. New York *Times,* May 23, 1982.
6. Interview, FBI, Miami, Aug. 17, 1982.
7. "Banks and Narcotics Money Flow," pp. 17–25.
8. Ibid., p. 229.
9. Ibid., p. 145.
10. Ibid., p. 146.

11. Interview, Alexander McW. Wolfe, Jr., vice chairman, Southeast Bank, Miami, Aug. 17, 1982.

12. "Banks and Narcotics Money Flow," pp. 69–95.

13. Ibid., pp. 62–63.

14. "Bank Secrecy Act Reporting Requirements Have Not Yet Met Expectations, Suggesting Need for Amendment," Report to the Congress of the United States by the Comptroller General (Washington, D.C.: General Accounting Office, July 23, 1981).

15. "Banks and Narcotics Money Flow," p. 206.

16. Ibid., p. 216.

17. Ibid., p. 208.

18. Miami *Herald,* May 24, 1981.

19. *Newsweek,* July 20, 1981, pp. 36–37.

20. Ibid.

21. Miami *Herald,* Feb. 28, 1981.

22. *The Wall Street Journal,* Dec. 14, 1982; New York *Times,* Dec. 14, 1982; Miami *Herald,* Dec. 14, 1982; Associated Press, Dec. 14, 1982; Miami *News,* Dec. 12, 13, 14, 15, 1982, and Jan. 4, 1983.

23. St. Petersburg *Times,* Oct. 16, 1982; United Press International, Oct. 15, 1982; *El Tiempo,* Oct. 17 and 18 and Nov. 17, 1982; *El Espectador,* Oct. 17, 1982.

24. Interview, Operation Greenback agent, Miami, Aug. 6, 1982.

25. "Analysis Relating to Large Currency Transactions Conducted at Five Banks in the Miami Area," U.S. Customs Service, Office of Investigations, Currency Investigations Division, 1978; Miami *Herald,* June 5 and 6, 1980, and Oct. 3 and 5, 1982.

26. Memorandum from George E. Gonzalez, national bank examiner, to John G. Hensel, regional administrator of national banks, Comptroller of the Currency, Aug. 3, 1978.

27. Miami *Herald,* June 6, 1980.

28. James V. Houpt, "Foreign Ownership of U.S. Banks: Trends and Effects," *Journal of Bank Research,* in press.

29. Statement of Doyle L. Arnold, Senior Deputy Comptroller for Policy and Planning, before the Subcommittee on Commerce, Consumer, and Monetary Affairs of the Committee on Government Operations, U.S. House of Representatives, Sept. 30, 1982.

30. Interview, Charles Kantor, president, Eagle National Bank, Miami, Aug. 4, 1982; *Latin America Weekly Report,* March 6, 1981; *El Tiempo,* April 9, 1980; Feb. 21, Nov. 5, and Dec. 2, 1981; and March 14, June 24 and 26, Sept. 29, Oct. 2, and Nov. 18, 1982; *El Espectador,* Feb. 26, March 11, Aug. 3, Nov. 5, 8, and 12, and Dec. 2, 1981; Feb. 21, April 11, May 17, June 29, July 3 and 23, and Nov. 18, 1982; Alberto Donadio, *Banqueros en el Banquillo* (Bogotá: El Ancora Editores, 1983), pp. 138–42; United Press International, July 15, 1983.

31. Interviews, economic and press attachés, U.S. embassy, Bogotá, Oct. 20 and Nov. 10, 1982; interviews, spokesperson, Federal Reserve, Atlanta branch, Oct. 15 and Nov. 2, 1982.

32. Miami *Herald*, March 17, 1981; memorandum from George E. Gonzalez, national bank examiner, to John G. Hensel, regional administrator of national banks, Comptroller of the Currency, Aug. 17, 1978.

33. Federal Reserve press release, Washington, Aug. 25, 1981; statement by Henry C. Wallich, member, Board of Governors of the Federal Reserve System, before the House Subcommittee on Commerce, Consumer, and Monetary Affairs of the Committee on Government Operations, U.S. House of Representatives, Sept. 30, 1982; statement of New York State Senator Carol Berman before the House Subcommittee on Commerce, Consumer, and Monetary Affairs, Sept. 30, 1982.

34. Memorandum from Connie See to Stephen M. Foster on Hearing by House Subcommittee on Commerce, Consumer, and Monetary Affairs, Sept. 30, 1982.

35. Berman statement, Sept. 30, 1982.

36. Interview, anonymous, Bogotá, Nov. 18, 1982.

37. *John Marcilla* v. *Chase Manhattan Bank*, 80 CIV 2336 (TPG), U.S. District Court, Southern District of New York, Foley Square, N.Y.; *The Nation*, Oct. 2, 1982, pp. 289, 302–4; Donadio, *Banqueros*, pp. 128–29.

38. Ibid.

39. Ibid.

40. Interview, Bogotá, Oct. 19, 1982; *El Tiempo*, Oct. 5, 1982; *El Espectador*, Sept. 22, 1982; letter from Alvaro H. Caicedo to Luis Alejandro Dávila Mora, superintendent of corporations, Cali, June 7, 1982; Donadio, *Banqueros*, pp. 122–29.

41. *El Espectador*, Sept. 17 and 23, 1982; Colprensa [Bogotá], Aug. 13, 1982; interview, Fernando Londoño Hoyos, Bogotá, Oct. 26, 1982.

42. Interview, Londoño Hoyos, Bogotá, Oct. 26, 1982; letter from Fernando Londoño Hoyos to Luis Alejandro Dávila Mora, superintendent of corporations, Bogotá, June 16, 1982; Commercial Registration No. 54.499 of the Bogotá Chamber of Commerce of Johannesson de Therrien and Company, with capital of 200,000 pesos (or U.S. $3,333.33), Bogotá, May 28, 1981; Commercial Registration No. 104.324 of the Bogotá Chamber of Commerce of Compañia de Negocios Mobiliarios La Sabana, Ltd., in which Johannesson de Therrien and Company is listed as a shareholder, Bogotá, May 27, 1982; Commercial Registration No. 47.413 of the Bogotá Chamber of Commerce in which Johannesson de Therrien and Company is listed as a shareholder, Bogotá, May 7, 1982; *El Tiempo*, Oct. 5, 1982; Donadio, *Banqueros*, pp. 124–25.

43. *El Tiempo*, Nov. 22, 1982.

44. Letter from Londoño to Dávila, Bogotá, June 16, 1982; *El Espectador*, Sept.

22, 1982; *The Nation,* Oct. 2, 1982, pp. 289, 302–4; Donadio, *Banqueros,* pp. 123–25.

45. *El Tiempo,* Nov. 14, 1982.

46. Account No. 642–10–23–8 at Banco de Comercio in Medellín. Source: Drug Enforcement Administration.

47. *El Espectador,* July 12 and Aug. 7, 1983; *El Tiempo,* Aug. 18, 1983.

Chapter 8

1. *El Espectador,* March 8, 1982; *El Tiempo,* Jan. 11, 1983; *Parapolitics/USA,* March 31, 1982.

2. John Cummings, "Miami Confidential," *Inquiry,* Aug. 24, 1981, pp. 19–24.

3. Ibid.; interview, R. Jerome Sanford, Miami, Aug. 4, 1982; Certificate of Articles of Incorporation of the WFC Corporation, Florida Department of State, Tallahassee, Sept. 29, 1982; *Who's Who in America,* 1982–83, p. 3262.

4. Hearings before the Select Committee on Narcotics Abuse and Control, U.S. House of Representatives, March 8, 1978; interview, anonymous, Miami, Aug. 12, 1982; interviews, Dade County Organized Crime Bureau, Aug. 13, 1982; *El Espectador,* May 14, 1978.

5. Interview, anonymous, Bogotá, Oct. 14, 1982; Henrik Kruger, *The Great Heroin Coup* (Boston: South End Press, 1980), pp. 8, 181–82; *El Espectador,* March 8, 1982; *El Tiempo,* Nov. 18, 26, 27, 28, 1981; interview, Sanford, Miami, Aug. 4, 1982; *Semana* [Bogotá], Nov. 16, 1982, pp. 26–29; Miami *Herald,* April 29, 1982; Miami *News,* April 28, 1982; St. Petersburg *Times,* June 1, 1982.

6. Hank Messick, "The Latin Connection," *Investigator,* September 1981, pp. 55, 70–72; interview, Sanford, Miami, Aug. 4, 1982; Cummings, "Miami Confidential."

7. Ibid.; memorandum from R. Jerome Sanford, assistant U.S. attorney, Southern District of Florida, Miami, to Robert L. Keuch, deputy assistant attorney general, Department of Justice, Washington, D.C., Aug. 1, 1977; Hank Messick, *Of Grass and Snow* (Englewood Cliffs, N.J.: Prentice-Hall, 1979), pp. 171–80.

8. Ibid.; Hearings before the Select Committee on Narcotics Abuse and Control, U.S. House of Representatives, March 10, 1978.

9. Messick, *Grass and Snow,* pp. 171–80.

10. Sanford memorandum to Keuch; Cummings, "Miami Confidential."

11. Ibid.

12. Miami *Herald,* April 29, 1982; St. Petersburg *Times,* June 1, 1982; *Newsday,* April 28, 1982.

13. Interview, Sanford, Miami, Aug. 4, 1982; St. Petersburg *Times,* June 1, 1982; Miami *News,* April 28, 1982.

14. Cummings, "Miami Confidential"; interviews, Dade County Organized Crime Bureau, Aug. 13, 1982; Miami *Herald,* May 11, 1980.

15. "The Castro Connection," segment on "60 Minutes," Feb. 26, 1978; *El Espectador,* May 14 and Oct. 19, 1978; *El Tiempo,* Aug. 30, 1982; St. Petersburg *Times,* May 31, 1982; *United States of America* v. *Guillermo Hernández Cartaya and Salvador Alderguía Ors,* Indictment No. 78–151, CR WMH, United States District Court, Southern District of Florida, May 4, 1978; Hearings before the Select Committee on Narcotics Abuse and Control, U.S. House of Representatives, March 8, 1978.

16. Interview, Sanford, Miami, Aug. 4, 1982.

17. Interview, anonymous, Miami, Aug. 12, 1982.

18. Cummings, "Miami Confidential."

19. Interviews, Dade County Organized Crime Bureau, Aug. 13, 1982; Donald Freed with Fred S. Landis, *Death in Washington* (Westport, Conn.: Lawrence Hill, 1980); Taylor Branch and Eugene M. Propper, *Labyrinth* (New York: Viking, 1982).

20. Interview, Sanford, Miami, Aug. 4, 1982; interviews, Dade County Organized Crime Bureau, Aug. 13, 1982; Miami *Herald,* May 11, 1980.

21. James Hougan, *Spooks* (New York: William Morrow, 1978), p. 208.

22. Interview, Fernando Capablanca, Miami, Aug. 12, 1982.

23. Hougan, *Spooks,* pp. 11–15, 19, 22, 25–48, 137–51, 195–99; Washington *Post,* June 6, 1976; Kruger, *Heroin Coup;* Philip Agee, *Inside the Company: CIA Diary* (Harmondsworth, Eng.: Penguin, 1975), p. 608; "Staff Study of the Frank Peroff Case," Permanent Subcommittee of Investigations of the Committee on Government Operations, U.S. Senate (Washington, D.C.: Government Printing Office, 1978); Miami *Herald,* May 11, 1980; "The Castro Connection."

24. Hougan, *Spooks,* p. 197.

25. Miami *Herald,* Feb. 28, 1978, and May 11, 1980; St. Petersburg *Times,* May 31, 1982; interview, Robert Serrino, director, Enforcement and Compliance Division, Comptroller of the Currency, May 18, 1982.

26. Interview, anonymous, Aug. 16, 1982.

27. Hearings before the Select Committee on Narcotics Abuse and Control, U.S. House of Representatives, March 22, 1978.

28. Sanford memorandum to Keuch; Hearings before the Select Committee on Narcotics Abuse and Control, U.S. House of Representatives, March 10, 1978; Messick, *Grass and Snow,* pp. 177–78.

29. Miami *Herald,* Jan. 24, July 3 and 10, and Dec. 3, 1981; interview, Sam Strother, lawyer with the Criminal Section of the Tax Division, Justice Department, Dec. 8, 1981; *United States of America* v. *Guillermo Hernández Cartaya et al.,* Indictment No. 18 USC 371, United States District Court, Southern District of Florida, March 16, 1981.

30. Miami *Herald,* Nov. 11 and 15, 1982; St. Petersburg *Times,* June 1, 1982; *Parapolitics/USA,* Oct. 31, 1981.

31 *El Espectador,* May 14, 1978; *El Tiempo,* Aug. 29, 30, 31, and Sept. 13, 1982; *La Republica,* Aug. 5, 1982; Alberto Donadio, *Banqueros en el Banquillo* (Bogotá: El Ancora Editores, 1983), p. 80.

32. Ibid., *El Tiempo,* Nov. 30, 1982.

33. "The Castro Connection"; Hearings before the Select Committee on Narcotics Abuse and Control, U.S. House of Representatives, March 8, 1978.

34. *El Tiempo,* Aug. 29, 30, 31, 1982; interview, anonymous, Miami, Aug. 16, 1982.

35. *El Espectador,* Aug. 5 and Sept. 16 and 26, 1982; *El Bogotano,* Aug. 10, 1982; *Latin America Regional Reports/Andean Group* [London], Aug. 27, 1982; Banco del Estado Statement of Condition, Dec. 31, 1979; Principales Grupos de Accionistas, Banco del Estado, Nov. 27, 1978.

36. *El Espectador,* Sept. 9, 1982; *El Tiempo,* Aug. 20, 21, 26, and 30, Sept. 9 and 22, 1982, and Jan. 9, 1983; *El Bogotano,* Aug. 12, 1982; *New York Times,* Dec. 25, 1982; Donadio, *Banqueros,* p. 69.

37. *The Wall Street Journal,* Aug. 19 and Sept. 13, 1982; Miami *Herald,* Aug. 12 and 18, 1982; *Flagship Banks, Inc.* v. *Inversiones Credival, C.A., and Juan Vicente Pérez Sandoval,* Civil Action No. 82–2540, United States District Court for the District of Columbia, Washington, D.C., Sept. 10, 1982; letter to Rep. Benjamin Rosenthal, chairman, Subcommittee on Commerce, Consumer, and Monetary Affairs of the Committee on Government Operations, U.S. House of Representatives, from Fried, Frank, Harris, Shriver & Jacobson, special counsel to Flagship Banks, New York, Sept. 24, 1982.

38. Ibid.; Miami *Herald,* Dec. 7, 1982.

39. Ibid.; Hearings before the Select Committee on Narcotics Abuse and Control, U.S. House of Representatives, March 10, 1978; list of shareholders in Sociedad Financiera Credival, May 1, 1981; *Guiabanca,* 1976, Venezuela; Registro Mercantil No. 53, Tomo 18–A AC, for commercial registration of Compañia Inversiones Fenix, now called Sociedad Financiera Credival, July 22, 1975; Registro Mercantil No. 6, Tomo 97A, for commercial registration of WFC of Venezuela, 1975; and Registro Mercantil No. 31, Tomo 5–A Sqdo, for commercial registration of UFASA, C.A., May 5, 1975, in Circumscripción Judicial del Dtto. Federal y Estado Miranda; Miami *Herald,* Dec. 5, 1982.

40. St. Petersburg *Times,* Oct. 21, 1982; Miami *Herald,* Nov. 9, 1982.

41. Barry Stavro, "Flagship Management's Latest Test—A Stockholder Takeover," *Florida Trend,* May 1981, pp. 47–51; Miami *Herald,* Aug. 18, 1982.

42. Interview, Janet Reno, Miami, Aug. 18, 1982.

43. Interview, anonymous, Miami, Aug. 9, 1982.

44. Ibid.

45. Interviews, anonymous, Miami, Aug. 12 and 16, 1982.

46. Interviews, FBI, Miami, August 1982.

47. Hearings before the Select Committee on Narcotics Abuse and Control, U. S. House of Representatives, March 8 and 10, 1978.
48. Interview, Lester Wolff, New York City, Dec. 15, 1981.

Chapter 9

1. United Press International, Oct. 11 and 12 and Nov. 5, 1982; *El Tiempo* [Bogotá], Oct. 11, 13, and 15, 1982; Agencia France-Presse, Oct. 12 and 13, 1982.
2. Ibid.; Henrik Kruger, *The Great Heroin Coup* (Boston: South End Press, 1980), pp. 8, 10–11, 183, 209, 214, 225; *Cuadernos para el Diálogo* [Madrid], Feb. 5, 1977, pp. 24–26.
3. New York *Times*, Aug. 31, 1981; United Press International, Oct. 12, 23, and 24, 1982; *Latinamerica Press* [Lima], Jan. 22, 1981; Ray Bonner, "Bailing Out Bolivia's Junta," *The Nation*, Nov. 29, 1980, pp. 573–76; *Cuadernos del Tercer Mundo* [Mexico City], August/September 1980, pp. 51–64; *Latin America Weekly Report*, Aug. 29, 1980, and Jan. 29, 1982; testimony of Stephen M. Block, deputy director, Office of Andean Affairs, State Department, n.d.; *El Tiempo*, Oct. 16, 1982.
4. Ibid.; according to Bolivian Interior Minister Mario Roncal, as reported by United Press International, La Paz, Oct. 12, 1982; *Latin America Weekly Report*, Oct. 22, 1982.
5. *Latin America Weekly Report*, Feb. 12, Aug. 13, and Oct. 22, 1982; *Newsweek*, June 8, 1981, pp. 28–29, and Nov. 23, 1981, pp. 18–19; *Latinamerica Press*, June 11, 1981; United Press International, Oct. 24 and 28, 1982.
6. *Semana* [Bogotá], Nov. 2, 1982, pp. 40–42.
7. *Newsweek*, Feb. 21, 1983, pp. 40–42; Associated Press [La Paz], Jan. 28, 1983.
8. *Newsweek*, Feb. 21, 1983, pp. 40–42; Minneapolis *Star and Tribune*, March 15, 1983; New York *Times*, June 10, 1982; Washington *Post*, Feb. 16, 1983; Martin A. Lee, "Their Will Be Done," *Mother Jones*, July 1983, pp. 21–38; Associated Press, Aug. 16, 1983; United Press International, Aug. 16 and 17, 1983.
9. *Newsweek*, Feb. 21, 1983, pp. 40–42, and June 8, 1981, pp. 28–29; Penny Lernoux, *Cry of the People* (New York: Penguin, 1982), pp. 224–25; Associated Press [Miami], March 14, 1983; Los Angeles *Times*, March 16, 1983; *Parapolitics/USA*, March 1, 1983; Toronto *Globe and Mail*, Feb. 7, 1983; *Tropic*, Jan. 2, 1983; New York *Times*, Oct. 17, 1982.
10. In January 1983 the government of Hernán Siles Zuazo charged Barbie with "organizing and advising a network of mercenaries and paramilitary" composed of former Nazis and Nazi sympathizers (Associated Press [La Paz], Jan. 28, 1983). See also *Semana*, Nov. 2, 1982, pp. 40–42, and note 5

above. *Newsweek,* Feb. 21, 1983, pp. 40–42; Minneapolis *Star and Tribune,* Feb. 6, 1983; Washington *Post,* Feb. 26, 1983; The *Sunday Times* (London), Feb. 6, 1983; *Latin America Weekly Report,* Feb. 4, 1983.

11. *El Tiempo,* Oct. 15, 1982.

12. Washington *Post,* Feb. 26, 1983; *Newsweek,* Feb. 21, 1983, pp. 40–42; New York *Times,* Feb. 25, 1983.

13. United Press International, Oct. 12, 14, and 27, and Dec. 4, 1982.

14. Lernoux, *Cry of the People,* p. 340.

15. Ibid., p. 196; Taylor Branch and Eugene M. Propper, *Labyrinth* (New York: Viking, 1982), pp. 305–20; John Dinges and Saul Landau, *Assassination on Embassy Row* (New York: Pantheon, 1980), pp. 117n, 196; Kruger, *Heroin Coup,* p. 10.

16. Ibid.; Washington *Post,* Feb. 23, 1982.

17. *Semana,* Nov. 2, 1982, pp. 40–42; *Time,* Sept. 27, 1982, pp. 26–27; New York *Times,* May 28, 1981.

18. *Semana,* Nov. 2, 1982, pp. 40–42; *Cuadernos para el Diálogo,* Feb. 5, 1977, pp. 24–26; Diana Johnstone, "P2 Revelations Are Startling Even by Italian Standards," *In These Times,* Aug. 12–25, 1981, p. 9ff.; Agencia France-Presse, Sept. 21, 1982.

19. *The Wall Street Journal,* Sept. 20 and Nov. 23, 1982; *Christian Science Monitor,* Sept. 15, 1982; *El Tiempo,* June 7, 1981, and Oct. 13 and 16, 1982.

20. United Press International, Nov. 26, 1982; *National Catholic Reporter,* Dec. 10, 1982; *Business Week,* July 19, 1982, pp. 63–64; *Financial Times,* July 17, 1982; *The Wall Street Journal,* Nov. 29, 1982.

21. Kruger, *Heroin Coup;* New York *Times,* May 27 and 28, 1981, and Dec. 27, 1982; *Parapolitics/USA,* Oct. 31, 1981; FBI transcript of interview with Michele Sindona, New York City, June 20, 1980. Lee, "Their Will," pp. 21–38.

22. Johnstone, "Revelations"; *National Catholic Reporter,* June 5, 1981; New York *Times,* May 24, 28, and 31, 1981; *Time,* June 8, 1981, pp. 33–34; United Press International, Sept. 14, 1982.

23. Joan Edelman Spero, *The Failure of the Franklin National Bank* (New York: Columbia University Press, 1980), pp. 51–57.

24. Ibid., pp. 51–59, 124, 198; statement of James E. Smith, Comptroller of the Currency, Washington, D.C., June 1, 1976; Charles Mann with Dale McAdoo, "Sindona: An Investigative Report," *Attenzione,* December 1979, pp. 51–58; Luigi DiFonzo, *St. Peter's Banker* (New York: Franklin Watts, 1983), p. 261; New York *Times,* Jan. 30, 1982.

25. *Securities and Exchange Commission* v. *Gulf & Western Industries, Inc., et al.,* Civil Action 79–3201, United States District Court for the District of Columbia, Nov. 6, 1980; New York *Times,* July 24, 1977; *The Wall Street Journal,* Nov. 27, 1979.

26. Spero, *Failure,* pp. 55–56; Lernoux, *Cry of the People,* p. 240.

27. Mann with McAdoo, "Sindona"; Kevin Coogan, "The Friends of Michele Sindona," *Parapolitics/USA,* Aug. 15, 1982.
28. *Time,* Sept. 13, 1982, pp. 8–15; *National Catholic Reporter,* Sept. 18, 1982.
29. Ibid.; *Time,* July 26, 1982, pp. 26–27
30. New York *Times,* Aug. 26, 1982.
31. *Time,* Sept. 13, 1982, pp. 8–15.
32. Spero, *Failure,* pp. 48–52, 57, 64–67, 95–99; Mann with McAdoo, "Sindona."
33. Lernoux, *Cry of the People;* New York *Times,* July 18, 1982; *Newsweek,* July 19, 1982, p. 19, and Sept. 13, 1982, pp. 62–69.
34. *National Catholic Reporter,* Sept. 18, 1982.
35. Spero, *Failure,* pp. 184–86; Mann with McAdoo, "Sindona"; appendix to statement by James E. Smith, June 1, 1976, House Subcommittee on Commerce, Consumer, and Monetary Affairs; DiFonzo, *St. Peter's Banker,* pp. 148 and 193–99.
36. Ibid.; Spero, *Failure,* p. 63.
37. Mann with McAdoo, "Sindona"; DiFonzo, *St. Peter's Banker,* pp. 222–23.
38. Mann with McAdoo, "Sindona."
39. *Newsweek,* April 12, 1982, pp. 62–69; *Christian Science Monitor,* Sept. 15, 1982; Agencia France-Presse, June 22, 1982; *The Guardian* in *Le Monde* international edition, Sept. 19, 1982.
40. Agencia France-Presse, June 22, 1982; *Time,* July 26, 1982, pp. 26–27; Luigi DiFonzo, "Justifiable Homicide," *New York* Magazine, April 11, 1983, pp. 30–33; Coogan, "Friends."
41. *Time,* July 26, 1982, pp. 26–27, and Sept. 13, 1982, pp. 8–15.
42. *The Wall Street Journal,* July 23 and Sept. 10, 1982; *National Catholic Reporter,* Aug. 13, 1982.
43. *National Catholic Reporter,* Sept. 18, 1982; Hearings before the Committee on Standards of Official Conduct, House of Representatives, 1976, p. 662, from report as printed in the *Village Voice,* Feb. 16, 1976, and addended to transcript of hearings; Kruger, *Heroin Coup,* p. 225; *Cuadernos para el Diálogo,* Feb. 5, 1977, pp. 24–26; Mann with McAdoo, "Sindona"; New York *Times,* Nov. 26, 1976; Johnstone, "Revelations."
44. Ibid.; DiFonzo, *St. Peter's Banker,* pp. 102–6; *Parapolitics,* Spring 1981, p. 9; Coogan, "Friends."
45. DiFonzo, *St. Peter's Banker,* p. 6; Jonathan Marshall, "The Business of Terrorism," *Parapolitics,* Spring 1981.
46. Kruger, *Heroin Coup,* p. 210.
47. Ibid., p. 48.

Chapter 10

1 *The Wall Street Journal,* May 31, 1981; *Time,* July 26, 1982, pp. 26–27.

2. *The Wall Street Journal,* Aug. 24 and 30, 1982; *Time,* Sept. 13, 1982, pp. 8–15; *El Espectador* [Bogotá], Sept. 25, 1982; José Luis Martínez, "La tenebrosa historia de 'El banquero de Dios,' " in *La Vanguardia* [Barcelona], reprinted in *El Espectador,* July 7, 1982; Leo Sisti and Gianfranco, Modolo, *El Banco Paga* (Barcelona: Plaza & Janes, 1983), p. 275.

3. *The Sunday Times* [London], Feb. 13, 1983.

4. Ibid.; PBS "Frontline" program, Feb. 14, 1983; *Parapolitics/USA,* March 1, 1983, citing *Corriere della Sera.*

5. *Time,* July 26, 1982, pp. 26–27; *The Wall Street Journal,* Aug. 30, 1982; *The Banker,* July 1982, pp. 67–69; Associated Press, June 19, 1982; United Press International, June 18 and 19, and July 3, 1982.

6. *Financial Times,* Aug. 22, 1982.

7. *The Wall Street Journal,* July 26, Aug. 19, Sept. 29, and Oct. 29, 1982; interview, anonymous, Sept. 22, 1982; Associated Press, Oct. 28, 1982; *Time,* Sept. 13, 1982, pp. 8–15; *The Sunday Times* [London], Feb. 13, 1983, and Nov. 14, 1982; *Parapolitics/USA,* March 1, 1983.

8. *National Catholic Reporter,* Sept. 18, 1982.

9. *Time,* Sept. 13, 1982, pp. 8–15; Martínez, "La tenebrosa historia"; *The Wall Street Journal,* Aug. 30, 1982.

10. *Newsweek,* Sept. 13, 1982, pp. 62–69.

11. *Time,* Sept. 13, 1982, pp. 8–15; *The Wall Street Journal,* Aug. 30, 1982; *Financial Times,* July 17, 1982; New York *Times,* July 27, 1982.

12. New York *Times,* July 27, 1982; *The Wall Street Journal,* Aug. 30, 1982; Sisti and Modolo, *El Banco Paga,* pp. 9–163.

13. *Financial Times,* July 17, 1982, and July 21, 1982; *The Wall Street Journal,* Aug. 23 and 30, Sept. 28, and Nov. 23, 1982; *Time,* July 26, 1982, pp. 26–27; Aug. 9, 1982, p. 47; Sept. 13, 1982, pp. 8–15; *Newsweek,* Sept. 13, 1982, pp. 62–69; Latin-Reuter, July 4, 1982.

14. Ibid.

15. New York *Times,* July 27, 1982; United Press International, Nov. 26, 1982; Associated Press, Nov. 22, 1982; *Financial Times,* July 23, 1982; *The Wall Street Journal,* Dec. 9, 1982; *National Catholic Reporter,* Dec. 10, 1982.

16. *The Sunday Times* (London), Feb. 13, 1983; *National Catholic Reporter,* March 18, 1983; Associated Press, March 7, 1983.

17. *The Sunday Times* (London), Feb. 13, 1983.

18. Ibid.

19. *The Wall Street Journal,* Dec. 9, 1982; *National Catholic Reporter,* Dec. 10, 1982.

20. *National Catholic Reporter*, Sept. 18, 1982.

21. *National Catholic Reporter*, June 5, 1981, and Oct. 29, 1982; United Press International, Oct. 19, 1982; Luigi DiFonzo, *St. Peter's Banker* (New York: Franklin Watts, 1983), p. 229; Kevin Coogan, "The Friends of Michele Sindona," *Parapolitics/USA*, Aug. 15, 1982; New York *Times*, June 4, 1981; Sisti and Modolo, *El Banco Paga*, p. 172.

22. Diana Johnstone, "P2 Revelations Are Startling Even by Italian Standards," *In These Times*, Aug. 12–25, 1981, p. 9ff.; *Newsweek*, June 8, 1981, pp. 28–29.

23. *Newsweek*, June 8, 1981, pp. 28–29; *Semana*, Nov. 2, 1982, pp. 40–42; *Latin America Weekly Report*, June 5 and July 17, 1981; New York *Times*, May 31, 1981; *National Catholic Reporter*, Oct. 29, 1982.

24. *The Wall Street Journal*, Aug. 18, 1982; *Topic*, June 1982, pp. 11–12; *The Guardian* in *Le Monde* (international edition), Aug. 10, 1981.

25. Penny Lernoux, *Cry of the People* (New York: Penguin, 1982), pp. 1–10, 332–50; *Encyclopedia of Latin America*, ed. by Helen Delpar (New York: McGraw-Hill, 1974), pp. 467–70; *Latin America Weekly Report*, June 5 and July 17, 1981.

26. New York *Times*, Oct. 3, 1982; *The Wall Street Journal*, Sept. 24 and Nov. 23, 1982.

27. *Latin America Weekly Report*, June 5 and July 17, 1981; *National Catholic Reporter*, Sept. 24, 1982; Associated Press, June 19, 1982; United Press International, Aug. 1, 1983.

28. *Latin America Weekly Report*, May 29, 1981, and Sept. 24, 1982; *Latin America Regional Reports/Southern Cone*, June 26, 1981; New York *Times*, Oct. 3, 1982.

29. *Latin America Weekly Report*, June 5 and 12, 1981; Associated Press, July 7, 1982; Agencia France-Presse, Sept. 21, 1982; letter, anonymous, Oct. 20, 1982.

30. *Financial Times*, Aug. 5, 1982; *El Espectador*, June 28, 1982; Latin-Reuter, July 7 and 9, 1982; *The Wall Street Journal*, Aug. 30 and Sept. 15, 1982; Martínez, "La tenebrosa historia"; *The Guardian* in *Le Monde* (international edition), July 19, 1982; New York *Times*, July 27, 1982; ANSA (the Italian news agency), Jan. 15, 1983.

31. Associated Press, Nov. 3, 1982; *Latin America Weekly Report*, Oct. 15, 1982; Agencia France-Presse, Sept. 21, 1982; *Semana*, Nov. 2, 1982, pp. 40–42.

32. *Semana*, Oct. 5, 1982, pp. 35–37, and Nov. 2, 1982, pp. 40–42; *Latin America Weekly Report*, Oct. 8, 15, and 22, 1982.

33. *Newsweek*, July 27, 1981; *Latin America Weekly Report*, June 6 and July 17, 1981; *Semana*, Oct. 5, 1982, pp. 35–37.

34. Taylor Branch and Eugene M. Propper, *Labyrinth* (New York: Viking, 1982), pp. 1–14; *The Leveller* [London], Oct. 31, 1979, pp. 22–23; Henrik

Kruger, *The Great Heroin Coup* (Boston: South End Press, 1980), pp. 183, 214.

35 *The Wall Street Journal,* Nov 23, 1982; *Time,* Sept. 13, 1982, pp. 8–15; *National Catholic Reporter,* Sept. 18, 1982.

36. *Time,* Sept. 27, 1982, pp. 26–27, *The Wall Street Journal,* Aug. 24, Sept. 15 and 20, 1982; *El Tiempo,* Sept. 25, 1982; United Press International, Sept. 14, 1982, and Aug. 10, 11, and 12, 1983; Latin-Reuter, Sept. 13, 1982; Associated Press, Aug. 10 and 11, 1983; Agencia France-Presse, Aug. 14, 1983

37 New York *Times,* May 24, 28, 30, and 31, 1981, *Time,* June 8, 1981, pp. 33–34.

38. *National Catholic Reporter,* Feb. 25, 1983; *The Wall Street Journal,* Feb. 14, 1983

39 See sources in note 36.

40. Johnstone, "Revelations", *Semana,* Nov 2, 1982, pp. 40–42, *National Catholic Reporter,* Oct. 29, 1982; *El Tiempo,* June 7, 1981

41 New York *Times,* July 28, 1982; *National Catholic Reporter,* Oct. 22, 1982.

42. *Financial Times,* July 17, 1982; *The Banker,* September 1982, p. 71, New York *Times,* July 14 and 18, Aug. 26, and Dec. 18, 1982; *National Catholic Reporter,* Aug. 13 and Oct. 29, 1982; New York *Times,* July 28, 1982.

43 *National Catholic Reporter,* July 17, Sept. 18 and 24, Oct. 22, and Dec. 3, 1982; interview, anonymous, Sept. 22, 1982; *Maclean's,* July 19, 1982, p. 19; United Press International, July 13, 1982.

44. Ibid.

45 *National Catholic Reporter,* Oct. 29 and Dec. 10, 1982; Associated Press, Oct. 6, 1982; United Press International, Nov 27, 1982.

46. New York *Times,* Nov 24 and Dec. 18, 1982; *The Wall Street Journal,* Nov 24, 1982; *The Wall Street Journal,* reprinted in Spanish in *El Espectador,* Aug. 13, 1982; *National Catholic Reporter,* Dec. 10, 1982; United Press International, Nov 23, 1982; *Business Week,* Dec. 13, 1982, p. 35

47 *National Catholic Reporter,* Aug. 13, Sept. 18, and Dec. 17, 1982; Associated Press, Oct. 2, 1981; *The Sunday Times* [London], Jan. 6, 1980.

48. Toronto *Star,* June 24, 1982; *Catholic New Times,* June 27, 1982; *National Catholic Reporter,* Dec. 3, 1982.

49 *Financial Times,* Aug. 22, 1982; *The Wall Street Journal,* Aug. 19, 1982; Agencia France-Presse, Oct. 7, 1982; *National Catholic Reporter,* Dec. 17, 1982; New York *Times,* Oct. 7, 1982.

50. *The Wall Street Journal,* Aug. 23 and 24, 1982; interview, anonymous, Sept. 22, 1982; *National Catholic Reporter,* Sept. 24, Oct. 29, and Dec. 10 and 17, 1982; *Semana,* Jan. 3, 1983, pp. 37–38.

51 DiFonzo, *St. Peter's Banker,* p. 259; Diana Johnstone, "The Ledeen Connections," *In These Times,* Sept. 8, 1982; *Parapolitics/USA,* March 1, 1983; New York *Daily News,* Jan. 25, 1983; *L'Espresso* [Italy], Dec. 12, 1982; *National Catholic Reporter,* Aug. 29, 1980; *Latin America Regional Re-*

ports/*Southern Cone,* July 31, 1981; Coogan, "Friends"; Sisti and Modolo, *El Banco Paga,* pp. 271–77.

52. *The Wall Street Journal,* July 14, Aug. 23, Nov. 29, 1982; United Press International, Oct. 8, 1982; *The Economist,* Oct. 16, 1982, p. 99; *National Catholic Reporter,* Aug. 27, 1982.

53. *The Banker,* August 1982, pp. 8–11; New York *Times,* Dec. 18, 1982.

54. *The Banker,* August 1982, pp. 8–11; Agefi Letter Nos. 426, 427, and 433 (London, 1982); *Financial Times,* July 20, 1982; New York *Times,* July 28, 1982; *The Wall Street Journal,* July 30, 1982; *Newsweek,* Aug. 2, 1982, pp. 35–36.

55. Ibid.

56. *Financial Times,* July 26 and Aug. 10, 1982; New York *Times,* Dec. 18 and 25, 1982.

57. *Financial Times,* July 18, 1982.

58. *Financial Times,* July 17 and 22, 1982; *The Wall Street Journal,* Sept. 1, 1982; *Business Week,* Aug. 16, 1982, pp. 87–88; Agefi Letter No. 433 (London, 1982).

59. *The Wall Street Journal,* Aug. 5, 1982.

Chapter 11

1. Interviews, São Paulo, Sept. 1983.

2. *El Tiempo,* Nov. 8, 1982.

3. New York *Times,* Sept. 13, 1982; *Business Week,* Dec. 20, 1982, pp. 43, 60, and March 14, 1983, p. 111; *Latin America Regional Reports/Mexico and Central America,* Oct. 29, 1982; United Press International, Dec. 30, 1982; *Time,* Jan. 10, 1983, pp. 4–11.

4. Carlos F. Díaz Alejandro, "Stories of the 1930's for the 1980's." Unpublished discussion paper (no. 376), Economic Growth Center, Yale University.

5. Among those to complain about the "loan pushing" was Manuel Ulloa, the Prime Minister of Peru, whose country had been broke in 1975 but became the toast of international bankers five years later during an IMF meeting in Washington. Said Ulloa of the crowd of bankers trying to press money on him, "I can hardly face going back to the hotel; there are six different banks waiting for me." Cited by Anthony Sampson, *The Money Lenders* (New York: Viking, 1982), p. 16.

6. Francisco Viana, "El modelo en un callejón sin salida," *Tercer Mundo,* No. 56 [Mexico City], Oct. 1982, pp. 32–37; *National Catholic Reporter,* March 21, 1980.

7. New York *Times,* Dec. 19, 1982; *The Economist,* Dec. 11, 1982, pp. 11–25.

8. *The Wall Street Journal,* March 25, 1983.

9 *National Catholic Reporter,* March 7, 1980; *The Wall Street Journal,* Feb. 18, 1983.

10. Ibid., *Development Forum,* United Nations Development Program, January/February 1978.

11 *National Catholic Reporter,* March 14, 1980; *Latin America Weekly Report,* Oct. 8 and Dec. 17, 1982; *Latin America Regional Reports/Brazil,* Oct. 22 and Nov. 26, 1982; *The Nation,* Nov. 6, 1982, p. 452.

12. Viana, "El modelo"; *National Catholic Reporter,* March 7, 1980; *Latin America Weekly Report,* May 28, 1982.

13. *Euromoney,* August 1982, pp. 20–52; *The Banker,* January 1982, p. 75.

14. Ibid.; *The Banker,* October 1982, pp. 80–82; Agefi Letter No. 427 (London, 1982); *The Economist,* Feb. 26, 1983; *Latin America Weekly Report,* Feb. 4, 1983.

15. Stephen Schlesinger and Stephen Kinzer, *Bitter Fruit* (New York: Doubleday, 1982); *Multinational Monitor,* Oct. 1982, pp. 18–21.

16. *Revista Diálogo Social* [Panama City], April 1982; *National Catholic Reporter,* Jan. 14, 1983; *Latinamerica Press,* June 10, 1982; *Update,* Washington Office on Latin America, Jan./Feb. 1983.

17. *Multinational Monitor,* May 1982, p. 9.

18 *Multinational Monitor,* Oct. 1982, pp. 18–21; *Update; Central America in Revolt,* CBS News Special, March 20, 1982.

19. *Multinational Monitor,* March 1982, pp. 14–15, and May 1982, p. 9; *Central America Report,* Oct. 1982; *NACLA Report on the Americas,* Jan.–Feb. 1983, p. 24.

20. *The Nation,* Oct. 16, 1982, pp. 364–66; *Inquiry,* March 15, 1982, pp. 4–5.

21. *The Wall Street Journal,* Aug. 20, 1982.

22. *Latin America Weekly Report,* Aug. 13, 1982; *Latin America Regional Reports/Brazil,* Nov. 26, 1982; *El Espectador,* Dec. 30, 1982; *Newsweek,* Feb. 21, 1983, p. 68; *The Wall Street Journal,* Sept. 13, 1982, and Feb. 8 and 25, 1983.

23. *The Nation,* Oct. 16, 1982, pp. 364–66; Richard J. Barnet and Ronald E. Muller, *Global Reach* (New York: Simon & Schuster, 1974), pp. 140–42; Isabel Letelier and Michael Moffitt, "Human Rights, Economic Aid and Private Banks," Institute for Policy Studies, Washington, D.C., n.d.; *El Tiempo,* Dec. 6, 1982; Maurice A. Odle, *Multinational Banks and Underdevelopment* (New York: Pergamon, 1981); *Latin America Regional Reports/Southern Cone,* Nov. 19, 1982.

24. *El Tiempo,* Dec. 6, 1982; *Euromoney,* August 1982, pp. 20–52; *Latin America Weekly Report,* Oct. 8 and 15, 1982; *Inquiry,* June 15, 1981, pp. 9–11.

25. *The Economist,* Feb. 26, 1983; *Business Week,* Dec. 6, 1982, pp. 28–30; United Press International, Dec. 12, 1982; *The Wall Street Journal,* Dec. 13, 1982.

26. *Business Week,* Nov. 15, 1982, p. 40.

27. *Euromoney,* August 1982, pp. 20–52; *Maclean's,* Dec. 27, 1982, pp. 20–22; United Press International, Dec. 11 and 15, 1982; Agencia France-Presse, Dec. 11, 1982.

28. *National Catholic Reporter,* Feb. 1, 1980; *Multinational Monitor,* October 1982, pp. 18–21.

29. *Business Week,* Feb. 21, 1983, pp. 128–33.

30. Ibid.; *Latin America Regional Reports/Southern Cone,* Nov. 19, 1982.

31. *The Wall Street Journal,* July 22, 1982; *Business Week,* Nov. 8, 1982, p. 11, and Nov. 29, 1982, p. 80; *Newsweek,* Dec. 20, 1982, pp. 43–44; *Latin America Weekly Report,* Nov. 19, 1982; *World Financial Markets,* Morgan Guaranty Trust Company of New York, October 1982, pp. 1–9.

32. *The Economist,* Dec. 11, 1982, pp. 11–25; *Business Week,* Dec. 6, 1982, pp. 28–30; United Press International, Dec. 1, 1982; *South,* January 1981, pp. 75–79; *NACLA Report on the Americas,* January/February 1983, pp. 40–44.

33. *Inquiry,* June 15, 1981, pp. 9–11.

34. Ibid.; *Newsweek,* Sept. 6, 1982, pp. 62–63.

35. *The Wall Street Journal,* Dec. 1, 1982; *Latin America Regional Reports/ Brazil,* Oct. 22, 1982.

36. *The Wall Street Journal,* April 6, 1983.

37. Dr. H. J. Witteveen, "Where Do We Go from Here?" *The Banker,* November 1982, pp. 17–23; New York *Times,* Feb. 27, 1983.

38. *Maclean's,* Dec. 27, 1982, pp. 20–22; New York *Times,* Dec. 19, 1982; Los Angeles *Herald Examiner,* Aug. 6, 1982.

Chapter 12

1. Samuel Eliot Morison, *The Oxford History of the American People. Volume Three: 1869–1963* (New York: New American Library, 1965), pp. 289–90, 308–9; Anthony Sampson, *The Money Lenders* (New York: Viking, 1982), pp. 59–61; *Business Week,* Sept. 3, 1979, pp. 32–37.

2. *Business Week,* Sept. 3, 1979, pp. 32–37; William J. Quirk, "The Big Bank Bailout," *The New Republic,* Feb. 21, 1983, pp. 17–21.

3. *Business Week,* April 21, 1975.

4. Quirk, "Bailout"; Emily S. Rosenberg, *Spreading the American Dream* (New York: Hill & Wang, 1982), p. 151; Sampson, *Money Lenders,* p. 56.

5. Rosenberg, *American Dream,* pp. 154–55.

6. Ibid.

7. *Business Week,* Sept. 3, 1979, pp. 32–37.

8. Interview, Alexander McW. Wolfe, Jr., Miami, Aug. 17, 1982; *The Banker,* August 1982, pp. 7–8; *The Economist,* Oct. 16, 1982, pp. 21–24.

9. "A Perspective on the Debt of Developing Countries," Brookings Papers

on Economic Activity, 2 (Washington, D C. Brookings Institution, 1977), pp. 507 and 509; *The Wall Street Journal,* Nov 10, 1982, *The Economist,* Oct. 16, 1982, pp. 21–24; *Multinational Monitor,* October 1982, pp. 9–15

10. Washington *Post,* March 10, 1983; Los Angeles *Times,* March 12, 1983; *The Wall Street Journal,* Feb. 2 and 16 and March 23 and 28, 1983; New York *Times,* Feb. 16, 1983; *Business Week,* March 14, 1983, p. 111, *Time,* March 14, 1983, p. 66.

11 *The Wall Street Journal,* April 11, 1983; *National Catholic Reporter,* Jan. 25, 1980; *Business Week,* Nov 15, 1982, pp. 89, 115

12. *The Wall Street Journal,* April 15 and 20, 1983; Los Angeles *Times,* April 20, 1983.

13. *Time,* Aug. 2, 1982, pp. 28–29, and Aug. 18, 1982, pp. 54–55; New York *Times,* July 19, 1982; *The Wall Street Journal,* March 21 and April 11, 1983.

14. *Time,* Aug. 2, 1982, pp. 28–29, and Aug. 18, 1982, pp. 54–55

15. *Business Week,* Oct. 4, 1982, p. 60.

16. *The Wall Street Journal,* March 21 and April 20, 1983; report by T J Holt and Company, Westport, Connecticut, Dec. 31, 1981, summarized by Dan Dorfman for the Tribune Company Syndicate.

17. *Time,* Aug. 2, 1982, pp. 28–29, and Aug. 18, 1982, pp. 54–55; New York *Times,* July 19, 1982.

18. Associated Press, April 10, 1983; *The Wall Street Journal,* Feb. 2 and 3 and April 8, 1983.

19. *The Wall Street Journal,* March 4 and 17, 1983.

20. *Business Week,* Dec. 13, 1982, p. 64; *Multinational Monitor,* Oct. 1982, p. 15; *The Nation,* Oct. 2, 1982, pp. 289, 302–4; Alberto Donadio, *Banqueros en el Banquillo* (Bogotá: El Ancora Editores, 1983), p. 128.

21. *Time,* Jan. 31, 1983.

22. Interview, anonymous, Federal Reserve official, Federal Reserve Board of Atlanta, Aug. 19, 1982.

23. *The Wall Street Journal,* Nov. 10, 1982; Dr. H. J. Witteveen, "Where Do We Go from Here?" *The Banker,* November 1982, pp. 17–23.

24. *The Economist,* Oct. 16, 1982, pp. 21–24; New York *Times,* July 19, 1982.

25. Witteveen, "Where Do We Go"; *Time,* Jan. 10, 1983, pp. 4–11

26. Thomas Braden, "I'm Glad the CIA Is Immoral," *The Saturday Evening Post,* May 20, 1967.

27. *The Wall Street Journal,* March 21, 1983; New York *Times,* April 1, 1983.

28. *The Wall Street Journal,* March 16, 1983; *The Banker,* April 1982, pp. 77–79.

29 *The Wall Street Journal,* April 6, 1983.

30. *The Wall Street Journal,* April 22 and 25 and June 15 and 28, 1983.

INDEX